*it*books

AN IMPRINT OF HARPERCOLLINS *PUBLISHERS*

*it*books

J U I C E D

Copyright © 2005 by *Jose Canseco*

Designed by Richard Ljoenes

Library of Congress Cataloging-in-Publication Data has been applied for.

ISBN: 978-0-06-0746414
ISBN: 0-06-074641-6

10 11 WBC/RRD 15 14

I want to dedicate this book to my fans, who have supported me and cheered me on for many years—and deserve to know the truth.

Contents

Introduction

A LOOK TO THE FUTURE

These past few years, all you had to do was turn on a radio or flip to a sports cable channel, and you could count on hearing some blowhard give you his opinion about steroids and baseball and what it says about our society and blah blah blah. Well, enough already. I'm tired of hearing such short-sighted crap from people who have no idea what they're talking about. Steroids are here to stay. That's a fact. I guarantee it. Steroids are the future. By the time my eight-year-old daughter, Josie, has graduated from high school, a majority of all professional athletes—in all sports—will be taking steroids. And believe it or not, that's good news.

Let's be clear what we are talking about. In no way, shape, or form, do I endorse the use of steroids without proper medical advice and thorough expert supervision. I'll say it again: Steroids are serious. They are nothing to mess around with casually, and if anything, devoting yourself to the systematic use of steroids means you have to stay away from recreational drugs. I was never into that stuff anyway, cocaine and all that, but if you're going to work with steroids, you have to get used to clean living, smart eating, and taking care of yourself by getting plenty of rest and not overtaxing your body.

I'm especially critical of anyone who starts playing around with steroids too early, when they are barely old enough to shave and not even fully grown yet. Your body is already raging with hormones at that age, and the last thing you want to do is wreak havoc with your body's natural balance. If you want to turn yourself into a nearly superhuman athlete, the way I did, you need to wait until you have matured into adulthood. That way your body can handle it. And you shouldn't fool yourself into thinking that all you need to do is just read a few articles on steroids, either. What you need to do is to absorb every scrap of information and insight on the subject—to become an expert on the subject, the way I did.

We're talking about the future here. I have no doubt whatsoever that intelligent, informed use of steroids, combined with human growth hormone, will one day be so accepted that everybody will be doing it. Steroid use will be more common than Botox is now. Every baseball player and pro athlete will be using at least low levels of steroids. As a result, baseball and other sports will be more exciting and entertaining. Human life will be improved, too. We will live longer and better. And maybe we'll love longer and better, too.

We will be able to look good and have strong, fit bodies well into our sixties and beyond. It's called evolution, and there is no stopping it. All these people crying about steroids in baseball now will look as foolish in a few years as the people who said John F. Kennedy was crazy to say the United States would put a man on the moon. People who see the future earlier than others are always feared and misunderstood.

The public needs to be informed about the reality of steroids and how they have affected the lives of many star baseball players, including me. Have I used steroids? You bet I did. Did steroids make me a better baseball player? Of course they did. If I had it all to do over again, would I live a steroid-enriched life? Yes, I would. Do I have any regrets or qualms about relying on chemicals to help me hit a baseball so far? To be honest, no, I don't.

We human beings are made up of chemicals. High school chemistry students learn to recite "CHOPKINS CaFe," which is all the chemical elements that make up the human body: carbon, hydrogen, oxygen, phosphorous, potassium, iodine, nitrogen, sulfur, calcium, and iron. Maybe it bothers some people to think of our bodies as just a collection of those elements, but I find it comforting.

I like studying the body and how it works. I like knowing all about what makes us stronger and faster. If you learn about the chemicals that make up life, and study the hormones coursing through our bloodstreams that give our bodies instructions, you can learn how to improve your health through controlled use of steroids. And you can do it safely.

Yes, you heard me right: Steroids, used correctly, will not only make you stronger and sexier, they will also make you healthier. Certain steroids, used in proper combinations, can cure certain diseases. Steroids will give you a better quality of life and also drastically slow down the aging process.

If people learn how to use steroids and growth hormone properly, especially as they get older—sixty, seventy, eighty years old—their way of living will change completely. If you start young enough, when you are in your twenties, thirties, and forties, and use steroids properly, you can probably slow the aging process by fifteen or twenty years. I'm forty years old, but I look much younger—and I can still do everything the way I could when I was twenty-five.

When I talk in detail about steroids and how I single-handedly changed the game of baseball by introducing them into the game, I am saying what everyone in baseball has known for years. To all my critics, to everyone who wants to turn this into a debate about me, Jose Canseco, let me quote my favorite actor (besides Arnold Schwarzenegger, that is) and say: You can't *handle* the truth.

That is the story of baseball in recent years. Everyone in the game has been hoping the lie could last as long as possible. They wanted steroids in the game to make it more exciting, hoping they would be able to build its popularity back up after the disastrous cancellation of the 1994 World Series. So when I taught other players how to use steroids, no one lifted a finger to stop me. When I educated trainers and others on how to inject players with steroids, there was nothing standing in my way. Directly or indirectly, nearly everyone in baseball was complicit.

How do I know that? I was known as the godfather of steroids in baseball. I introduced steroids into the big leagues back in 1985, and taught other players how to use steroids and growth hormone. Back then, weight lifting was taboo in baseball. The teams didn't have weight-lifting programs. Teams didn't allow it. But once they saw what I could do as a result of my weight lifting, they said, "My God, if it's working for Jose, it's gotta work for a lot of players."

So all of a sudden ballparks were being built with brand-new, high-tech weight-lifting facilities, and at the older ballparks they were moving stuff around and remodeling to make room for weight rooms. I definitely restructured the way the game was played. Because of my influence, and my example, there were dramatic changes in the way that players looked and the way they played. That was because of changes in their nutrition, their approach to fitness and weight lifting, and their steroid intake and education.

If you asked any player who was the one who knew about steroids, they'd all tell you: Jose Canseco.

Who do you go to when you want information on steroids? Jose Canseco.

Who do you go to if you wanted to know if you were using it properly?

Jose Canseco.

If you picked up this book just for a few juicy tales about which players I've poked with needles full of steroids, or what it was like when Madonna sat on my lap and asked me to kiss her, that's fine with me. I've lived a colorful life, and people have always been curious about the things I've done. If you want to flip through the chapters looking for the highlights, I have no problem with that (as long as you pay the cover price, of course).

But let me be clear that I'm writing this book for people who are ready to think for themselves. That's all I'm asking. Hear me out, listen to what I have to say about baseball and other things, and come to your own conclusions. That might sound easy, but believe me, coming to terms with a true picture of what has been going on in baseball in the past ten years or so might not be what you really want.

Do I expect some skepticism from people? Of course I do. I've made some mistakes in the past. I've made mistakes in my personal life, and I've made mistakes in public, too. There have been times when I spoke out without realizing how my comments might sound to people. That's all water under the bridge. Now, I'm looking to the rest of my life, not dwelling on what might have been.

I'm telling the truth about steroids in this book because someone has to do it. We're long overdue for some honesty and, as any ballplayer will tell you, I know the real story of steroids in baseball better than any man alive. I'm also in a position to tell you the truth because I no longer have any ties with Major League Baseball, and I have no interest in the politics and double standards of Major League Baseball. I'm my own man and always have been.

Back when I first started using steroids, I tracked down as many books as I could find on the subject, and I studied the science behind steroids. I started becoming something like a guru. I wanted to know everything about each steroid and what it did, especially pertaining to athletes and sports and baseball. Could it make me faster? Could it make me stronger? Could it make me injury-free? I started experimenting on myself, using my own body to see what steroid could do what. Today, I probably know more about steroids and what steroids can do for the human body than any layman in the world.

I believe every steroid out there can be used safely and beneficially—it's all a question of dosage. Some steroids you cycle off and on, depending on the dose. You just have to make sure you give your liver enough time to filter them out. There are other steroids that have very low toxicity levels. Those can be taken continuously by most healthy people. It just depends. Growth hormone? You can use that all year round. Same thing with your Equipoise, your Winstrols, your Decas—taken properly, those are fine all year round. But something like Anadrol, and some high dosages of testosterone—those have to be moderated, taken more selectively. This is all important because when ballplayers talk about steroids, they really mean a combination of steroids and growth hormone, and that requires some serious planning if you don't want to get yourself in trouble.

Believe it or not, I first found out about the benefits of growth hormone in a book. That was when I was first educating myself, years ago. There were certain bookstores that had a big selection of books on body building and related subjects, and you could go into the stores and flip through the books, or buy them and bring them home like cookbooks full of recipes to try. Or you could just go talk to bodybuilders. They were always on the lookout for the latest information themselves, so often they would sell the books or magazines with the newest tips. It took me some time, and a lot of effort, but I educated myself. I read and I listened to bodybuilders talk about the subject. Little by little, I turned myself into an expert and that gave me a huge edge as a baseball player.

There's always that competitive angle in baseball: The pitchers trying to stay in front of the hitters, the hitters trying to stay in front of the pitchers. As hitters, we were always looking for better equipment and for any other edge we could gain. We may keep a video camera on a pitcher, trying to find out if he's tipping his pitches. The game has become so technical. You can go back during a game after every at-bat to look at what you just did. You have five computers with ten different camera angles, and you can slow it down, fast-forward it, break it down, this and that. You can use the computer to break down where your hot zone is and know exactly what you're doing wrong pitch by pitch.

You feel like a damn scientist back there: They play back every one of your at-bats, watching them in slow-mo, and from every different angle. It's just incredible. You can reexamine each at-bat to analyze every element of your performance: where your hands were, how your feet were placed, the speed of your swing. This radical new technology has taken over baseball, and all of sports. It's awesome, really—but it makes sense, given all the money at stake now. And that applies to every kind of technology, running the gamut from digital video and high-powered software to steroids and growth hormone, and whatever comes next.

Remember back when Mark McGwire and I were called the "Bash Brothers" during our time together on those memorable Oakland A's teams from the late 1980s to early 1990s? I didn't always like that tag, but people were right that McGwire and I spent a lot of time together. Of course, we didn't talk much.

What we did, more times than I can count, was go into a bath-room stall together to shoot up steroids.

That's right: After batting practice or right before the game, Mark and I would duck into a stall in the men's room, load up our syringes, and inject ourselves. I always injected myself, be-cause I had practiced enough to know just what I was doing, but often I would inject Mark as well.

It helps to have a partner to do the injecting for you. It's diffi-cult to inject yourself, especially when you're first starting out, because you have to get the needle at just the right angle to hit the glute muscle in the ideal spot. Whenever you're going to in-ject into muscle tissue, you have to hit your spot just right. I don't recommend injecting steroids into yourself in the early going. Get a friend, or a doctor, to do it.

Growth hormone is a little different. For best results, you want to inject growth hormone into your abdominal mus-cles—you just pinch a thin layer of fat and inject yourself right there. It's pretty easy, and you can get good at it quickly. Some of the players were injecting growth hormone every day, or every third day. It all depended on how big you were and what results you wanted.

As a rookie, McGwire was a skinny kid with hardly any mus-cles on him at all. There's no doubt that Mark was always a great hitter, even before steroids: He hit forty-nine homers in his first season, 1987, which is still the rookie record for home runs. He always had a smooth, compact, and powerful swing; he had amazing technique. But the steroids made Mark much bigger and much stronger; perhaps most important of all, I personally observed how they made him feel more confident and more comfortable with his own body. All of that definitely helped him break Roger Maris's record in 1998. I don't know of anyone in baseball who won't tell you that's true, so long as they're talking off the record and in private and don't have to worry about being quoted in a splashy headline somewhere.

Have other superstars used steroids? If you don't know the answer, you've been skimming, not reading. The challenge is not to find a top player who has used steroids. The challenge is to find a top player who *hasn't*. No one who reads this book from cover to cover will have any doubt that steroids are a huge part of baseball, and always will be, no matter what crazy toothless testing schemes the powers that be might dream up.

Is it cheating to do what everyone wants you to do? Are players the only ones to blame for steroids when Donald Fehr and the other bosses of the Major League Players' Association fought for years to make sure players wouldn't be tested for steroids? Is it all that secret when the owners of the game put out the word that they want home runs and excitement, making sure that everyone from trainers to managers to clubhouse attendants understands that whatever it is the players are doing to become superhuman, they sure ought to keep it up?

People want to be entertained at the ballpark. They want baseball to be fun and exciting. Home runs are fun and exciting. They are easy for even the most casual fan to appreciate. Steroid-enhanced athletes hit more home runs. So yes, I have personally reshaped the game of baseball through my example and my teaching. More than that, I am glad that soon enough the work I've done will help reshape the way millions of you out there live your lives, too. Why should only top athletes with huge salaries reap the benefits of the revolution in biotechnology that will define our times? Why shouldn't everyone get to ride the wave?

I hope this book will help you get over any biases you may have about steroids. I will do my best to help you unlock your own potential, so that even if you are not a professional athlete, you can look like one and feel like one and, in some ways at least, perform like one.

Prologue

THE FIRST TIME HURTS MOST

I was really scared the first time I used steroids. It all started for me late in 1984 when I was twenty years old. I had vowed to my mother that I would become the best athlete on the planet, no matter what it took, and I was totally focused on making that happen. I came back to Miami after playing minor-league baseball in the Oakland A's system for the 1984 season, and I was more determined than ever to turn myself into an amazing physical specimen. Fortunately for me, I had a friend from high school (I'll call him Al) who knew a lot about steroids and had experimented with them. He had enough firsthand experience to know what the hell he was talking about.

After I finally decided it was time, I looked him up when I got back to Miami. I had asked him a few general questions before, but now it was like I was cramming for a test. I pressed him to give me as many details as possible about how steroids actually worked and what they actually did to you. I was always thinking about trying to make myself better and stronger and faster, and since I was still a runt at that stage, five foot eleven and one hundred and ninety pounds, I knew I had a lot to gain from dabbling with steroids.

The first time I injected steroids was in Al's room, over at his house. We'd been talking about steroids so much, I knew it was just a matter of time before I gave it a try, and one afternoon we went to get something to eat at this pizza joint near Coral Park High and had one more discussion about what I would need to do, and how long it would take to work, and what sort of increases I could expect in size and strength.

I remember being very nervous as we went back to his house. I was worried about allergic reactions and things like that, but at the same time I had my doubts about whether steroids really worked. That may not seem like so long ago, but let me tell you, it was another era as far as knowledge about steroids goes. Nowadays, you can hop on the Internet and dive right into a mass of information about steroids and find out anything you want. There are tons of Web sites that offer precise breakdowns on every steroid imaginable. Twenty years ago, there was not much to go on. You always heard stories about fake steroids, and I was wondering about that, too. Would it be something fake I was injecting? I had no idea. It could be anything. Back then, nobody even knew if steroids were illegal at all.

The first time is strange. You're so scared; your nerves are heightened and you kind of exaggerate the feeling. I'm serious. You actually feel the needle penetrating your buttock muscle that first time. Then the needle is pulled out, and you expect that to hurt, too, but it doesn't. And then it takes about eight to ten seconds for the oil-based steroid to get into your body.

From then on you pretty much know what to expect, and the next time it doesn't hurt nearly as much. Soon you're totally used to it and it doesn't feel like anything, at least no more than pulling off a Band-Aid. I was always trying to learn more by talking to other people who injected themselves, asking them for the details of how they did it right. If someone does it perfectly, you don't feel anything at all. Al was pretty good, and that was lucky for me.

Steroids don't do you any good unless you're working out hard, and that afternoon when Al injected me for the first time, we headed straight for the gym and did an upper-body session, working on the shoulders, back, and triceps. Back then, I was bench-pressing only around 200 pounds, usually five reps. Those first injections were with an oil-based steroid, so it took about two weeks before there were any noticeable effects.

The first thing you notice is an increase in strength. If you stand there in front of the mirror and really check yourself out, you won't see any actual differences for a good two weeks. But you start to feel stronger much sooner. That's partly psychological, but I remember noticing about ten days after that first injection that I really felt stronger, especially when I was lifting. The first injection hurt a little, and so did the others that followed every two weeks or so after that, but to me the pain felt almost good, because I was so determined to live up to that promise I had made to my mother.

Chapter

"YOU'LL NEVER ADD UP TO ANYTHING"

I always told Jose and Ozzie,
"Do better next time."
I'm obviously a very serious man.
I never fool around with anything.
But I was never stern or a dictator.

JOSE CANSECO SR.,
My father

My dad earned a good living in Cuba during the Batista years, working as a territory manager for Esso Standard Oil. He also picked up a little extra cash working nights as an English teacher at the Professional School of Commerce in Havana. He worked hard and was a good provider for our family. As soon as Fidel Castro came to power in 1959, though, my father was smart enough to know that before long the new leftist system would control the entire country, and that would not be a good thing for people like my father. He figured that everything he had worked for in Cuba would be lost, and he was right, too. Soon after Castro came to power, my father lost his job. Then he lost his house. And then his car.

He was in an unusual position in that he had already spent time in the United States studying English. He had gone to Shreveport, Louisiana, as a teenager and lived with an uncle there for several years, starting in 1940, and his time in American schools gave him enough of a grounding in the language to teach it in Cuba. As much as he would have liked to stay in Cuba, his country, he was also comfortable with the idea of diving into a new life in the United States—if that was his only choice.

So my father notified the Cuban government that he wanted to leave the country, and the government basically answered: Tough luck. There was a serious shortage of skilled professionals, and Castro could not afford to lose white-collar workers like my father. The government announced that such workers would only be allowed to emigrate if a specific replacement could be found to handle their particular job. But no one was available who was qualified to take over my father's job with the oil company. The government wrote him a letter saying that because of his professional ability and expertise, he was not allowed to leave the country until further notice. He would have to wait years for them to change their minds.

My dad was born in 1929, in a town called Regla, on the outskirts of Havana. Both my father's parents had come over from Spain and his father, Inocente, had a big, light-green Packard car that he used to earn a good livelihood. He would load six or seven tourists into the Packard and drive them all over the place showing them the sights of Havana. Back then, baseball and boxing were the top sports in Cuba. My dad used to listen to New York Yankee games on the radio; his favorite players were Babe Ruth and, later, Roger Maris and Joe DiMaggio. But my father was not much of a baseball player himself. He shagged a few balls when he was a boy, but that was about it.

My father met my mother, Barbara, when they were both teenagers in Regla. He had come back from Louisiana and was studying at the Institute of Havana, from which he graduated with a degree in English. They used to go ballroom dancing or take strolls together around the town's central park. Sometimes they would go to the movies to catch the latest Errol Flynn picture or sweeping sagas like *Gone With the Wind*.

My parents and older sister, Teresa, were living in Regla in July 1964 when my mother gave birth to me and my twin brother, Osvaldo. People like to say that Ozzie and I were like pocket-sized atom bombs when we were babies, but my father says we were actually nice and quiet. People were always fussing over us. They usually had trouble telling the two of us apart because we looked the same and were the exact same size and weight. But I had a birthmark on the back of my hand, so that helped family members know which of us was which.

Those were bad times to be living in Cuba, especially since the government knew my father did not support their system. My father had to wait until the year after Ozzie and I were born for a chance to leave. The Castro government announced in 1965 that it would allow an airlift of people from Varadero, Cuba, to Miami. Ozzie and I were just babies when my parents took us and Teresa to the airport, where we climbed into a small propeller plane. There was only room for about twenty people inside, and apparently it was stuffy. I don't remember any of that, but it was an important day for the family and we heard about it later.

"It was very, very hot inside the plane," my father used to tell us, looking back on that momentous day.

He would always tell us how sad he was, leaving behind his home country and his parents, and the rest of his family. But he knew he had to do it, and he was eager to start a new life, making the most of his knowledge of English. We were also lucky to have family members living in south Florida, ready to help us out. My Aunt Lilia was there at the airport, waiting to meet us, but first my parents had to go through an inspection. They had no money or identification, but they stripped my father and searched him, and then stripped my mother and searched her, too.

"We had nothing," my father would tell us.

But he had English, and the work experience to land a good job soon after he arrived in America. He found work as a territory manager for Amoco Oil, which was a good position, but to him it was only a start, and he was always looking for other ways to bring in extra income. He also worked nights as a security guard at two different places. We grew up in an average environment, in the southwest section of Miami, but my dad was always working like crazy to improve our position. He always had dreams of bettering himself and took some college courses, and was always studying something.

He never had much extra time, but sometimes he would take a break from his work in the afternoon and drive Ozzie and me to a nearby school in Opa-locka so he could teach us baseball. He started this when Ozzie and I were real small, just three or four years old, and continued for years, helping us develop. We would wait until school was out for the day so we could use the school building as a backstop. We just needed a bat and a ball.

"Jose, see this bat here?" my father would ask me.

"Yes, Dad," I'd say.

"You put that bat on your shoulder and I'm going to pitch the ball to you." "And when I say 'Swing!' you swing, so you can hit it."

Each of us would get ten hits. One would take his swings, and the other would stand behind my dad to field any balls that made it that far. My dad says that Ozzie learned faster than I did, and used to hit the ball farther when we were both little kids, but I don't remember.

Ozzie and I started playing organized baseball when we were twelve or thirteen. You could say we were both late bloomers. We were always just average baseball players, and that was really frustrating for my father. He had worked so hard to give us a good life in America, and he wanted us to do great things. Average was never acceptable, and my dad would criticize us a lot because we weren't better. He would come to all of our games, and every time we would play badly, my dad would scream at us in front of everybody. It was embarrassing and really hard to take. Sometimes we'd leave the game crying.

"You're going to grow up and work at Burger King or Mc-Donald's!" my father would scream at us. "You'll never add up to anything!"

Ozzie and I were both pretty lousy baseball players at that time, and we gave my dad plenty to scream about. But we were just kids, twelve or thirteen years old, and his yelling was pretty hard to take. I guess it kind of stuck with us, even today.

"You stink!" he would shout.

My father was a real perfectionist. He was tough on himself, always trying to do everything in life perfectly. And he was hard on us, too. But my father was expecting too much of us, and we couldn't live up to such high expectations. Now he says he hopes he did not push us too much.

One day, in an effort to help us get better, my father made a deal with us that he would give us five dollars for every home run we hit. He stuck with that long after I had made the major leagues and was hitting plenty of homers every year.

But early on, after he first made that offer, I didn't get many chances to collect. I don't know if it was because my father was always pointing out everything I did wrong on the baseball field, or if it was because I was skinny and weak at that age, but I never felt like I had any real talent as a baseball player. I did love to watch the game, though.

I used to watch the Cincinnati Reds a lot, and on Saturdays I would catch the television show *This Week in Baseball*. Back then, Reggie Jackson was the big hero; he was my favorite player—the big power hitter—and I used to watch him whenever I could and try to study what he did. But I never tried to imagine myself in his shoes. That was just not for me. Guys like me didn't make it.

As a little kid, I played with Rafael Palmeiro and Danny Tartabull, two guys who you just knew were automatic major leaguers. You could just take one look at them and see that they had what it took to become some of the best baseball players in the world. You could tell from watching their swings or checking out the little details about the way they played the game. They were so talented, it was incredible. Palmeiro had the sweetest, most compact swing. Both of them stood out among us kids.

Raffy went on to hit more than 500 home runs. Tartabull finished with 262 homers. Between the three of us, we've hit more than 1,250 major-league home runs. But back then, when we were boys, those guys were way ahead of me. They were already superstars, confident and physically developed at thirteen or fourteen. I was so puny, it was a joke. Now it turns out I'm probably twice their size and twice their strength. Life's funny that way.

Baseball was such a struggle for me. I never even had a set position until I got to high school and started playing a lot of third base. Basically, when you're a kid you just play everything. You catch. You pitch. You play some outfield. You play some infield. You're trying to find what position you'll actually do well in, so you play all over, waiting for something to click.

Ozzie and I kept plugging away, and my dad kept criticizing us. For both Ozzie and me, it would have been a lot harder to handle my dad's constant criticism and yelling if it weren't for our mother. She was always there for us, taking care of us, feeding us. If we got beat up by some other kids—and believe me, that happened from time to time when we were little—we'd go to my mom and she'd make everything better. She was a stay-at-home mom and a great cook. There was always something on the stove, usually Cuban food, and she would look after that and look after us, and she always maintained an even disposition. I don't remember her ever being angry with us, not once, even though sometimes we definitely deserved it. My father took care of supplying the anger.

My mother came from a quiet family back in Regla, the Capas family, and she was just the quietest, nicest lady in the world. All of my memories of her are set in the house. My mother was always restrained in her emotions; she loved Christmas, and I'll always remember the half-smile she had as we decorated the tree. That smile was how you knew she was really enjoying herself. On Christmas Day, when we woke up to find a pile of toys under the tree, my mother sat there beaming at us. She was so giving. I think it must have been her favorite day of the year.

My mom never learned much about sports. My father was the one who took us to practice, telling us what we needed to do to improve. My mother almost never came to our games; she just wouldn't have understood what was happening out there, and anyway that was my father's domain.

My mother was very old-fashioned and hardly spoke any English. She loved to sing to us in Spanish. I remember when we were little, she would put us to bed and sing us Spanish lullabies. My mother was our rock.

She was our protector when my dad had a bad day at work or was after us for some other reason. Don't get me wrong. Ozzie and I were not what you would call little angels. Sometimes we would misbehave and we probably did deserve to get spanked for it. But that was only some of the time. My mom was the one who was always trying to soften the blows or the issues with my dad. From the time when we were young boys and all the way up until high school, Ozzie and I would always run to mom for protection if my dad criticized us or spanked us. We loved her very much.

People always laugh when I tell them what ordinary kids Ozzie and I were growing up, but it's really true. We looked forward to the same things as any other kids, like going to the movies. A lot of times, we would head up to the Jerry Lewis Theater in Carol City, which was a little to the north of Opa-locka, to check out the double features they were showing. I always loved the movies and as crazy as it might sound, I always thought about being in movies myself. That was a dream that seemed more real to me than playing professional baseball.

One weekend, when Ozzie and I were about eleven, we went with our two cousins to see Bruce Lee in a double feature of *Enter the Dragon* and *The Way of the Dragon*. I don't remember much about the plot of *Enter the Dragon;* what I do remember was the action. Bruce Lee was so fast, nobody could touch him, and that was long before computer-generated special effects.

That first time we saw Bruce Lee and all the amazing things he could do, we came out of the theater into the bright sunlight of South Florida and started messing around, kicking each other in an attempt to recreate what we'd just seen. We knew we had to try to learn some of his tricks, and from the beginning we were pretty good at it. It was fun, too. Bruce Lee was so cool; we all wanted to be like him. Back then, he was the foremost martial artist in the world, and not only because he was extremely fast, but also because of his ideas and philosophy. Once we had seen Bruce Lee on screen, it kind of stayed with us. I remember every now and then, Ozzie and I would play around, either kicking each other or trying out some of Bruce Lee's other moves. It didn't take long before we found a way to get some actual lessons to learn how to do some of these things properly. We didn't have enough money to go to a dojo, of course, but a friend knew someone who was an instructor and we were able to arrange private lessons for a group of us, two or three times a week.

I enjoyed those lessons a lot. We were learning Tae Kwon Do, and I took to it quickly. Finally, something I was good at! I was the highest kicker in the group, almost right from the start, and as I practiced more, I got better. The lessons were sporadic, but even when we weren't taking lessons, Ozzie and I practiced by ourselves. We turned into serious students of the martial arts. Later on, as we got bigger, we put that on the back burner, but I knew we would get back into it when the time was right.

A J.V. PLAYER AT CORAL PARK HIGH

Staring down at this poor sap from the pitcher's mound,
his uniform flapping loosely in the breeze,
I remember thinking, Jesus Christ, this guy could
Hula-Hoop inside a Cheerio.
The toothpick's name was Jose Canseco,
and before this game was over, I'd beat him for four
dribbled groundouts and a nice, fat K.

DAVID WELLS,
Perfect I'm Not

You hear many players say that they'd been dreaming about the majors since they were old enough to hold a bat. Not me. I was always a scrawny kid, not very athletic, and in my wildest dreams I couldn't see myself playing at the major-league level. I never, ever thought that I would make it, or that I was good enough. After all, I was so shy and wimpy-looking back in high school, everyone ignored me most of the time, especially the girls. Seriously, I was probably the ugliest kid at my high school. I did have a girlfriend in high school for a while, a beautiful girl named Anna, and I don't even know what she saw in me. I was the ugly duckling.

I remember having a crush on a cheerleader named Dawn Alba, who was drop-dead gorgeous. Every guy at the school must have had a crush on her. She was Cuban, of course, but looked kind of Italian, with dark hair, dark eyes, and an incredible body. You know how high school crushes are. My jaw would drop when I saw her, but I never talked to her. I was basically too dweeby and yucky-looking to approach her.

I never really said much of anything to anyone. I kept to myself, rather than having to deal with communicating with other people. Every week in social studies, the teacher made some of the students go up to the front of the class to give a verbal presentation on something we had been studying. I couldn't do it. It was too scary for me. I would just take the bad grades on the verbal presentations because I knew I didn't have the courage to talk in front of the class. Not once did I go up there. The idea of speaking in front of people made me too nervous. You could have offered me a million dollars to go up to the front of class and speak, and I still could never have done it. I just refused and took a failing grade.

My high school physical education teacher, Glenn Dunn, was also one of our baseball coaches, and he made an effort to bring me out of my shell. We still talk about those days. He'd tell me that if I had more confidence in myself, good things would happen. My brother was always more confident than I was, and that might have helped him make a better impression on people, including the coach. But Ozzie was also more aggressive than I was, and tended to mix it up in a way I didn't.

Coach Dunn remembers that I got in more than one fight at school. But he also remembers how reserved I was. "You were usually laid back," he says. "If four guys started a fight, you would be right in there, kicking butt, but you would never be the aggressor. That was never your style. You never went and picked fights."

He coached me in a lot of ways. "You're a smart person, Jose," he would tell me. "You could be a tremendous student if you just applied yourself, but you really don't care about school."

I'd just nod my head and try to get out of the spotlight.

He was right, though. I didn't care about school because I never felt like I was a part of things. I'm not going to say it was because of my father, and the way he was always so hard on Ozzie and me, but let's just say I was used to having the feeling that I was always doing something wrong. I always felt a little out of it, like I never quite felt the same way about things as the people around me.

I always liked sports, though. I remember sometimes we would have three-on-three basketball games, the coaches against whichever students wanted to challenge them. Sometimes Ozzie and I would play together in those games. Since our father wasn't around, it was just us, so I could relax and have a little more fun. I was still a runt, five foot eleven and 155 pounds, and I wasn't much of a basketball player, either. Coach Dunn told me I was a good natural athlete, but I thought he was just trying to be nice. The one sport I was excited about playing was football, but my parents forbid me from doing that because on my size.

"They'll kill you out there," my dad told me. "There's no way we're going to let you play football."

So I stuck to baseball, even though I was too small to be very good at that, either. I didn't even make the varsity team until my senior year of high school. How many future major leaguers can you say that about? If you're going to be skinny, like I was, you needed to be quick, and I wasn't especially quick, either. It was hard to find a good position to play.

"You're too skinny to play third base," my father would tell me.

The one thing I started doing pretty well was hitting the baseball. I guess I just had good hand-eye coordination or something. Even with that skinny, lanky body of mine, I showed some talent for hitting some baseballs pretty far. That's what people remember who knew me back then.

One time, we had a practice game where half our team was going against the other half. A guy named Val Lopez was on the opposing team, and he was a friend of ours. A lot of times, he would pick us up and give us a ride to practice or to games. He was a pitcher, and that day he threw me a fastball up and in, and I hit that ball as hard as I'd hit a ball up to that time.

"You crushed it!" Val told me.

He couldn't believe it. You almost never saw someone hit a ball on that field that made it to Twelfth Street, which marked the edge of the school. The houses beyond the street were considered untouchable.

"You hit it so far, it nearly hit a house in the air," Val said.

Back then, Ozzie was more outgoing than I was, and we were together so much, it made it easy for me to hang back and let him do the talking. Val, who is now a CPA in Miami, says he remembers me having some kind of presence.

"You always had charisma," he tells me. "When you would enter the game, even at the age of fifteen or sixteen, we knew you were there."

It was true that by then I could drive the ball, and pitchers worried when I would come up. But I was a limited baseball player. I really had no foot speed, and my throwing arm was only decent to average. I never knew where baseball was going to take me. To me, it was psychologically out of my reach to consider playing at the major league level.

Even so, I guess they were impressed by my home runs, because they named me most valuable player of the junior varsity team during my junior year. That, and the fact that the varsity team had lost a bunch of guys to graduation, meant the varsity coaches had no choice but to put me on the team my senior year. I had a good year in varsity, and was named MVP again. I still had a long way to go as a baseball player, but at least I had improved enough to where my father couldn't find as many things to criticize.

He was there at all the games, screaming at us the same way he had been doing ever since we were little boys. If you did something wrong, you always knew you would hear from him. I had a lot more positive games than negative games in high school, and he didn't scream at me quite as much. But even many years later, after I made it all the way to the big leagues and did things no one had ever done in the history of the game, it was never enough for my father.

Think I'm kidding? Let me give you an example: In June 1994, I had a monster game for the Texas Rangers, hitting three homers and finishing with five hits and eight runs batted in. We crushed the Seattle Mariners that day, 17-9. So I talked to my dad after that game, and what do you think he said?

"How'd you do on your other at-bats?" he asked me.

I was dumbstruck. I felt like saying, "Gee, I don't know, I was probably still out of breath from my *three home runs!*"

I don't think I was ever good enough for him. Later on, I could handle that. But back in high school, it was really tough. I was just happy they let me play baseball at all, because I had so little confidence and the whole time I was out on the field, I was always bracing myself to hear some jab from my father. That was definitely the worst part of playing baseball for me.

"Don't scream at us!" Ozzie and I would yell back at my father sometimes, and even though we would be crying, it never made any difference. He didn't listen. You know how parents are.

To me and Ozzie, it seemed like each of our teammates heard every single thing our father said, and we cringed every time he'd rip us for not doing something or just for doing something different than the way he thought we should. But I guess to some of these other guys, whose dads didn't come to games very often, it seemed like it would have been nice to have a father so involved with what you were doing.

"Your dad is dedicated," Val Lopez used to tell me. "He's at games, he's at practices—and you always know he's there."

Another guy from that high school, Pedro Gomez, ended up as a sportswriter in California, covering the Oakland A's when I was in my heyday there, and now he works as an on-air reporter for ESPN. He says I was kind of a character in high school, which just goes to show that different people have different recollections.

"You were like the Judd Nelson character in *The Breakfast Club*," Gomez tells me now. "You know how the assistant principal kept turning the knife into Judd, inside the library, and he would respond by saying things like, 'Does Barry Manilow know you raided his wardrobe?' You just never knew when to turn it off. You were a smart ass."

Gomez was kind of a smart ass, too, the way I remember it. And maybe I did like to goof off back then. It was only high school, you're a different person for every class.

The Oakland A's ended up drafting me in the fifteenth round of the 1982 amateur draft, and that came as a surprise to me. I didn't think I was going to get drafted, and I was amazed even to be picked in the fifteenth round. The scout who drafted me was Camilo Pascual, a star pitcher for the Minnesota Twins in the 1960s, who won twenty games two years in a row.

Pascual's son Bert was one of my teammates at Coral Park High, so he had seen me swing the bat quite a few times, and thought that I had potential. Pascual thought I should have been picked sooner in the draft, and he actually got into kind of a fight with the A's about signing me. I was only asking for a $10,000 signing bonus, which was not much money at all, compared to what other players were getting, but they didn't even want to pay that much.

Pascual couldn't believe it. He thought they were crazy, and he let them know just where he stood. He was in a meeting with the A's general manager, Sandy Alderson, and all the scouts, and maybe an owner or two, and he reached into his pocket very dramatically and pulled out his wallet.

"You don't want to give this kid his bonus?" Pascual asked them. "I'll pay the extra amount from my own pocket. That's how sure I am that Jose is going to make it."

They decided to sign me, and to be honest, I wasn't that thrilled by the news. People always assume that if you get signed to play professional baseball, you must be unbelievably excited, like it's one of the best moments of your whole life. I didn't feel that way. Probably a lot of ballplayers have the same feeling, but don't talk about it. Basically, I was too scared to be very happy. I had no idea what to expect, and it seemed totally obvious to me that I didn't belong, and soon enough they would realize it had been a mistake to sign me at all. I just had no confidence in my abilities. I was always waiting for bad things to happen.

So when I talked to people about my future, I tried to play down what baseball meant to me. My attitude was more like, *Hey, I have nothing better to do.* I figured that once my brief experiment in professional baseball ran its course, and I had shown the whole world that I didn't have what it took, I could go to college and figure out what kind of work I wanted to do for the next forty or fifty years. My plan was just to give baseball a shot for a few years to make sure I wouldn't have any regrets later.

I played in Idaho Falls in the Pioneer League that first season as an eighteen-year-old, and that was a big change. A predominantly Mormon community, Idaho Falls was a long, long way from South Florida. We hardly had any money, so seven or eight of us all lived together in a place that was almost condemned, it was such a dump. It had no heater, no nothing, and if you wanted to use the bathroom, you would have to wait until you went to the ballpark.

A lot of us slept on the floor there, and we took to calling that place the "Animal House." I was making six hundred bucks a month. I'd send some of that back home to my dad, because I had hardly any expenses. I had two pairs of jeans I wore all the time, when I wasn't in uniform, and only paid thirty bucks a month in rent. People in town felt sorry for us, because we were living on so little, and they would give us coupons so we could eat two breakfasts for the price of one and stuff like that.

You could say I was the mascot in the Animal House. I was a scrawny young kid, so a lot of times the other players would pick on me, telling me I was stupid, that I sucked as a baseball player. That was an old tradition, the older guys hazing the younger guys, picking on them and running them down. You expected it as the natural order of things, but still, as a skinny eighteen-year-old kid, I got picked on more than anyone. They would just throw me around from one to the other and ridicule me all the time.

"What are you thinking?" they would all yell at me. "You're never going to make it to the major leagues!"

We had some fun times there. One player I knew there, a heavy-set guy named Greg Robles, was probably the funniest person I've ever met. He never made it to the major leagues, but a couple years later he did hit three home runs in one game, playing minor-league ball in Madison, Wisconsin. He was definitely the funniest guy in baseball. He had these dumb magic tricks that he would do, and those always busted everyone up. You have to see it for yourself, but to give you an idea, we would be having a family party, with kids and everything, and Robles would set up a whole gag involving a slice of pizza.

"I'm going to eat a slice of pizza now," he would tell everyone.

He would eat it, and then drop his pants and bend over—and a slice of pizza would fall out of his ass. It would hit the floor—whap!—and no one could believe their eyes. He'd set it up beforehand, of course, wedging it between his ass cheeks, but even if you knew that, it was still funny. I know it's pretty revolting, but I've got to admit, it still makes me laugh, thinking about that crazy guy.

Idaho Falls made a big impression on me, and not because of anything having to do with baseball, either. That was the first time I ever drank liquor. Back home in Miami, I had tried beer and wine, but I was not a big drinker at all. I'd never touched the hard stuff. So one night at the Animal House, there was a bunch of guys and girls drinking and they invited me to take part and join them. I didn't realize until later that the reason they had invited me was so they could get me drunk and laugh about it when I made a fool out of myself.

I was young and innocent. It sounds funny now, but it's true. Like any kid, inexperienced and shy, I was just trying to be part of the crowd, so I started drinking and trying to keep up with them. The thing was, they gave me this bottle that was just nasty. I think it was something like 120 proof. At the time, I had no idea what I was drinking. I just drank—and then I noticed that everyone around me couldn't stop laughing.

"Come on, drink another!" one of them would say.

So I drank one or two.

"Come on! One more!' someone else would cry out, and so I drank one or two more.

That didn't last very long, as you can guess. Pretty soon I was in really bad shape. I almost died of alcohol poisoning. I was sick the next three days, and on the fourth day I was still recovering. That's how bad it was. It traumatized me so much; it gave me a lasting distaste for liquor.

To this day, I don't really drink much, especially not hard liquor. Maybe it was good that I had that traumatic experience because it really shook me up; I never forgot it.

As for baseball, I didn't make much of a mark playing in Idaho Falls. I played in twenty-eight games in the Pioneer League, and only hit two homers. I think I barely hit .260 there, and I could not have been less impressive. I still didn't have any meat on my bones; I'm sure I looked like just another kid who wasn't going anywhere.

Things turned out a little differently.

A VOW TO MY DYING MOTHER

One year later . . . Canseco and I would cross paths again . . . and I was stunned to find that "the Idaho skinny guy" had somehow grown up to become a freaking Macy's balloon. Brand-new biceps ripped out from under his uniform sleeves. Thick slabs of beef padded his formerly bony frame. A pair of tree trunks now connected to his ankles. Seven innings and two 450-foot moon shots later, I still had no idea what to make of this new improved mutant. Was this kind of super-size growth spurt even possible? What the hell was this monster eating?

DAVID WELLS,
Perfect I'm Not

So much has changed since then: Now there are so many huge Latino stars in the game, it's totally common to have several Latino players on your team, or a lot more than that. But I remember as a Cuban kid in the A's farm system at that time, I was very aware that baseball was closed to a young Latino like me. That was only twenty-three years ago, but for baseball it was a completely different era.

There were no Cuban players at the major-league level at that time. Previously, there had been some great Cubans, like Luis Tiant, who actually pitched in six games for the California Angels that year, before finally retiring at age forty-two. That same year, another great Cuban, Tony Perez, turned forty—and was still playing, too. Perez had made his name with the Cincinnati Reds, but he had become more of a part-time player by the end, and bounced around from team to team. Still, he could always hit and actually batted .328 in 1985, not bad for a forty-three-year-old.

But they were the exceptions that proved the rule. Many talented young athletes were playing street baseball in Cuba, Puerto Rico, the Dominican Republic, and many other Latin American countries, but the barriers to breaking into the major leagues were almost impossible for most to get around. Later, it made me mad that there was such a pervasive double standard for Latinos, especially compared with an all-American boy like

Mark McGwire. But back when I was eighteen, I just figured it was the way it was. If there were no Cubans in baseball, there must be a reason. Who was I to think that I was going to make it to Major League Baseball?

My second year in the minor leagues, 1983, I was still a long way from making any kind of mark in baseball. I was kind of sleepwalking through games at that point. I played in almost sixty games for Class-A Medford in Oregon that summer, and I had almost two hundred at-bats—but I still only hit eleven home runs, and my batting average was less than .270. True, I was considered the most powerful hitter in the Northwest League, and I did make the All-Star team, but I was a long way from looking like a major leaguer. I also played some games that year in Madison, Wisconsin, which was also Class A, and I had three homers in thirty-four games, and my batting average was .159. How's that for impressive?

Even during that off-season, I was still in a fog when it came to baseball. If you had asked me at the time what I was doing, I wouldn't have known what to tell you. But looking back, I can see I was just going through the motions. The next season, 1984, they sent me to Class-A Modesto, the next step up. And I got off to a pretty good start there—until a call from my sister brought that period of my life to an abrupt end.

My mom had been sick for years, going back to a bad blood transfusion in Cuba in 1964 that infected her with hepatitis. She had to take medicine for the hepatitis, and that was bad for her diabetes. My whole life, she was sick with hepatitis and diabetes. A lot of times she was really weak and had to stay in bed. But in 1984 I got a call from my sister, Teresa, and I knew that this time it was different.

"Come home," she said. "Mom is sick."

"What's wrong?" I asked her.

But that was all she would say. I knew it was really bad. My mother had been suffering so much, just getting weaker and weaker. She had a blood clot in her back, and it had somehow worked its way to her head. They admitted her to Miami's Cancer Research Center that weekend, but the terrible headaches she was having only got worse. I flew back to Miami to see her and went right to the hospital, but by then she was in a coma. She had never seen one of my minor-league games, and when I got there, the doctor told me she never would.

"The brain is dead," the doctor told us. "That's it."

We stayed with her in the hospital, but there was absolutely nothing we could do. Once the brain dies, that's it. Her body was being kept alive artificially with some machines, and we had to make the decision to disconnect her from life support.

I went into shock and cried for hours. I just couldn't believe that my mom was dead. Out of nowhere, overnight, she was suddenly taken away from me, and I would never be able to talk to her again. She had protected me and my brother all those years, and gave us so much love and support and encouragement—but she would never see me play professional baseball. I was a wreck. I was just devastated, and all my family members knew it.

We went through the whole process of burying my mom, remembering her, honoring her, and mourning her loss together as a family. I needed a few weeks afterward before I could even think about playing baseball again. By the time I got back on a plane to fly west and rejoin the Modesto club, I had gone through a complete transformation.

I'd had some time alone with my mother, there in the hospital, and even though I knew she was already gone, that was my mother lying there, and I sat close to her and looked at her and had one last heart-to-heart talk with her.

"I'm going to be the best athlete in the world, no matter what it takes," I told her, and I choked up and had to fight back tears.

"I promise you, Mom, that I will be the best."

The doctors can say what they want about her brain being dead, but still, I know she heard me make that promise, wherever she was, and I have always taken that promise every bit as seriously as if she had responded, "Yes, Jose, I know you will."

So from that moment on, I dedicated my life to living up to that vow, and I didn't care what it took. No matter what the price, it didn't matter, I was going to turn myself into the best athlete in the world.

Up until that time, I'll be the first to admit I didn't always work very hard. People thought it was because I was lazy, but actually, it was really just a question of me not seeing a future in baseball. I like to think things through, and baseball looked like it would lead to nothing but disappointment, like almost any Latino could expect to experience. But after that promise, I stopped thinking like that. I just willed myself to put everything I had into improving.

I finished out that season with Modesto, playing decent but not great ball, with fifteen homers and an improved batting average. Then I was invited to instructional league. That was when I really got down to business. I started an extensive weight-lifting program, and that was the beginning of a whole new approach for me. I just ate, drank, and slept baseball.

That was it for me, nothing else. There were no girls. There was no going out. There was nothing. The only thing that went through my mind every single day was constantly thinking: How can I become better? How can I become faster and stronger? How can I gain more knowledge of the game? How can I learn more about my body and its potential and what I can do to unlock that potential?

I was hitting the weights hard at the 24-Hour Nautilus Gym, which was five miles away from where I was living. Every day after practice I would walk the five miles, lift weights until I couldn't lift my arms in the air, and then I would walk another five miles back home, every day. That was hard, but soon it didn't feel like enough of a challenge, and then I actually started jogging it, both ways, to get faster and stronger.

At that time, I hardly had any money and couldn't even afford to buy myself a car. Maybe that was good in a way, because all that jogging back and forth helped me get into great shape, but I remember how every time I would jog one way or the other, I would pass this particular Chevrolet dealership. I'd look at all those shiny new cars, lined up in rows, and that gave me one more reason to work hard and get bigger and stronger. As I went by, I would say to myself: One day I'm going to buy myself a Corvette. And later I did—I actually got two Corvettes at once, and all just for doing a TV commercial for a dealership in California.

To give you an idea of how insignificant I was to the organization back then, one time during instructional league that year I had a first-hand look at the way racism and the double standard worked in baseball, at least at that time. I was a nobody to the A's, a fifteenth-round pick and a Latino. There was a huge contrast between how they saw me and how they saw their golden boys, like Rob Nelson, a big, left-handed power-hitter who was a dumpy-looking six-four, with 220 pounds of soft muscle. You could tell he had never worked out, never lifted weights, but the A's picked him in the first round of the 1983 draft.

I remember one day we were working on a drill where the pitchers would make a move over to first base and throw the ball, trying to pick you off, and we were supposed to get our leads and then dive back to the base ahead of the throw. I took my lead, and when it came time to dive, I did, but this guy Rob

Nelson caught the ball and slammed his mitt down, hitting my elbow. I couldn't believe that he would make a big, awkward tag like that, even if it meant hurting a teammate. He struck me so hard on the elbow that it started swelling up right there.

"What was that?" I asked him. "Look what you did to my elbow. It's swelling up."

Nelson didn't like me calling him on it like that, and he and I got into it, talking back and forth. But that didn't last long.

"What the hell are you doing?" one of the coaches yelled at me, and gave me a real strange look.

"That's our No. 1 draft choice," he told me. "Who are you to talk to him that way?"

He seriously said that to me. I wasn't allowed to tell someone he shouldn't act like a thug, that's how little the organization cared about me. They decided to show me how ticked off they were with me, too. They weren't content just to yell at me a little. They wanted to make sure I got the message that I wasn't good enough to speak to this big, dumpy-looking, inconsiderate guy. So they got together, talked it over, and cooked up what they thought was a really clever scheme.

Then came the humiliation. They decided that for a couple of days, I would have to be a bat boy. For a couple of days, I didn't play at all, just fetched bats. I was the first one they had ever tried to ridicule like that, making me run around to pick up after them. They all taunted me the whole time, like I was some kind of animal.

"Wow, you really make a good bat boy, Jose," someone would say.

"You missed one, Jose," another would add. "Come on, right here, come on, right here, boy, hurry up."

Nothing could explain treating a person that way. I remember even some of the head guys laughing at me, telling me I should consider making a career out of being a bat boy.

If my father had taught me anything, it was pride, and they were trampling on that. I did my best to ignore what they were saying, trying not to let it bother me. Somehow I got through the first day as a bat boy, hoping they would relent and one day would be enough. But I came back the next day and found out they were serious about making me be a bat boy again for another day.

"Hurry up and pick up that bat," one of them said.

And finally, it was too much. I didn't say anything to anybody. I just walked off the field, went straight into the clubhouse, sat there by myself, and started to cry. I decided then and there that I was going to quit baseball. I couldn't believe they were doing this to me. It felt as if I had no choice but to quit. It seems short-sighted now, but at the time, it felt like they wanted me gone and I didn't want to be there. I'd just have to find some other way to live up to the promise I had made to my mother.

Then I heard something that made me stop crying. I was in the clubhouse all alone and I heard someone coming. I had wanted some time to myself, and I didn't want to talk to anyone. But it turned out to be Howard Ashlock, a minor-league pitching coach in the A's organization at that time and one of the few people who really took an interest in me.

"Listen, Jose, they're just testing you," he told me.

Ashlock had been paying close attention. He'd been watching them pushing me, trying to see how much I could take.

"It's ridiculous," he said. "They know you're an emotional, volatile kid, and they want to make an example of you."

I was packing my stuff as he talked to me. I was going to leave and never look back. I'd made a vow to my mother to be the best athlete on the planet, but it was my mother who taught me that if someone is treating you like dirt, you have to stick up for yourself and protect your dignity. I was sure she would have wanted me to walk away rather than take any more of that. But Ashlock helped me think it through; he helped me realize that if I walked away, those jerks came out the winners.

"Don't quit the game," he told me. "You have a lot of talent and ability. Go back out there and don't let them get to you."

I went back out and finished the day as a bat boy. Then I went home and tried to put it behind me. The next day, I was playing again. We had a game at HoHoKam Park against the Cubs and my first at-bat I hit a shot to dead center, 500 feet over the center-field wall. My next at-bat, I hit another home run over the center-field wall. That was a real turning point for me and my future in baseball. From that day on, the Oakland A's treated me as a serious talent. They had seen what I could do. They even named me the No. 1 prospect in the A's farm system. I was also rated as one of the top two or three prospects in all of baseball at that time. I had come a long way in instructional league.

"By 1984 Jose's name was already buzzing throughout the organization," says Pedro Gomez of ESPN. "The only prospect everyone was talking about was this Cuban kid from Miami."

But what happened that day at HoHoKam was no accident. It was the result of a lot of hard work and dedication. I was really focused, and I was determined to show everyone in the A's organization what I could do. I wanted to make it clear to them what kind of ability I had. That was my way of living up to the promise I had made in that hospital in Miami.

I wasn't going to stop there. I wanted to become faster, stronger, better, more powerful than any other athlete. I did it all for my mother, and the promise I made her, but hitting home runs never made me feel any better about losing my mom. I'd trade it all away in a second if it could bring my mother back. Even now, not a day goes by when I don't think about her.

"THE NATURAL"

*Jose was the buzz of all of baseball that year. Everyone
in the game was aware of him and what he was doing
at Double-A Huntsville and then later that year at
Triple-A Tacoma, and finally his September call-up.
It was truly one of the most amazing single seasons in
the history of the game, especially considering
he did it at three levels.*

PEDRO GOMEZ,
ESPN

I t's just human nature to feel awkward and afraid when you first experience something, and when I had my first couple shots of steroids, I was so nervous it was just ridiculous. I was so scared of putting this external liquid in my body. I didn't know what it was going to do to me. But after a while it becomes so easy, it's incredible. Steroids become like a friend. You come to understand them and how to benefit from them and how to use them properly and mix them with other chemicals, whether oil-based or water-based. You start seeing the effect that using steroids has on your body with the proper exercise and proper nutrition.

I guess you could say it was kind of ironic. I was doing steroids to live up to the vow I had made to my mother, but my mother would never have understood if she had found out that I was using steroids. She was an old-fashioned mom; I'm sure she never heard of steroids. If I had told her about it, she would have no idea what I was talking about. She would have assumed they were just some sort of supplement.

I gained weight little by little. But I was always sure to be careful. Some people go crazy with steroids, and just bulk up absurdly. But from the beginning, I was trying to use steroids more for strength and stamina than for size. I didn't want to go overboard. I was also careful not to talk about steroids with people, except for a very small circle, mostly Al and my brother. The three of us talked about it a lot. Ozzie was curious, too, but he didn't start using steroids until later. As I mentioned, Al injected me the first few times, and my brother injected me sometimes, too, and later on other baseball players injected me sometimes. I was dating this girl Linda during my rookie year, and sometimes she would inject me.

People always talk about how steroids can't give you hand-eye coordination, and in a sense that's true. If you've got no natural ability, steroids aren't going to give it to you. But if you are naturally athletic, steroids can enhance whatever you have, both in terms of strength and stamina, and also in terms of hand-eye coordination and performance. For example, I noticed that during the season, most athletes get tired. You start out great, but you lose 20 or 30 percent of your strength and bat speed. A player who started out hitting a lot of home runs would taper off toward the end, because he was just physically tired. Since I was new to it all, I didn't know that steroids could help you with that.

One by one, I gained an education into what various steroids could do. I did a lot of experimenting, since that's how I learned things. I started with the light stuff that off-season before the 1985 season, your basic testosterone, liquid form, combined with some Deca Derbol. I lifted weights seriously all the way through to spring training the next February. Coming back from Modesto the previous year, I'd weighed only 180 pounds. A few months of work at the gym—and my new steroid regimen—made all the difference: I arrived at spring training in 1985 twenty-five pounds heavier than the year before, and it was all solid muscle.

"Wow, you've been really working hard in the off-season," the general manager, Walt Jocketty, told me. "You've really been working the weights."

"Thank you," I said.

What else was I going to say? I had started transforming my body, and already looked more like a bodybuilder than your typical baseball player. The strength gains were just incredible, and I was really creaming the ball. I had a great spring training, and thought I was going to make the A's Major League roster right then, even though I had only played as high as Modesto in the Class-A California League. I almost did, too. But they decided that I wasn't quite ready, so I was sent to Huntsville, Alabama, which is Double-A.

To be blunt, I disagreed with them about my not being ready. I knew I was, and I didn't feel like wasting any more time in Double-A before I got to the only place where I could prove they had been wrong. That was the Oakland A's. If you look at my stats in Huntsville, they were incredible. I hit .318 with twenty-five homers and eighty RBIs, all in only fifty-eight games. I set so many minor-league records, it was a joke. I bounced up to Triple-A Tacoma, Washington, and just kept hitting. I hit the ball clear out of the stadium in Washington, something no one had ever done before, and nothing gets people talking like long home runs.

The organization pretty much had to call me up to the A's, and I made it there in time for the last twenty-nine games of the season. Between Double-A, Triple-A, and the major leagues that season, I hit forty-odd homers with 140 RBIs, and batted over .300—and that was even though I broke my finger and missed four weeks.

And I can tell you now: Steroids were the key to it all. I was such an improved player, and I think it was because steroids not only give you a lot of physical strength and stamina, they also give you a mental edge. Think of it this way: whenever you drink one of those energy drinks or eat one of those health bars, even before you finish the thing you're feeling better. It could just be sugar water and a candy bar, but mentally, you're feeling like you could run up a wall. It pumps up your confidence like you wouldn't believe, and for any athlete, that's a very potent combination. When your physical ability is there, your strength and stamina are there, and when your confidence level is up as well, the combination can carry you a long way. Wow, I realized, these chemicals *work*.

Soon I was injecting myself, and getting good at it. You learn to turn your leg at an angle, to give yourself a better target, and you become an ambidextrous injector, because you definitely are going to want to hit both sides of your glute. One week you would hit your right side, the next week you would inject the left side. If you keep hitting the same spot, you're going to regret it, and I mean in a big way. It can get nasty.

There are others muscles that can be used, like the quad or shoulder muscle, but if you're a baseball player you don't want to use the shoulder muscle, because you're constantly catching and throwing. You don't want to use your quad muscle, because you're running around too much. Some athletes have injected themselves in the shoulders, the quads, and the calves, but I don't do that and I don't recommend it. One time, I tried injecting myself in the shoulder, and it was very painful. It gives you a bruise and you end up with lasting pain. You only shoot yourself in the shoulder with water-based steroids, which allow you to use a smaller-gauge needle, as opposed to oil-based steroids with their larger-gauge needles.

As I experimented more, I started trying different categories of steroids. Different types do certain things to the muscles, the skin, the hair, the eyes, and your quick-muscle-twitch fibers. Every steroid played a different part. And when you combined them with growth hormones, the effect was just incredible.

It was actually pretty funny that year, 1985, when I was having such a great run at three different levels. Back when I was at Double-A Huntsville, the fans were so excited about what I was doing, the home runs I was hitting, and my whole style of play that they started flashing THE NATURAL—you know, like the Robert Redford movie—up on the scoreboard whenever I would come up to bat. It was ironic, but the name stuck: Later, when the A's put me on the cover of their media guide for 1986, the headline was THE NATURAL.

I was the first to use steroids in baseball in a serious way, and no one in the organization had any idea what was going on at that point.

"I know I never thought: 'Oh, he must be using steroids,'" says Howard Ashlock, the A's minor-league coach who convinced me not to quit when they made me work as a bat boy.

"It never entered my mind. That was 1985. I don't think people started talking about steroids until much later—probably not until 1991, when Lyle Alzado, the former Oakland Raider, died of a brain tumor after speaking out in public about the risks of steroid use. That was when steroids became more of a social issue."

So off to the big leagues I went. Lucky bat, lucky syringe—luck had nothing to do with it. My first big-league homer was off Jeff Russell of the Texas Rangers, who was only twenty-three at the time, just starting out like I was. Back then, before they rebuilt the Oakland Coliseum to make room for the Raiders, it was probably the most difficult ballpark to hit a homer out of. Russell threw me a fastball, and when I connected with that, it nearly landed in the ice plants out in dead-center field, one of the few balls that ever made it that far back.

I hit .302 for the A's during my September call-up, and had thirteen RBIs to go with five homers, all in only ninety-six at-bats. I was just a twenty-year-old kid, tall and lean, but what I noticed was, I was far stronger than someone my size should have been. My strength and my stamina were just incredible. I really had the feeling that I could hit a baseball six hundred feet.

Back in Miami, the Cuban-American community got really excited about everything I was doing, and about what I might accomplish in the future. There are a lot of very passionate, very smart baseball fans among the Cubans in Miami. But even in the 1980s, we Cubans felt almost as if we weren't even part of the game, once Tiant and Tony Perez got older. As a young minor-league player, I had been convinced I had no chance of making a mark in baseball as a Latino, let alone making it all the way to the major leagues. But here I was, a big Cuban, and I was doing these things that had people talking.

"If you went into any of the little Cuban coffee shops in Little Havana, that's all *anyone* was talking about. It was 'Jose this' and 'Jose that,'" Pedro Gomez remembers. "Nobody was talking about Palmeiro or Tartabull."

You can imagine what it was like after the season when I went back to Miami. People would stop me everywhere I went. The way they saw it, everything I was doing was for them. Gloria Estefan was huge at that time as an entertainer, but in the world of sports, I was the biggest thing to come out of Miami. They were so proud, they even invited me to take part in the annual Eighth Street Parade (Calle Ocho), and I stood up there on one of the floats, waving to people.

"You're the best athlete I've ever seen," people would tell me all the time.

One funny thing about that year: I got back to Miami and my father lived up to the promise he had made years before to pay me five dollars for every homer I hit. So that year, I hit forty-one home runs. When I saw my dad after the season, he handed over $205 in cash. He kept doing that for years after that, too.

I worked really hard that off-season, lifting weights at least once a day and learning more and more about steroids. I was doing more experimenting with different types of steroids: Winstrol, Equipoise, Anadrone, Anavar, and more. I started realizing that, using the proper combinations of steroids, there was almost no limit to how much I could continue to improve as a baseball player.

I was educating myself on all aspects of steroids—from why they were invented, to their chemical makeup, how to use them properly, what dosages, how to cycle off, how to cycle on, which steroids did what for the body, which one was good for strength, or for quick-muscle-twitch fiber, or for foot speed. I wanted to keep getting better and better every year, and I was seeing that the steroids could help me do that.

It was almost like I was becoming a machine, built for baseball and nothing else. I could never slack off. There was too much to absorb, too much to learn, and too much to do. I learned all about the proper technique to become a better runner. As I got bigger and heavier I actually got faster, because I knew how to run the right way. The weight I put on was pure dense muscle with hardly any fat, and every exercise I did was fast and explosive. I was working out like a sprinter, not a baseball player. I was built like a football player and had incredible strength. I concentrated on putting on weight by doing only exercises that incorporated quick muscle-twitch fibers. I was training the way no other baseball player had ever trained. And the results were starting to show.

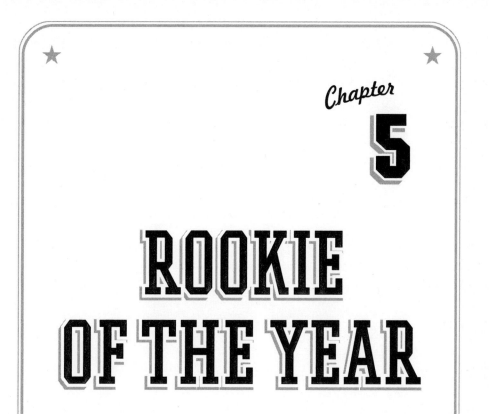

ROOKIE OF THE YEAR

The A's unquestionably have power. In Canseco, they feel they have a new Mantle.

RON FIMRITE,
Sports Illustrated, *April 14, 1986*

One of the most important things that happened to me during my rookie year had nothing to do with baseball. That February, just before I flew out to Arizona to start spring training with the Oakland A's, I was at my favorite spot in Miami, the Scandinavian Health Club, doing one of my last workouts of the off-season. I was feeling pretty good, knowing I was in the best shape of my life, and I was looking around the gym during my workout, the way I always do. Steroids aren't the only thing that can boost your testosterone levels, let me tell you. So can seeing a beautiful woman—and believe me, in Miami there were as many stunning women as you will find in any city in the world.

I've always had a thing for women who are fit and strong, and the Scandinavian Health Club offered a smorgasbord of possibilities. Tall women. Short women. Blondes, brunettes, redheads. Latinas, white girls, black girls, Asians. You would see every kind of beautiful woman in there, but I had never seen a woman quite like the one I spotted that February just before spring training. Damn, I get weak in the knees just thinking about it now.

She had green eyes and dirty blonde hair and an incredible body, and she stood out so much from all the others, it was like she was traveling at Mach 4 and they were all at a standstill. She was spectacularly beautiful and had an exotic quality, especially in her eyes. It was only later that I found out that Esther (that was her name) was Lebanese on her father's side and Cuban on her mother's. As shy as I was, I still knew I had to meet her. I kept waiting for an opportunity to walk over and talk to her in between her sets, but the right moment never presented itself.

All of a sudden she was gone. When I realized she had walked out into the parking lot, I went after her. She probably thought I was crazy, but mostly she was just doing her best to ignore me. I asked her out, and she didn't say yes, but she didn't say no, either. I had to wait to follow up, though, since I had a long base-ball season ahead of me and wouldn't be back in Miami for any length of time until the next October. By then she had been voted Miss Miami, 1986, and I had been voted American League Rookie of the Year.

I remember sitting on the plane taking me out to Arizona, and having a lot of questions about the year ahead. I figured I had a good chance to make the team. I'd shown some talent in my performance the previous September, when I hit over .300 with five home runs, including some of the longest home runs ever hit at the Oakland Coliseum.

The whole Oakland A's organization had embraced me, but I wasn't taking anything for granted. That was never the way I thought. To be honest, I was really nervous going into spring training that year. I had these huge doubts about whether I be-longed. I also wondered if I was going to be accepted by the other players, especially the veterans.

I find it funny how people think they know just what you're thinking and feeling, even when they are way off. It became a cliché in the media to say that I was conceited and arrogant, but in fact, I was never that type of individual. My whole time in the major leagues, I was never completely convinced that I be-longed there. I was never sure that I was good enough to be on the same level as all these amazing athletes I was competing against every day.

I was probably more insecure than every other athlete there, and that was especially true my rookie year. I felt like a kid who had been let out on the field by mistake. I would see these great athletes walking by, as if it was no big deal, and I would just be gawking at them.

"Wow, there's Dave Kingman," I'd say to myself.

Then a minute later I'd be staring again.

"Wow—that's Reggie Jackson."

Sometimes, it was all too much. *Look at these guys!* I'd be saying to myself. *What am I doing here?*

I was just a young kid, twenty-one years old that spring, and in a lot of ways, a young twenty-one. I'd been such a late bloomer, it was still a huge shock to me just to be taken seriously as an athlete. I'd watched all these guys on TV. I'd seen all these famous ballparks on TV. I just couldn't help myself; no matter how much I tried to be calm, I was in awe of the stadiums and starstruck with the players.

People would laugh if they could hear the kind of pep talk I was always giving myself back then.

"Slow down, Jose!" I'd say.

"Try to control your emotions."

"Your adrenaline is flowing too fast."

"Easy!"

If you let your adrenaline take over, everything seems too fast and too out of control. You have to slow everything down to your pace. When you're hitting and everything seems slow and easy, you're locked in. When you're hitting and everything seems like it's accelerating superfast, beyond your control, then you're in trouble. It took me a long time to understand that, and in my rookie year, I was all over the place. I would hit a huge home run that had everyone talking, and then I would swing so hard at a bad pitch that I would almost injure myself. When you're working with steroids and your muscles are so dense, you're strong enough to swing your shoulders right out of the sockets.

No one really showed me the ropes, either. A lot of times a veteran will kind of take you under his wing and tell you what's what. I never had that kind of relationship with a veteran when I was an A's rookie. I didn't have the nerve to bother any of the veterans with questions, for starters. I was just a quiet kid and kept to myself whenever I could. Nobody really knew anything about me. They might have been surprised to know that I was too scared to ask these players for advice, but that's how I was. I'd see someone like Dave Kingman, who had been hitting mammoth homers for years, and I'd think about getting his autograph more than asking him about his stance.

Later in my years with the A's, we had a group of guys who had been together for a while and knew each other really well. You might not like everyone. Someone like Carney Lansford and I were never going to click, for example. But you knew where you stood with everybody, and they knew the same about you. But in 1986 we were in a rebuilding mode, trying to accumulate new players, so it was like musical chairs. The team looked different all the time.

It wasn't like we were all the same age, either. We had a lot of younger guys and a lot of older veterans at the same time. Everybody was just getting to know each other, so you really didn't have that much fun together, or play practical jokes on each other, or anything like that. Usually, you don't play practical jokes on someone you barely know. That stuff comes later.

We were just trying to crawl out of the cellar in our division, and even though I was a very quiet kid, very shy, I was supposed to be like the savior of the organization. They had already built me up so much when I was in the minor leagues, before I ever put on an A's uniform, because they wanted to generate some excitement and bring some fans out to the ballpark. In some ways, I was never fully accepted, but because of the buildup, it was kind of understood that I was a part of the mix. Everyone was like, "Okay, now Canseco is here. Get on with the show."

Fortunately, I got off to a good start that year, and the veterans seemed to be impressed.

"Damn, this guy knows what he's doing," I'd hear them say to each other.

But I was just getting by on my raw ability. It was going to take me a long time to learn how to hit consistently at the major-league level. Much later in my career, I became much more knowledgeable about the game and became a guess hitter who studied pitchers on videotape carefully. I thought long and hard about what a given pitcher was likely to do in a given situation. But that only happened after years of soaking up as much information as I could as a hitter, watching and learning and picking up any extra advantage I could.

Back in my rookie year, it was *see ball, hit ball.* I was a pure re-action hitter. You hear that term all the time, reaction hitter, but what does it mean? Just that you react to the pitch in flight. You never pick up any signs beforehand. You never really see the rotation of the ball. You never say, "In this situation he's going to throw a breaking ball down and away, so look for it down and away." I was on the edge, winging it, but because I had so much physical ability, and so much strength, I was able to get away with it. Swinging the bat and hitting home runs was fun, but it was also nerve-wracking, trying to prove myself, and then watching how the media tried to figure me out. At that point, I was just trying to figure myself out.

That first year in the major leagues went by fast. Maybe it was because everything was so exciting and new to me. I got off to a great start; I was selected for the All-Star Game, even though I was a rookie. The game was at the Astrodome in Houston, Texas, that year. I walked around trying to take it all in. There I was, an All-Star, and I just couldn't believe it.

Roger Clemens pitched three perfect innings for the American League and ended up as the most valuable player of the game. The manager that year was Dick Howser of the Kansas City Royals. The American League hung on for a 3-2 win, but it was so close, Howser never even put me into the game. It felt weird to make the trip to Houston and never even do anything but sit around and watch. But later it turned out that Howser was really sick, which put it all into perspective.

"I remember the indignation all of Miami had after the 1986 All-Star Game," says Pedro Gomez, my classmate back at Coral Park High in Miami. "A few months later, it was revealed that Dick Howser had a brain tumor and died, and all the old Cubans in Miami pointed to that as the reason Jose did not play—because the guy had no brain."

I was glad to get back to Oakland after the All-Star break and rejoin the A's, but I got off to a terrible start. I had one bad game and then another and another and another. The whole thing just snowballed on me. I started the second half going 0-for-40, which if you think about it is pretty hard to do. It was the worst slump of my life, hands down, one of those times when everything went bad all at once.

Every time I hit the ball hard, it went right to someone. It felt automatic, like the whole thing was out of my hands. Let's say there was a guy on first base, and he'd take off to steal, and the second baseman would break to go cover second base, and then I'd hit a line shot that would be a base hit up the middle nine times out of ten, or ninety-nine times out of a hundred, only this time the second baseman would be right in the path of the ball, so he'd catch it and instead of a base hit, it would be a double play.

I was striking out plenty, too, believe me, and finished that season with 175 strikeouts, which ranked third in the league and was far and away the most strikeouts I've had for one season in my whole career. I didn't know how to handle it.

"What's going on here?" I would say to myself. "This is crazy. Does this happen to other players?"

It was also a great learning experience. My stock had gone up so high so fast, and then just like that, it came down again. You can never get too comfortable in baseball or the game will find a way to shrink you back down to size. Slumps are just part of baseball, and all you can do is find a way to work through them. Fortunately for me, the A's organization believed in me and gave me the chance to stay in the lineup to work my way out of it— which I did.

We went to Detroit for a series against the Tigers. Walt Terrell gave me a good pitch to hit. I took a big swing and hit a home run to center field that ended up in the Tiger Stadium upper deck. They told me afterward that I had already hit a home run in every American League ballpark as a rookie. After that, the slump was behind me.

That September we played the New York Yankees in Oakland, and I had four hits in what ended up being a 9-8 win for us. One of those hits was a home run, which gave me 100 RBIs, making me the first player in baseball with 100 RBIs at that point. I finished with thirty-three home runs, which was fourth best in the league, and 117 RBIs, which was second best.

Back then, hitting thirty homers in a season was like hitting fifty nowadays. But at the time, I didn't think of it as a lot. I knew I still had a lot of work to do. There were so many aspects of my game I had to improve. I couldn't really enjoy my successes as a rookie when I knew I had so many weaknesses that I would have to work on before I could live up to my ability.

Everything about me needed improvement. I needed to get bigger, stronger, smarter, and more patient at the plate. But the thing I was most focused on was speed. Even though I stole fifteen bases as a rookie, and only got thrown out seven times, I knew I had the potential to steal a lot more bases. But I could only do that if I learned how to harness my speed and develop a more explosive first step, which makes all the difference when you're trying to get a good jump down to second base. I was so rough back then, I was focused on everything from cutting down on my strikeouts to psychological strengthening.

People forget, but even for a home-run hitter like me, the mental part of baseball was always important. I was still nervous at times, or overexcited. What you find out as you play more games is that the more knowledgeable you become, the more insight you have into playing in a certain ballpark or facing a certain pitcher, the more it helps you focus and become that much more intensely involved with the game.

That came with time, but it was a hard lesson, believe me. As I said, I never had anyone to train me or show me the way. That might have helped me a lot, especially since I was so much younger than most of the other players, even though I was expected to help carry the team from my rookie year onward.

I always had the feeling that I was doing everything my own way. I was basically creating my own road as I went. There was no paved road for me to follow—it was like I was down in the Amazon, using a machete to cut my own way through to where I wanted to go. It was a slow process doing it that way.

The more years I had under my belt, the more I learned how to be myself without trying to break rules all the time. My strike zone refined and got smaller. Early on, I would swing at just about anything—high, low, inside, outside, you name it. I remember one time swinging at a pitch way up over my head. I had to reach so far for it that when it ricocheted off my bat, the ball slammed into my helmet. I swung at balls in the dirt all the time, and the funny thing was, I couldn't figure out why. I was so reactive at that time, and often so nervous, I was just a wild swinger. I wasn't concentrating on the right area.

But that was part of what got people excited about watching me. People used to say that watching me swing and miss was more entertaining than watching other hitters swing and hit a home run. I was swinging so hard, like there was no tomorrow, and they knew that if I got all of a ball, it would do things they had never seen a baseball do before.

Probably the funniest example of that was a game in Anaheim early in my career. I still have this play on tape. Mike Witt threw me a slider down and away, and I took a big swing and made good contact, but off the bat it looked like a low liner to the shortstop, Dick Schofield. He actually jumped up in the air, thinking he was going to catch it, that's how low to the ground it was. But it sailed over his head, and as it headed toward the outfield, it just kept rising. I hit it with such good backspin that it hydroplaned like a golf ball, and just rode the wind all the way out of the ballpark.

"There's a line drive over short," A's announcer Bill King said over the radio. "It's in the gap! It's gone!"

It was freakish. I ran hard down to first base, thinking it was a line drive just over the shortstop's head, but all of a sudden I saw it go out.

"Did that ball really go out?" I asked someone.

I couldn't believe it. That was probably one of the best technical swings I've ever had in my life, and I guess it proved that you
can hit a home run that never gets higher than twenty feet off
the ground. As I ran the bases, the other players were all giving
me shit about it, saying they couldn't believe it went out. We
were all laughing. It just goes to show, you never know what
you're going to see any one day at the ballpark. I like to think I
made people feel that way a lot of times in my career.

As soon as I got back to Miami that off-season, I started
thinking about Esther, that half-Cuban, half-Lebanese exotic
beauty I had met in February just before I flew out to Arizona
for spring training. I was hoping I'd run into her at the Scandinavian Health Club, but no such luck. I was not someone to go
out of my way to run after a woman, but this was different.

"You remember that girl Esther I met?" I asked a Miami friend.

"You kidding me?" he said. "She's Miss Miami. How could I
forget her?"

"Where does she live?"

Lucky for me, he knew Esther's address. I went by her house
and introduced myself again and started talking to her. As soon
as we started dating, it was all over with. I was crazy in love with
her. But the thing was, she was worried about what her father
would think of me.

"I can't tell my dad I'm in love with a drug dealer," she told me.

She was serious—she thought I was pushing drugs. After all, I
wore expensive clothes; I drove an expensive car; I was big
enough that no one would want to mess with me. I had never
talked to her about being a professional baseball player. I wasn't
big on conversation when there were so many other ways to
spend our time together. Esther's father, who had been one of
my baseball coaches in junior high school, was not about to let
her move in with me unless we were married. Two years later, we

had a big ceremony with three or four hundred people. That was the year I hit forty home runs and stole forty bases and was the most valuable player in the American League. The media wanted to get involved. They had helicopters in the air, trying to find us, as if we were a Hollywood couple. It was crazy, which was how things were through most of my marriage to Esther.

Dave Stewart, my teammate with the A's, had bet me that I wouldn't really marry Esther; if he lost, he had to pay for the wedding. So once we announced the date, he started getting nervous—especially as we kept inviting more and more people. Eventually, I let him off the hook: I only made him pay ten thousand dollars.

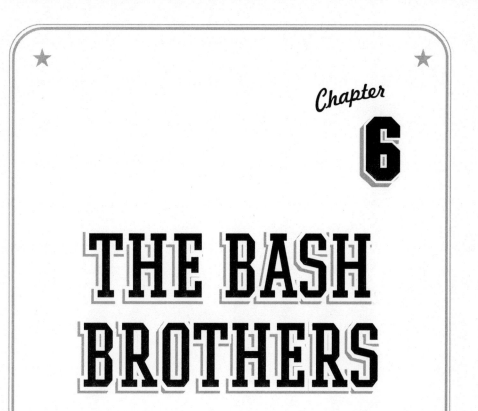

THE BASH BROTHERS

If Mark McGwire belongs in the Hall of Fame, so does Jose Canseco.

JOHN WILLIAMS,
Slate *magazine*

Mark McGwire showed up as an Oakland A's rookie in 1987, my second full year in the major leagues, and I'll never forget what he looked like back then. I remember going down to Arizona for spring training that year and seeing this tall, skinny kid with basically no muscle on him whatsoever. He was six-five and weighed only 220 pounds.

But McGwire had one of the best—if not *the* best—right-handed power swings I'd ever seen in my life. I thought: *Wow, this guy has technique.* He proved it was a great swing when he went out that season and hit forty-nine homers. He was named American League Rookie of the Year, so he and I were back-to-back Rookies of the Year.

Mark and I were a lot different, but from his first season with the A's, we became friendly. We were never really buddies, though. One of the main things we talked about was steroids—about how to tailor your doses and cycles to achieve the best results. We had access to the best steroids; it was like shopping from a high-end catalog.

Like me, Mark was curious about what different types of steroids could do for him, and how they could make him bigger and stronger. But he needed a little time to get used to the idea of actually using them, and so far as I know, he didn't actually start using steroids until after his rookie season. So the forty-nine home runs he hit that year probably came without any chemical enhancement.

The next year, 1988, Mark and I started talking about steroids again, and soon we started using them together. I injected Mark in the bathrooms at the Coliseum more times than I can remember. Sometimes we did it before batting practice, sometimes afterward. It was really no big deal. We would just slip away, get our syringes and vials, and head into the bathroom area of the clubhouse to inject each other.

Nobody knew that much about steroids back then and nobody really knew what we were doing. As the years went on, more and more players started talking to me about how they could get bigger, faster, stronger, but at that time, as far as I know, Mark and I were the only ones doing steroids.

The media dubbed us the Bash Brothers, but we were really the 'Roids Boys. Eventually, based on all that hype, I realized that people actually believed that we were living together, that we always hung out together, that we ate together, that we slept together. "Where's your other half?" people would ask. "Where's your brother?" It was laughable the way people built up these ideas in their minds based on a gimmicky slogan.

We hung out here and there, but Mark didn't like to go out with me because the girls wouldn't pay any attention to him. They would all pay attention to me. That was mostly because of Mark. He was never the best-looking guy in the world. He felt awkward and out of place at clubs, plus he would never talk. I was quiet, too, but compared to Mark, I was a social dynamo. Mac just didn't like to go out because it felt like he was being overshadowed.

I always had a presence, and at the time, I was the most famous athlete in the world because of the way I looked, what I did to a baseball, and what I accomplished in the game. Also, I was a rebel and a rogue, and some people liked that edge. Mark was kind of a second-level star in those years, not nearly as famous as he would become later in the summer of 1998, but even so, he had things I did not. For starters, as a white all-American boy, he was accepted in a way I never could be as a Cuban. I guess at that time in the United States of America, it was taboo to have someone like me as an all-American hero.

There was this contrast between us, and from the very beginning, they pitted us against each other as competitors. Who's better? Who's stronger? Who hits the ball farther? Who is more dangerous? Mark always hated those comparisons, even more than I did.

I think it was only through using steroids and giving himself a new body that Mark really became more comfortable with himself, and stopped being quite so awkward around other people. I was the godfather of the steroid revolution in baseball, but McGwire was right there with me as a living, thriving example of what steroids could do to make you a better ball player.

Early in Mark's career, he went through the same transformation that I did. Suddenly, he was enormous. He developed these huge, muscular arms; his whole body was just massive. He kept with it and added more and more muscle mass. Later on, the year he and Sammy Sosa were both going after Roger Maris's single-season home-run record, McGwire would set the record, weighing in at 270 pounds.

In recent years, as the public has come to understand how widespread steroid use has become in baseball, there's been a lot of speculation about where Mark's natural talent left off and the steroids kicked in. The answer is that steroids gave Mark strength and stamina—but they also gave him a more positive attitude.

The psychological effect of steroids is very dramatic. Using steroids properly can do wonders for your confidence. You look good. You're big and strong. McGwire was a twitching mass of muscle, and he had great technique. If that combination doesn't help you feel confident, I don't know what will.

The mind is a very powerful thing; if you convince yourself that you're a great player, and you have the basic ability, you're going to be a great player. You can have the perfect body for baseball and perfect ability, but if your brain is telling you "You have no chance!" you're not going to be successful. For Mark, steroids helped send his confidence level sky-high.

McGwire was a good twenty pounds heavier than I was, but guess what? For some reason, where McGwire was concerned, nobody ever mentioned steroids. What was going on? McGwire was already being groomed for superstardom. Baseball has always been on the lookout for players who could be packaged and marketed as all-American heroes, and McGwire was perfect for that: a big, awkward redhead with a natural home-run stroke. As all of us in baseball knew, McGwire was an untouchable. He was so protected by the powers that be in the game, it was incredible. No media outlet would even think of calling him into question, because there's no way they'd ever get an inside source.

To McGwire's credit, he was a little slow to understand what it was all about. I remember one time in the late 1980s, we were all sitting down together in the A's clubhouse talking about something that had appeared in one of the papers, declaring that Mark McGwire was the all-American boy and the all-American athlete. We mentioned it to McGwire, and I looked at him to see what he would say.

"Jose, I didn't want to be labeled like that," Mark told me.

I think he meant it, too.

"Mac, you know what?" I told him. "Now you're protected. You're protected by America. Nobody is going to touch you no matter what you do wrong."

It started to sink in with him that I was right.

"It's great to have that kind of backing by America," I told him. "You are set. You can never do anything wrong. You could rob a bank while raping a cheerleader and nothing would happen to you."

That's how the system works. There are some players who are protected by the system, and other players who the system abuses and takes advantage of, hanging them out to dry and turning them into scapegoats. It's disgusting the way baseball really works sometimes.

Walter Weiss, the shortstop who became the A's third straight Rookie of the Year in 1988, after me (1986) and McGwire (1987), once told me a story about the day when Mark and Walt were racing their cars after a game at the Coliseum, and this old lady was driving along really slow, and they forced her off the road. But what happened? Where was the media frenzy after that? Nowhere. After all, this was Mark McGwire, the golden boy, so everybody covered it up—the organization, the police, the media, everyone.

Just imagine how an incident like that would have been handled if I had been involved. That was the pattern throughout our entire careers. Whether it was on a personal or professional level, you never heard the media breathe a bad word where it came to Mark McGuire. Everything was whitewashed. Meanwhile, my divorce was on national TV. That was how the deck was stacked, and Mark knew it and we all knew it: He could do no wrong, and I was always going to be the subject of controversy.

Think about if for a minute. How much of what people think they know about me goes back to the image of me portrayed in the media? How much of that feeds on itself, with people assuming they know what I'm like, and turning that into new controversies that convince more people that I'm all these bad things people say I am? Where does perception start and reality end? When does perception create reality?

The truth is, no one wants to face the fact that there was a huge double standard in baseball, and white athletes like Mark McGwire, Cal Ripken Jr., and Brady Anderson were protected and coddled in a way that an outspoken Latino like me never would be. The light-eyed and white-skinned were declared household names. Canseco the Cuban was left out in the cold, where racism and double standards rule.

Let's be honest: Back in 1988, no one wanted a Cuban to be the best baseball player in the world. Maybe it's different today, because there are so many great Latino superstars out there. But in 1987 and 1988, who were the great Latino ball players? There was only one; it was just me.

And when I became the first player ever to hit forty homers and forty stolen bases in one season, I was hands down the best player in the world. No one even came close. But who wanted a Cuban to be the best player in the world? Imagine doing something that had never been done in a major sport like baseball. I remember at the beginning of the 1988 season, the media guys asked me if I had any goals for the upcoming year.

"Well, I plan on doing the forty-forty—stealing forty bases and hitting forty home runs," I told them.

They laughed at me. I couldn't understand why.

"What's so hard about it?" I asked them.

"You know, no one's ever done it before," one of the reporters told me.

So what? I thought it was no big deal. "Well, I have the ability to do it," I said. "So why not do it?"

People always cite that example to prove I was ignorant. But who had the last laugh? I knew something the reporters didn't. I knew that all my hard work, and the right combination of steroids, had already made me a much better athlete than I had been before. I knew I was far beyond what any of them could conceive of in terms of my body and its capabilities.

Already by that point, I had become much faster, and even though I was up to 235 or 240 pounds, I had learned how to move that weight quickly. I incorporated technique with explosive speed, and I had enhanced my muscle-twitch fiber to be able to move much more quickly. Also, I knew that steroids would improve my stamina and keep me strong and explosive throughout the long baseball season. I incorporated all of that and did the forty-forty.

"That was great," my father finally said, but mostly he told other people that, not saying it to me directly.

The double standard began to kick in that year, at least when it came to media coverage. We won our division and went to Boston to play the Red Sox in the American League Championship Series, which we ended up sweeping. But suddenly you heard a lot of talk in the media: *Oh, Canseco had this forty-forty year because he's doing steroids—Oh, he's an obvious steroid user.*

I remember one time Harmon Killebrew was doing commentary for a game between the A's and the Twins. When I came up to bat, he said: "I saw Canseco in the minor leagues and I've never seen a player change so much so drastically."

What a joke. How about McGwire? He went through an even more dramatic change than I did—you could see that just by comparing him in his rookie year with the A's, when everyone saw him, to how he looked a few years later. But nobody even cared what McGwire was doing.

He used to hide behind big, oversized shirts, but McGwire had the largest arms in baseball—twenty-one inches, and forearms like you wouldn't believe. But no one ever made an issue of it.

That was the pattern, from that year on. It started circulating a little bit that I might be doing steroids, and more and more reporters were criticizing me for gaining all this weight and stacking up the home runs. McGwire just kept getting bigger and bigger, but he was always protected by the media and by the organization.

And me? I was left out to dry.

MY FIRST LAMBORGHINI

Dangerous car. What if you're doing a mere 50, do you have the illusion of being parked and try to step out of the car?

SPORTSWRITER SCOTT OSTLER,

After I was pulled over for doing 125 in my Jaguar and said the car was so smooth, I thought I was only doing 50 mph

As long as I can remember, I've always loved cars—especially fast cars. So many baseball players drive sports utility vehicles now, rather than sports cars, but I don't really understand it. If I had two weaknesses in my life, they would have to be fast cars and women. I never spent that much money on other stuff. Some baseball players were into piling up a lot of diamonds and jewelry and expensive clothing and shoes. Other guys had a passion for houses and wanted to have them all over the place. But cars and women were really enough for me. When I drove fast, it would be at nighttime on a deserted road. I never put anyone in danger. Nowadays, you see guys driving fast in heavy traffic and swerving in and out. I never toyed with death—not that way.

Most of all, I loved the power and the look of a really fast car. It was such an adrenaline rush, knowing you had six or seven hundred horsepower under your hood, and at any time you wanted, you could just step on it and shoot past any other car on the road. That was a great feeling. I was never into long car trips. That didn't make much sense with those high-horsepower cars. I don't know how they could take traveling over a hundred miles. I'd mostly just use my sports cars to go back and forth to the ballpark, or out to dinner, or to a club.

Nothing can quite match the first time you buy yourself a brand-new sports car. Esther and I drove down to Santa Cruz, about an hour south of Oakland, to Bruce Canepa Motors. I was really excited driving through the Santa Cruz Mountains.

The car was a custom-built Porsche 911 Turbo Slant Nose, and I'd heard a lot about what a great car it was. We pulled up and I got my first look at the 911, a white-and-black convertible, and it was so beautiful, I just stared at it endlessly. Bruce told us all about the car and how it handled. He used to race cars on the circuit, and he was very knowledgeable about high-performance cars.

We got in to take a spin through the Santa Cruz Mountains, and Esther decided she'd stay put rather than squeezing into the small back seat. It was a good thing she did, too. We were driving through hills and mountains and Bruce was taking these turns so fast, the back end would spin out. This man made me shit my pants; I thought I was going to die. But he was in complete control of that machine.

I had to buy it, no two ways about it. It cost me ninety grand, but driving the 911 back home that day was such a great feeling. I loved that car. It had the perfect engine and the perfect combination of speed and handling, and I liked that it was a convertible so I could just let the wind blow. That was the first sports car I ever owned, and I really should have kept it; today the Porsche 911 Turbo Slant Nose is considered a classic. But later on, I ended up selling that car to Ivan Rodriguez. I wonder if he still has it today.

My second sports car was a Ferrari; then I picked up a Corvette, the car I'd been thinking about for so long, jogging past the dealership on my way to the gym. (Actually, I got two of them.)

A white Lamborghini came soon, and later I bought another. There was also at least one Jaguar in there, metallic red with twelve cylinders, and a BMW.

I think at one point I had twelve cars. Soon after I met Jessica, who became my second wife, she came to see me in Texas, and in the garage I had a '93 Testarossa, a Lamborghini, a white Ferrari, and my 930 Porsche—not to mention the Chevy Suburban parked out on the street. When Jessica needed to drive to Arlington Stadium, my housekeeper, Vera, told her to take her pick.

"Just go in the garage and take one of the cars and meet him at the game," she told Jessica.

So Jessica went out into the garage and just stood there, looking at all these sports cars. Then she turned back to Vera.

"I can't drive any of those cars," she said.

But Vera insisted, and Jessica ended up driving my Porsche to the ballpark that night. (She did fine.)

At that time, I had built up a pretty nice collection of modified Porsches. I had one of them custom-made with 820 horsepower; that car was probably the fastest street-legal Porsche in the state of Florida, if not the whole United States. I used to race motorcycles on the highway with that thing. I'd be out on I-75, and motorcycles would want to race me. They thought they could beat me easy, but that Porsche could do about 240 miles an hour. I'd be racing those motorcycles going almost 200 miles an hour in third gear, and they'd freak out. They couldn't believe how fast the car was. I took it up to 200 miles an hour one time, just to see what it could do, but never faster than that.

The fastest I've ever gone in a car was 202 miles per hour. That was in my Lamborghini Diablo, which cost me about $225,000 and had license plates saying "40-40." Once, when I first moved to Weston, Jessica and I took the car down I-75 in Florida—which was a new road back then. There were no cars out there at all, and we were all alone with all that newly paved highway.

"*Wow, how fast is a Diablo?*" I started thinking. "*I wonder if it can really do 205 the way they said it can.*"

So I decided to find out. I took that Lamborghini up to 202 miles an hour—I remember watching the needle creep just past 200. The Diablo is wide and low, flat to the ground; the faster you go, the more you hug the road. It's basically a detailed race car and handles the speed like a dream.

Once I hit 202, we passed a cop, and he flashed his lights at me. I didn't want to take any chances and was going to slow down.

"Listen, the exit is only about three or four miles up," Jessica said. "Why don't you just keep going?"

Like an idiot, I listened to her. We kept going, blowing right out of the cop's reach, but then only a mile farther down the road, there was a bunch of cops waiting for me. I had slowed down, but I was still going about 120 when I reached them.

They pulled me over, and I sat there waiting for these cops to walk up to the car. I was so worried, I started sweating and shaking. "My God, these guys are going to put me in jail," I told Jessica. "My career is over. I'm going to be arrested. I'm done, completely done."

These two young officers walked to the side of the car. I reached over to roll down the window to talk to them; I was so jumpy, my hand was shaking. They saw that, and they knew I was nervous.

"Don't worry, Mr. Canseco, we're not going to arrest you," they told me. "We just wanted to see the inside of your car." The Lamborghini Diablo had just come out then, and these young cops had never seen one before.

I sat there staring at them for a minute.

"Here, take my car," I said after a minute. "You can have it."

Then I started joking with them.

"Go ahead, take it for a ride," I told them. "You can do whatever you want." Apparently, I could, too; those cops let me off the hook.

Another time, I had that Diablo with me at spring training in Arizona. I parked it at the team hotel and was off with the team when someone staying at the hotel backed his Ford Escort into the Lamborghini, causing twenty thousand dollars in damages. But what can you do? I came back later and talked to the driver of the car and even autographed a baseball for his son. As I've said, despite my reputation, I'm basically a calm person.

I think with age certain things change in your life. I'm forty years old now, and my main priority is my daughter, so I don't need fast cars. I still have my Bentley and my Escalade, my Mercedes, and so forth, but I really don't need ten or twelve cars anymore. I think my favorite car right now would be my Bentley, for its combination of luxury, looks, and sports-car power. It's a 450-horsepower turbo, it's all handmade, and it weighs two and a half tons. Not bad for a practical family car.

I loved the feeling of going fast, but some other players would get scared if you took them out on the open road and let it fly— which made for some pretty hairy episodes. One night back in 1990, I was back in Florida for the off-season, and Frank Thomas was one of several players who had come down there for a card show. We did what we had to do at the card show, pocketed the cash, and decided to go out afterward.

Frank rode with me in my Ferrari. We were leaving the restaurant, and two Porsches pulled up and wanted to race me. That happened a lot in Florida. If you had a car like that, people always wanted to see what it could do. So the next thing you knew, Frank and I were racing these two Porsches—or I guess I was doing the racing and Frank was just holding on for dear life. He was already really nervous at that point.

We had the Ferrari out on the highway doing about 130 miles an hour, and I didn't realize that up ahead, the highway was turning right on the short side. Frank, sitting in the passenger's seat, had a better view. I could feel him tensing up.

"Jose!" he said.

"Frank, I got it," I told him.

"Oh shit!" he said.

I downshifted and braked hard and the Ferrari went into a spin. We almost hit the railing, but I pulled out of it easily enough, and once I did, I glanced over at Frank. I've never in my whole life seen such a big guy look so scared. Frank thought for sure I'd killed us both. He was white, just stone-cold white—which is kind of unusual for a black man.

IMPORTS, ROAD BEEF, AND EXTRA CELL PHONES

*If you're really interested in finding out
about a city's pro athletes, go straight to
where they hang out...strip clubs.*

ZEV BOROW,
ESPN The Magazine

Here's something you probably don't know about Roger Clemens: He's one of the very few baseball players I know who never cheated on his wife. I was amazed by him, to be honest. His wife should be very proud of him. You see all these other guys—oh, my God, every chance they got, they would be hitting the strip clubs. They would have extra girls staying in the team hotel, one room over from their wives, so they could go back and forth from room to room if they wanted. They would have their choice of women in damn near every city imaginable.

Roger was the exception to that. I went out with him a bunch of times when there were beautiful women around, and he had a lot of opportunities and never took them. I was with him enough times to realize: This man never cheated on his wife. He was one of the rarities, the anomalies, in baseball. I can hardly think of anyone else who *never* cheated on his wife. I wish I could count myself as an exception, but I can't.

Sex is a big part of the game. The main reason is that it's just so easy to find. Wherever baseball players go, women want them. The women let the players know they want them and they make themselves available. I truly believe that if it weren't made so easy for them, 60 percent of baseball players wouldn't cheat at all. But it's just made too easy for us. We're men; we have egos and libidos, and that's a tough set of forces to combat.

The women I was involved with were always drop-dead gorgeous; you just couldn't turn them down. You never lost any love for your wife at home. But men are men, and many of us want something different than our wives back home. That's just human nature, even if your wife is spectacularly beautiful and you're truly in love with her. Men can cheat at times without having it mean anything at all. The only problem is that you might find a girl, realize that you really like her, and start to have a real relationship with her—that kind of thing tends to damage your marriage.

When I was out on the road, men I'd never met before were trying to hook me up. On two different occasions, I went to do a card show and, at the end, when they were supposed to be paying me, one of the organizers pulled me aside and made me an offer.

"Jose, for your payment, you can have sex with my wife—and I'll watch," each of these guys said.

"I'll take the money," I said.

But I was no prince. Sometimes, when I was down in Anaheim hanging out in my hotel suite with a few friends and business associates, and we would organize beauty contests with twenty or thirty girls. We would have these great-looking women all gathered in the suite, and they would parade around in bathing suits as we played the part of the judges, with an elaborate rating system and everything. Based on those ratings, we would choose the top fifteen girls—and then later, after the game, we'd take all fifteen out with us in a limousine to hit some clubs.

I always saw myself as more of an entertainer than a baseball player, and I was always very up front about it. Some people didn't like to hear that back then, but now I think most people have accepted that baseball is as much an entertainment business as a game. I never had a problem with thinking of baseball as entertainment. Actually, I always enjoyed that part of it.

People used to like to come out to the ballpark just to watch me during batting practice. When *People* magazine named me one of their fifty most beautiful people, I just laughed—but I think it was because they saw me as an entertainer, too.

I was a novelty. I was six four, 240 pounds, and I could run the forty-yard dash in 4.3 seconds. I was unusual looking for a baseball player, and I think that kind of fed the public's curiosity about me. That was definitely true of women. They wanted to meet me, and talk to me . . . and see where things led from there.

Did I sleep with a lot of those women? Sure I did. But I'm not talking about outrageous numbers of women. That was never my style, trying to work on my personal statistics. I know Wilt Chamberlain says he slept with thousands of women, but that sounds crazy to me. I don't keep count, but if I had to guess, I'd say maybe a couple hundred. I know a lot of ballplayers who have slept with far more women than I did in my years on the road. It's an ego booster to have women wanting to be with you, and there's always a natural need for companionship on the road.

Strip clubs were always very popular with baseball players. You had plenty of money for tips and drinks, and didn't have to think twice about it. And people usually don't bother you in a strip club the way they would in a regular bar. Every city had a quality strip club where all the ballplayers would congregate.

There were always sex acts going on in the strip clubs. Any players could get a blow job, and plenty of them had sex with strippers. I never had sex in a strip club myself—not in any way, shape, or form. I may have fondled a girl in there, but I was always too scared that there would be cameras around to try anything more serious. It was much better to hook up with a beautiful stripper and then go back to your place. As I mentioned, I happen to have a specific taste for women who are very fit. I'm in great shape, and I've maintained my body, so I respect people who stay in shape, too. I like fitness models—not to the point where they are bodybuilders, but lean and ripped. It's just what I enjoy. I don't like women who are too tall, or too fat. I'm very picky when it comes to women. They can be blonde or brunette or redheads; that part doesn't matter to me. But they have to be a certain type—around five foot three to five seven, and with a good lean physique and a real appetite for exercise. I've never really deviated from that.

There was kind of a code among baseball players about how you got away with things on the road. We always looked out for each other. Let's say I went out and ended up bringing three or four women back to the hotel. I'd call up my friends on the team.

"Meet me in the room," I'd tell them. "I've got three or four girls here. I can't handle all these girls, so come and hang out with us."

Usually these girls travel in packs, so you'd make sure that her girlfriends would hook up with your baseball buddies. Most of the time, I'd have a big suite; we'd have some fun there, and then guys would disperse, going back to their own hotel rooms with one or two women.

Sex is such a big part of life on the road, baseball players have some techniques and habits that most people don't know about. Here are a few.

SPECIAL TREATMENT

If a girl is gorgeous and I want to impress her and make sure she comes back, I call it *special treatment.* That involves catering to her—you know, completely tending to her needs, not your own. That can mean anything, from a little massage or a foot rub to licking the toes you're massaging—really taking care of her, and for a long period of time. The idea is to do everything per-fectly—which helps to make sure you'll get a second date.

OTHER PLAYERS' WIVES

I can't mention any names, but it wasn't at all unusual for players to sleep with other players' wives. I can remember several occasions where a player would bring his wife or fiancée out with the rest of us to a nightclub when the team was on the road. If the player knew he had a big day ahead of him—say, a pitcher who knew he'd be on the mound—he would go back to the hotel early, and his wife or fiancée would stay out with the other girls. Then, if she was feeling a little lonely and had a few drinks, she would come on to you.

Some players in that situation were only too happy to take the wife or fiancée up on such an offer. That kind of thing happens a lot in baseball, especially when the woman wants to get back at her husband or fiance for sleeping with another woman. Some players even exchanged wives. I was never into that kind of thing, but there were plenty of other guys who were willing to pick up the slack.

SLUMP BUSTERS

As everyone knows, baseball players are very superstitious. Players who are struggling start talking about how they need to go out and find something to break their slump. And often enough it comes out something like this: "Oh my God, I'm 0-for-20. I'm going to get the ugliest girl I can find and have sex with her."

That was never for me. I'd rather go 0-for-40. I never believed in the superstitions of baseball, like the idea that if one day you go four-for-four, you have to do all the same exact things the next day. I never bought into any of that—and I sure never went out and looked for a slump-buster. But it was a term you heard a lot. It could mean different things to different players, I guess. It could mean the woman was big, or ugly, or a combination of both. One manager I used to play for described a slump-buster this way: "She's so big, you don't even know if you're in there or not."

Mark Grace defined a slump-buster as the "fattest, gnarliest chick you can uncover, and you lay the wood to her."

However you slice it, it was bound to be unpleasant.

Sometimes players used the slump-buster line as an excuse: If their teammates started razzing them—"We saw you with that girl last night and she was ugly as hell"—the player would say, "Hey, she was just a slump-buster." But as often as not I think the players just couldn't do any better.

But there were always some players who believed in the power of a slump-buster. They were ready to try everything they could to get out of a slump, and if that's what it took, they would go out and find it.

ROAD BEEF

This one is pretty simple: Any girl you met on the road and had sex with was referred to as "road beef." I wouldn't say the term had any special meaning or special connotation. It just meant a piece of meat, a piece of ass for the player to enjoy while he was away from home. Just about every player I ever knew used that term.

IMPORT

What's an import? Let's say you got a hankering for your favorite road beef, one of your quality girls. If you decide you want to see her before you're scheduled to be in her town, you just pay for a plane ticket and fly her in. That way, you spend time with her, get to know her better, not just in her city but anywhere you want. That's an import. I know one player who went on a family trip with his fiancée, broke up with her, and returned from the family trip with a different girl. That's why most organizations have forbidden girlfriends, even fiancées, from flying on family charters any more—they don't want to be in the adultery shuttle-bus business.

SECOND CELL PHONES

Most baseball players keep a Little Black Book, like guys have been doing for years and years. But technology has changed this, too: Nowadays more and more players keep a separate cell phone in their locker, registered to a John Doe alias, which they use to call all their girls.

This kind of thing can get a little tricky. Some players have tried keeping two numbers registered on the same phone; just punch in a special numerical code, and the second number would pop out. I did that myself for a while, but I got caught with it. One day I called my second wife from the wrong number by mistake, she looked at the caller ID, saw it was a slightly different number, and realized what was going on. That was pretty stupid of me, and she wasn't happy about it.

Before I wrap up this chapter on men, women, and baseball, there's one other, er, little matter I want to set straight.

In general, I would say I've noticed very few side effects from my steroid use. I've had my system completely checked. I'm perfectly normal. But that's because I know exactly how to use steroids—what combinations to use and for how long. But people still hear all kinds of strange things about the side effects of steroids. For instance, I've always had a little nervous twitch—even when I was younger—but people are constantly jumping to conclusions and saying, "Look—he's so juiced up he's twitching." I just tell them, "I've been married twice and divorced twice. That's enough to give anybody a nervous twitch."

But one definite side effect of steroid use is the atrophying of your testicles. I can confirm that. Whatever size they start out, they will definitely shrink if you are taking steroids over a period of time. But here's the point I want to emphasize: what happens to your testes has nothing to do with any shrinking of the penis. That's a misconception. As a matter of fact, the reverse can be true. Using growth hormone can make your penis bigger, and make you more easily aroused. So to the guys out there who are worried about their manhood, all I can say is: *Growth hormone worked for me.*

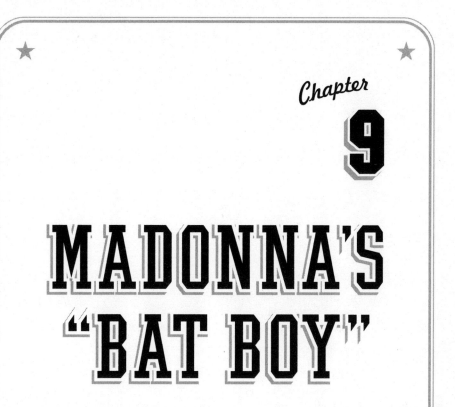

Chapter

9

MADONNA'S "BAT BOY"

He was Michael Jordan, Steve Young and Dennis
Rodman all rolled into one. He was a Hollywood star,
and the playing field simply was his stage.

BOB NIGHTENGALE,
The Sporting News

I always thought Madonna was very sexy, and I always wanted to meet her. I'd listened to all her records and saw her in *Desperately Seeking Susan* when it hit the theaters in 1985. By that time, she had pretty much become the Marilyn Monroe of our time, not just a sex symbol but a larger-than-life personality. The whole world was infatuated with her.

Later on, once I had established myself with the MVP Award in 1988, I found out that Madonna was as interested in meeting me as I was in meeting her. Of course, I found that intriguing. Madonna heard about me through her publicist, who checked me out one day when I was playing against the Giants during spring training in 1991. She couldn't wait to call Madonna after that.

"There's this guy you gotta meet," her publicist told her.

By then Madonna had decided that she wanted to have a baby; specifically, she wanted to have a baby with a Latino man. She had developed a real infatuation for Cubans—all Cubans— and she put out the word that she was on the lookout for interesting Cuban men to meet. Somehow our representatives contacted each other, and right away all these rumors started flying that Madonna wanted to meet me, even though at the time I was still married to my first wife, Esther. To me, it was all hard to believe.

"Who am *I*?" I kept asking myself. "This *athlete* is going to meet *Madonna*?"

But I did want to meet her. I was sure it would be interesting. So when the A's headed off to Anaheim on a road trip, I decided to go see Madonna. I brought along my agent at the time, Jeff Borris, and we drove up into the Hollywood Hills the day of a game to meet her and get acquainted. I remember parking in front of her house and honking the horn, then watching as the door opened up for a minute. This head popped out to take a look at us, and then disappeared again.

"Was that Madonna?" I asked my agent. "It didn't even look like her."

We both kind of stared at each other, not sure what to think. Madonna at that time had black hair in an unusual style, parted down the middle; she didn't look anything like what we were expecting. We sat there in the car, waiting for something to happen, until finally she came out and brought us back into her house.

She looked at me, then over at Jeff, and then back at me. "Does your agent follow you around everywhere?"

"No," I said.

So Jeff just sat there on the couch, and Madonna gave me a tour of her house. We walked around for a few minutes and wound up in her bedroom. Right away, she walked over and closed the drapes. I knew she had something in mind, but I didn't know what.

"Sit down," she told me.

So I sat down. Who wouldn't? She hit the remote control on her VCR and started showing me parts of *Truth or Dare,* her documentary, which hadn't yet hit the theaters. I think you can guess which scene she showed me. It was the famous masturbation scene on that big bed.

"This is crazy!" I was thinking to myself.

There I was, sitting about a foot away from Madonna as she played that part of the movie for me. A million guys would give anything to be in a situation like that, but the truth is actually kind of funny: Mostly I was just scared. I had a kind of blank feeling; as sexy as it all was, it was hard to be turned on when I was busy wondering what Madonna was going to say or do next. She can be a very intimidating presence—and we were in her territory, so she was very much in control. I wasn't used to that.

My eyes were glued to the TV, but eventually I realized that she was watching me even more closely. There was a long, awkward silence, but I could tell she was getting ready to say something.

"So what do you think?" she asked after the scene ended.

I looked back at her for a minute.

"It's very interesting," I told her.

She smiled, but didn't say anything. It was like I could hear the gears working, she was thinking so hard. She seemed to be checking me out, studying my body like I was a champion race-horse, inspecting me to see what sort of potential I had for stud service, and what sort of genes I'd be passing on.

We walked around the house some more after that, then went back to see how Jeff was doing. Madonna kept asking me questions, one very specific question after another, as if she had drawn up a list beforehand. She wanted to know about my background, and my family, my personal philosophy, what I thought about every subject you could think of.

"Why do you wear that big diamond ring?" she asked, looking down at this six-carat diamond ring I had then. "Do you feel like you need more attention?"

"No," I told her. "I just like jewelry."

There were so many questions, Jeff and I stayed at her house longer than we should have, and when we got back into the car to drive to Anaheim Stadium for the game, we realized there was no way we were going to make it in time. I was going to be late, and that meant I would have to confront Tony LaRussa, my manager, who was going to be mad. I decided that I'd better tell him the truth.

"Tony, I was at Madonna's house, talking to her, and I'm late," I told him. "So I missed batting practice." Tony was pretty pissed off, but he let me play, so that was the end of that.

With Madonna, though, that was just the beginning. Before long, she was calling me every day, wherever I was. She was amazing. She knew exactly what my schedule was and exactly where I was.

A lot of the times, she would call the clubhouse, using the code name Melissa. But all of my teammates and other people around the team figured out who it was, and they were always talking about it. You can just imagine what it was like. I didn't tell them much. I wasn't the type of guy to brag about anything. But they'd always be bringing it up and giving me shit.

"Jose, *Melissa* is on the phone," they'd say all the time, whether she was really calling or not.

For a while, Madonna and I would talk just about every day, although I have to say it was always kind of strange. I wouldn't say we ever really got to know each other. Usually she just called to ask about my schedule, and when we could see each other. She never asked about baseball or anything related to that. She never talked about her own work or career. She would just ask me questions about my marriage to Esther and the details of our separation, and would try to figure out a time when we would be in the same city so we could meet again.

Madonna doesn't fool around. She's a woman who knows what she wants, and goes after what she wants, and for a few weeks that year she had decided I was what she wanted: I was Cuban, I was a superstar baseball player, and she liked the way I looked.

She never really got a good look at my body when I visited her house in California, and on the phone she kept asking me a lot of questions about how different parts of my body looked. So I had the A's team photographer take a shot of me wearing nothing but some tight riding shorts, and sent that to her.

"It looks nice," she said. I didn't ask what she meant by "it."

The rumors got heavier and heavier. For some reason, there was an awful lot of curiosity about what happened between Madonna and me. I guess it's no surprise: I was the bad boy of baseball at that time and she was the bad girl of music, so we made kind of an interesting combination. There was all this talk about how she was in love with me, and how she wanted to be with me. I tried to tune it all out, but at the same time, it was a big compliment.

That May, the A's went on the road for a series against the New York Yankees, and when I arrived at our hotel in Manhattan I gave Madonna a call over at her penthouse apartment overlooking Central Park.

"Why don't you come up to my apartment?" she asked me. "I've got to see you."

I took a taxi over to her apartment on the West Side, and as soon as I got out of the cab, I realized there were paparazzi out in front of her apartment building. She also had her own personal security guard down at the front gate. He was huge, almost seven feet tall and easily 350 pounds.

"Hi, I'm Jose," I told him.

"Yeah, I know who you are."

So as I'm walking past him toward the elevator, I can hear people talking in the background.

"Who was that?" one voice asked.

"Wasn't that Canseco?" someone else said.

I forgot all about the photographers and went up to see Madonna in her penthouse apartment. In some ways seeing her this time was a lot like the first time I'd met her, back in California. She showed me around her place, the way she had in the Hollywood Hills. But this time she didn't play any videos. Mostly, we talked. She's a very smart woman, and when she talks, you want to listen closely. I felt like I could learn from her. We talked for more than an hour and a half, and then she came over and sat on my lap. Like I said, she was a woman who knew what she wanted and went after it.

"You want to kiss me, don't you?" she asked.

"No," I told her.

Yeah, that's what I told her. Sure, I wanted to kiss her. But I was trying to play it cool, since she'd caught me off-guard. Madonna's a very intelligent woman, someone who knows a lot about business. She's also very intuitive and very knowledgeable about life. I was impressed by the business side of her personality, but on that trip I also got to know another side of her, the little-girl side. She was very relaxed that night, and showed more of a sense of humor. Everything changed, even the tone of her voice; she wasn't Madonna-the-businesswoman or Madonna-the-pop-culture-icon. When Madonna lowers the wall around her, she's a very nice lady. So after a while, I kissed her, and we made out for a while. As curious as I was, though, I just wasn't that into her. She was pretty, but not really my type; to be honest, I didn't find her attractive enough. I was a big fan of hers, but as I sat there with her, I realized I was infatuated with the idea of it more than anything. There was no real chemistry there.

As I left her apartment that night and went downstairs, it was late, maybe two in the morning, but the paparazzi were everywhere out in front of the apartment building. None of them got past the huge security guard, but there were more than a hundred of them standing there behind him. And as I walked out, all their cameras were flashing. It was insane—like a light show at a dance club.

I woke up the next day, and there it was, the headline on the back cover of the *New York Post:* MADONNA'S BAT BOY.

They had a picture of me walking out of her apartment building—and before I knew it everyone was talking about it. Up at Yankee Stadium, I was playing the outfield and the fans were just going nuts. They were throwing coins and batteries at me; someone even threw a bullet. You have to watch out when stuff like that comes flying out of the upper deck. At various times that season, they also threw an inflatable doll, a transistor radio, and a head of cabbage. And they spent most of the game chanting at me: "Esther and Madonna and Jose, do-dah, do-dah!" (The papers had been quick to note that Esther and I were still officially married at that time.)

The next day Madonna and I talked again, and this time she got down to business: Basically, she was tired of waiting for me.

"I want you to leave your wife," she told me. "I want you to be with me. We can get married."

To be honest, I didn't know what to think. She heard me hesitate, and couldn't believe it.

"What's the problem?" she asked. "Why don't you leave your wife? Are you worried about the money you're going to have to give her if you get divorced? Don't worry about that: I've got money enough for both of us."

I'll never forget that. I was thinking to myself: Damn, that's pretty impressive.

But the news of my visit with Madonna in New York was causing me all kinds of trouble. When Esther heard about it, she went berserk on me. Even if you're separated, no girl wants you to be dating someone else—or at least they don't want their faces rubbed in it on the covers of newspapers around the country.

"I can't believe what you did!" Esther screamed at me over the telephone. I wished I could make her believe the truth: The whole thing with Madonna was just a friendly deal. I never had sex with her. *Never.* I was quiet and shy at that time in my life; I didn't really know how to handle her. Maybe if we'd spent more time together, I might have had sex with her—eventually. But it just didn't happen.

Ultimately, I just kind of left the whole Madonna thing alone, because I was still in love with Esther. Sure, I'd been curious about meeting Madonna, but it never really developed into anything. Every time she pushed to have me come see her, I kept pushing it back; it was like I was playing hard to get . . . except that I really didn't want to be gotten.

There was one last time when Madonna and I did try to see each other. After the end of that season, I was back in Miami at my home on Cocoa Plum Beach. I had two boats on my dock, one a speedboat that could do about 115 miles per hour. Madonna and I were talking on the phone, and she said I should come get her; at the time, she was living nearby at Star Island, maybe fifteen minutes away on the water.

So I got in my boat to go pick her up at her dock and headed off toward Star Island, until saw a helicopter above me. It started following me, and I could see a camera pointed down at me. I had this boat going 100 miles an hour, easy—probably 110—and I just couldn't shake this helicopter. So I had to call Madonna up and tell her what was happening.

"Listen, they're following me with this helicopter," I said. "I don't think I'm going to be able to pick you up. If I did, it would be all over the news."

I was more worried about Madonna's privacy than about my

own. After that day, she and I completely shut down communication. We talked briefly when she was shooting *A League of Their Own,* and she wanted me to fly in and give them some instructions on how to make a baseball movie. I would have, if my schedule was clear, but I couldn't make it at that time, and that was the last time I spoke to Madonna.

It's amazing, though. Ever since then, my whole life, people I meet are always asking me about Madonna. "Jose, how was she?" they'll ask me. Or they ask me about all the crazy rumors they've heard—like the idea that she used to have a trapeze in the bedroom of her Manhattan penthouse apartment. They always ask about having sex with her. And all I can tell them is: I don't know. Ask someone who has.

I had a lot of respect for Madonna, and I didn't want to mess it up at the time by trying to have sex with her, like any ordinary guy would do. I didn't want to do anything stupid. As I got to know her, I really became more interested in her for the person she was and the things that she had accomplished.

Even now, I think about her sometimes. I guess that's only natural. Eventually, she married another Cuban, Carlos Leon, and had a baby with him, but that didn't last. I've heard she goes through phases that way, and I guess that's what her infatuation with me was. But still, when Madonna had her first baby, Lourdes Maria, it did cross my mind to wonder what it would have been like. I thought to myself, *Can you imagine being married to Madonna right now? Or having kids with her? What would your life really be like?*

Obviously, I'll never know.

THANK YOU, TOM BOSWELL

*When Canseco wore the uniform of the A's
or the Rangers, he was just the colorful
black-hat wrestling villain, the way Charles
Barkley has always been a black-hat villain
at Madison Square Garden.*

MIKE LUPICA

I f I had five minutes to talk to a twenty-year-old version of myself, I wouldn't warn him off taking steroids or dating pop stars. The one piece of advice I would give him is that as much as players like to laugh at sportswriters—accusing them of being jock-sniffers or wannabes, for wearing ridiculous clothes, for not taking care of their bodies at all—the simple fact is that the media can make or break you. And let me tell you, there are some guys out there who really know how to work the angles. I can just throw up watching the total phonies go to work, guys like Cal Ripken or Alex Rodriguez; everything out of their mouths sounds like it was tested by some kind of focus group beforehand.

Alex, in particular, leaves most corporate spokesmen looking unpolished and overly sincere. He's better at politics than any politician I've ever seen. After all, he's been groomed that way. He's been taught just to make money, money, money. As a player, he has no entertainment value; he fades into the background, and he bats second in the lineup. But he has mathematical value, and for that they pay him ridiculous money. And when it comes to dealing with the press, Alex and the other politicians in baseball just know how to say the correct thing, right on cue. They have the media eating out of their hands. So what if it's all totally false? Who cares about that? The point is, he'll always give you a sentence or two to put on TV or in your newspaper. Sure, it'll be pure drivel. There won't be a spontaneous word there. But it sounds like ballplayer talk, and that's what matters.

The media reward players who talk a lot of B.S. It used to be Cal Ripken Jr. who was most obvious about play acting for the media and projecting a bogus image; today, it's Alex who's playing that role. That's not surprising, I guess, since Alex has said that he's looked up to Cal from boyhood as some kind of hero.

The perception of Alex is that he's the clean boy—that he doesn't do anything wrong. He's always careful and does everything right. I know some reporters don't like him because he's such a boring interview, the one guy who always gives a politically correct answer. So why do they keep coming back? Because they're waiting for him to make a mistake and slip up. And someday he could: He's not the saint he's perceived to be. Eventually the media will find something nasty to write about Alex Rodriguez, because trust me, they're looking for it.

Throughout his career, Cal Ripken Jr. was completely protected by the media. With his family history in baseball, he was one of those untouchable players, the guy who could do no wrong. He even got a pass on the way he dealt with the other players. He used to stay at a separate hotel from the rest of the team, and take a separate car from the team bus. The official explanation was that it was for security reasons, but we minority players couldn't help feeling otherwise. Now, if some minority player ever tried taking a separate car, you know what the media would say: "They're not team players. They don't care about the team." But a guy like Ripken can do whatever he wants, no questions asked. The double standard strikes again.

As a player, it's hard not to get frustrated with reporters who aren't smart enough to trust their own eyes. I don't know how many times I watched a pitcher who was just firing on all his cylinders—his fastball crisp, his slider nasty, everything right over the plate—only to watch a reporter come in after he shuts out the other team and ask what he had going for him that night. Well, EVERYTHING! Sure, it may be a little easier for those of us inside the game to know what's going on. Still, you'd think that after so many years on the job these guys would pick up on what it takes.

What really gives me a laugh, though, are the numbers geeks. There are a lot of guys who have never played the game—never even been around the game—and still try to use mathematics to figure it out. That's a joke. It's impossible. Mathematical equations can't tell you if a player has an injury—not to mention if he's having troubles at home. Stats can't account for the human factor. And yet these guys all act like they're the smartest guys around; some of them act so superior it's almost embarrassing. (We'd have some fun with them if they ever showed up in a clubhouse, but usually they're too scared to talk to a player face to face.)

An awful lot has changed in the sports business in the past twenty years. Back then, media competition was nothing compared to what it is now—and believe me, as a player, you notice the difference. The competition among the media now is just savage—so what happens? Reporters make stuff up. I'm not saying they do it all the time, but I know from painful experience that sometimes they do. I've sold millions and millions of newspapers and made some media people's careers, but a lot of what they wrote was a pack of absolute lies.

I was created by the media. Back in the 1980s, I was like a rock star. Everywhere I went, I had to have bodyguards. I had it all: the body, the personality, everything. I was Hollywood. When most fans thought of me, they didn't think of me playing baseball; they thought, "He's dating Madonna," or "He's got a great ass." Forget about how I played on any given night; I knew my role was to give the media and the fans what they really wanted—which was to be colorful and larger than life. And the media could always be counted on to magnify everything I did. I always answered questions honestly and spoke from the heart, but I never got the feeling the reporters understood me (most of them probably weren't trying that hard); most of them were happy to present me as a caricature and a clown, partly because it was what their editors wanted. And it sold papers.

Part of it was that most of these guys just didn't understand where I came from. Miami Cubans have come a long way in the past twenty years, but when I was first making my mark in baseball, there was still a lot of quiet racism. I'm talking about people who don't even know they're racist, but who make easy assumptions based on little or no knowledge of a person's background. Sure, I'll say it: Latinos aren't dead fish. We like to talk, and sometimes we like to yell. That's just how we communicate. Believe me, to us, long silences seem a lot more awkward than a few flat-out shouts now and then. But whenever my first wife, Esther, and I were overheard yelling at each other, you can bet your life some reporter would write it up as if we'd been swinging at each other with machetes.

The most glaring example of the double standard that I faced as a Latino, compared to the treatment the Ripkens and McGwires of the world received, was a column Thomas Boswell of the *Washington Post* published on me in 1988. Boswell apparently decided that I was the player he wanted to make an example of as a steroid user, but he offered no evidence—and he never explained why he was singling me out and saying nothing about Mark McGwire, even though Mac was bigger than I was.

Why? No one cared about what good-boy McGwire was doing—or they didn't want to know. But I was always made out to be the bad boy, so I was treated differently. The rest of the media jumped on me; hey, it was fun. But it was twelve years after Boswell called me a steroid user before anyone made any serious claims in print about McGwire and steroids.

So why did I care about being exposed that way? Well, for one thing, Boswell cost me a million-dollar endorsement with Pepsi. The deal was all lined up: There I was, Jose Canseco, a big Cuban kid all set to be pitching Pepsi on TV. But when Boswell's article came out, Pepsi took a walk. Snap your fingers: that's how fast Boswell pulled that million bucks out of my hands.

After the Pepsi deal fell through, so many endorsement opportunities went with it. Once the rumor went around that I was on steroids—though nobody presented any smoking guns—I was persona non grata. I wanted to sue Boswell, but in the end, it just didn't seem worth my time.

Soon after that, we were in Boston for the playoffs, and something funny happened: All around me, I heard the fans start chanting: "*Steroids! Steroids!*"

When I heard that, I paused a moment to think about how to respond. Then I just turned sideways, flexed for them, turned the other way, and flexed again.

The crowd went nuts.

Looking back now, I realize that it all came naturally to me, being an entertainer. But in a lot of ways, I was pretty stupid about the media. To put it simply, I didn't understand how powerful the media were, and how important they were to a player's career. Maybe that's not so surprising, since I think a lot of individual sportswriters I've dealt with over the years have also tended to lose sight of how powerful the media are, how much influence they have over shaping a player's public image.

I was never close to Albert Belle, but there's another guy who got a raw deal. No doubt he did some stupid things, like back in

1996 when he got mad at a *Sports Illustrated* photographer and threw a baseball at him. Not a good move. I never did anything like that. But here's the thing: Just ask yourself how the media would have reacted if Ripken or McGwire had done such a thing. They would have called it a joke: *Ha-ha, funny-funny, that ol' boy sure does like to clown around.*

A lot of great baseball players, from Ty Cobb on down, have been jerks. I can understand that. Sometimes, players need to maintain their intensity on the field by being intense off the field. But white guys who are that way get called *gritty* and *tough* and *a real competitor.* If it's a black guy or a Latino, then the white media reports on the player's difficult side as if it's proof positive that he's a bad person.

I learned too late in my career about the importance of the media, not only when it comes to endorsements (thank you, Tom Boswell) but also when it came to negotiating a long-term contract. When you're working on building a serious long-term commitment with a team, you've got to be extremely careful about how you treat the media—instead of bitching and complaining and trying to belittle reporters. McGwire used to call reporters "faggots." I think he thought that was clever. And, like me, he never grasped why they didn't understand him better.

It sounds obvious enough, but it has to be said: More reporters need to stop for a minute and keep in mind that baseball players, even the richest superstars, are just human beings with families and emotions, just like anybody else. Some days you feel like laughing. Some days you feel like crying. Different individuals are always going to have different opinions; some people might have different opinions from day to day, or even hour to hour. You can't be a happy-go-lucky guy all the time— not if someone in your family is sick, or you're having family or financial problems. At some point, you're going to say something you shouldn't have said, and then you get jumped on. I don't think you can really judge an individual on one instance. You have to know them over the course of years—just like you would a family friend or coworker—and watch how they act under different circumstances.

Reporters are always talking about objectivity and fairness, but who are they kidding, anyway? Everyone knows the media can portray an event however they want to, positively or negatively. They have that power, that degree of control. They can make your career, if they like you, or they can destroy you.

I'm not saying that the reporters who covered me wrote only bad things about me. In August 1990, Rick Reilly did a big piece on me for *Sports Illustrated* that tried to knock down a few of the false assumptions people were making about me.

"Jose Canseco is the subject," Reilly wrote, "and *San Francisco Examiner* columnist Bill Mandel, a man who has never met him, offers this: 'I'm from New York and in New York there is a word for guys like Canseco, and that word is schmuck.'

"Okay, so if Canseco is such a schmuck, why does he spend so much time at the Miami Youth Club, playing basketball with the kids, staying for their spaghetti dinners, donating hundreds of pairs of sneakers at a time?

"If Canseco is such a schmuck, why is he so deeply involved in the Make-a-Wish Foundation, which fulfills the fantasies of dying children?

"If Canseco is such a schmuck, how come he paid for a kid with leukemia to be flown from Sacramento to Scottsdale, Arizona, for the A's spring training?

"If Canseco is such a schmuck, how come he drove to Pleasanton, California, to raise money for a paralyzed kid called J.O. by signing autographs for four and a half hours?

"And if Canseco is such a schmuck, why did he give his brother a house and a brand new Porsche 911 and his father a new Cadillac?

"Jose Canseco is a baseball virtuoso, an athletic flower that blooms once a century. We know this because he mentioned it the other day."

That article was published back in the day when people still read *Sports Illustrated* the way they watch ESPN now—as the be-all and end-all of sports reporting. I wish some of Rick Reilly's good vibes toward me had caught on. But Reilly was the exception to the rule. The truth is, too many reporters and analysts really don't know what they're talking about. The public may assume everything they read or hear in the media is the truth. But half the time, these reporters or journalists don't do their homework. Way too often, they're basically misquoting an athlete, or relying too much on opinion and emotion.

Having had a good close look at the media during the seventeen years of my major-league career, I've come to the conclusion that when a reporter or journalist uses his own opinion, he's slipping into the danger zone. It's too easy to go overboard, instead of just telling the truth about an actual incident the way it really happened. To me, the mark of a good reporter is not confusing one's own emotional feelings toward an athlete—or toward a race or a color or a creed—with the facts. It's a shame, because some of the reporters out there are racists, and if you give these people free rein, they can destroy an athlete. Does that sound paranoid to you? Time to grow up. Anyone who tries to claim that not one out of a thousand media personnel is racist, is speaking out of pure ignorance. There's racism everywhere in this world, in any profession. Why should the media be different?

What reporters need to understand is that the public has only one vehicle for learning about these players, and that's through the media. The media is notorious for misquoting individuals, and for writing whatever they want, especially if they can't get interviews. But it's the public that suffers, by getting confused between opinion and fact.

I'll give you an example. Everyone remembers the Loma Prieta earthquake of 1989, which struck the Bay Area the day we were supposed to play game three of that year's World Series against the Giants. We were down on the field when it hit, around five in the afternoon, and I remember leaving the ballpark with my wife Esther. We were in my Porsche, driving back to the Blackhawk area in the East Bay; I was still wearing my baseball uniform, because the clubhouse was blacked out, so we couldn't change back into street clothes.

I was low on gas, so I stopped at a gas station, but it was the only one open at that time and there was a long line of people waiting for gas. We waited there about half an hour, and when it was our turn, Esther told me she wanted to pump the gas.

"Listen, you'd better stay in the car," she told me. "You're dressed in full uniform, and there are people all over the place. If you get out, who knows what's going to happen? People are going to get out of their cars. They're going to want autographs. It's just going to make matters worse."

So she got out and pumped the gas herself. Makes sense, right?

Not so fast. Esther pumped the gas, and we left, but what we didn't notice is that there there were a few media people there. So the next day, in the paper, all you heard was: "Jose Canseco, the male chauvinist pig, makes his wife Esther put gas in the car."

You hear about *Girls Gone Wild*. They ought to call it *Media Gone Wild*.

Here's another example of how the media can twist things and turn everything around. I'll call it the Case of Jose Canseco,

Famous Gun-Toting Maniac. It all started with another episode that happened in 1989, the year after I made MVP. During spring training, I cracked the hamate bone in the heel of my left hand. It's a small bone in the hand; you really don't need it, but it's very painful if it breaks. So I had surgery to repair it, and for a while I had to wear a cast.

Late that April, Esther and I drove over from the East Bay, in the modified candy-apple red Jaguar I had at the time, to have the bone checked and make sure it was healing properly. We pulled into the parking lot at the University of California at San Francisco Medical Center, way up California Street in Laurel Heights, and the whole thing was empty. It was a Friday; there wasn't a single car in sight.

Esther and I went into the medical center; I had a magnetic-resonance imaging test, and they told me everything was healing fine. But as we were heading back out to the parking lot, four or five police cars pulled up, two of them unmarked, the others squad cars.

"Is this your car?" one of the policeman asked me.

"Yeah," I said.

"Well, you're under arrest," the policeman said.

"Under arrest for what?" I asked.

"For carrying a gun on campus property."

It was true that I had a gun, a 9 mm automatic pistol—but it was registered. It was something I felt I needed for my own protection, and for the protection of my loved ones, because by that point I was very much a public figure. There were all kinds of wackos out there ready to take a run at me and steal some gold or do something worse.

To me, the real question wasn't what I was doing with a gun. It was, how did the cops know about it? And what was wrong with it, anyway?

Well, the answer was pretty revealing. I kept the gun in a pouch underneath the front seat of my car, and when I stopped to park the car, the pouch slid forward a little. After we left the car, apparently, someone was walking by and checking out my Jaguar—with its "40-40" license plates—and as they were snooping around, they caught a glimpse of the pouch. So they called the police, and before you knew it I was being interrogated by the FBI. All for a completely legal gun that no one would have known was there if it weren't for somebody snooping by.

But that didn't stop the media from blowing the whole thing out of proportion. When the *San Francisco Chronicle* wrote the story up, they didn't just lead the sports section with it; they stuck it right out there on the front page of the whole newspaper:

CANSECO ARRESTED—LOADED PISTOL IN HIS JAGUAR

And as bad as the *Chronicle*'s story seemed, there were others that were a whole lot worse. By the time you were done reading them, you'd think I'd been waving the gun around, shooting at kids or something. (When reporters talked to Esther when she came to the sixth floor of the county jail, she just told them the truth: "This is all bullshit.")

One bad story like that, and you're set for life. The whole rest of my career, people always mentioned that gun arrest, as if I was running around campus waving a gun in the air. Now I hate to think what would have happened if Cal Ripken Jr. had landed in the same position; "Excuse me, Mr. Ripken, sir. We're so sorry, but we got a call about a gun in your car, and we just have to check it out. Strictly a formality, we're sure. Oh, what's that? You say you've got it taken care of and there's no problem? Okay, fine. Go get 'em, slugger."

Even the simplest stereotypes can be revealing. I remember when I was playing for Double-A Huntsville and I heard a reporter in the background asking one of the coaches, "Can he speak English?"

I almost broke down laughing, it was so ridiculous. Just because my name is Canseco and I'm Latino, it automatically means I can't speak English? Yeah, right. Try that on Arnold Schwarzenegger.

But I shouldn't give the minor-league reporters too much trouble. In general, I found that they were a lot different from major league reporters; they're more interested in what happened during the game itself—in keeping it on the field. Major league reporters are far more interested in your private life, in trying to dig up what you do off the field—at least if you're not on the off-limits list.

I was always, from day one, the evil guy of baseball. Reporters were always trying to pit Mark and me against each other, to contrast us—Jose Caneco the aggressive, Latin lover with his fast cars, and Mark McGwire, the all-American boy.

In general, I was able to handle the media pretty well early in my career. I was still shy, but interviews were no big deal. The real problems started when I came up in 1985 from Triple-A Tacoma to Oakland. The team was struggling. No fans were coming out. The organization wasn't even on the map. So at that point the organization decided to try to sell me as the future of the A's. I was the new power hitter, the new young stud who was going to save the team. That's how they portrayed me, and the media picked up on it, too. Once I came up, the organization started restructuring, adding other players like McGwire and Walt Weiss. Little by little, the team started winning. But I'd been the one who was supposed to be the team savior—to carry the whole burden on my back—and when it didn't quite work out that way, the media never let me forget it.

I'm not saying reporters always have it easy. Once baseball started becoming more popular again, not just in Oakland but everywhere, the competition among them media became just overwhelming. There were so many media personnel covering the teams that each of them had to struggle to scrape up a different story to stand out from the crowd and draw attention (and readers) to themselves.

So what happened? I became the guy who was always the butt of the joke, the easy target for controversy. Each new reporter tried to dissect my personal life and my marriages, everything they could find about my background. From 1987 on, I was attacked all the time by the media. Every little thing that would happen to me—right down to getting tinted windows in my car—was national media. It was just crazy.

It was only during the last two or three years of my career that I felt the press beginning to treat me differently, after I'd learned to socialize with them a little more and I was less shy. Until then, I spent years being made fun of, lied about, exaggerated about— you name it. And I couldn't help but notice that every negative story that came out about me was by a white reporter. Never once in my entire career do I remember seeing a negative article from a minority paper or minority writer or minority producer.

Of course, I didn't take all this mistreatment quietly. I spoke out against the double standards I saw, and sometimes made an issue of it when I saw that black athletes weren't being treated fairly and getting the right contracts. For example, when contract renewal time came around, Will Clark had the same service time as Kevin Mitchell, and Kevin Mitchell had performed better. All of a sudden, Will Clark was getting a four-year contract for a good amount of money—and Kevin Mitchell wasn't.

I spoke out about that. And the media hammered me for it—the white media, that is. But I had no qualms about speaking out against the injustice. Why? Because a lot of us minority players felt like we got the cold shoulder from Will Clark. Clark was a country boy, and from the way he acted and the comments he would make, we had reason to believe he had no respect for us. But who was going to complain? He was white, he was Will Clark, and he was protected by the system.

After I made some comments to the press about Mitchell and Clark, in every ballpark I'd go to, the minority athletes would greet me with a thumbs-up and a high five. They knew I had the power to challenge the double standard, and they loved watching me use it.

In the end, of course—though I didn't realize it until after I retired from baseball—all those controversies worked against me. If I hadn't been political, and spoken out and fought for what was right, maybe the owners would have wanted me around in baseball a little longer.

The public has to realize that the good guys in baseball aren't as perfect as the media says they are—and the bad guys aren't as bad, either. The truth is always somewhere in between. Yes, the media can portray you as an angel even though you're a devil, and vice versa. They can completely control what is brought to the public. It's just like political propaganda, only on a smaller scale. No one knows what goes on in the political world unless the media covers it and carries it accurately back to the public. But what if the media is really deceiving the public? That kind of thing has happened before, it's happening now in certain areas, and it will continue to happen. It's left to the public to make a choice about what to believe.

As I've asked myself for years: If you can't trust a sports reporter to tell the truth, who can you trust?

11

TEXAS-SIZED SLUGGERS

There are trades in sports, and there are TRADES in sports, and this was definitely the latter. Out of the blue, the biggest celebrity in baseball had been sent flying from the Oakland A's. This was the kind of deal—the bolt-of-lightning trade—that just wasn't supposed to happen anymore.

LEIGH MONTVILLE,
Sports Illustrated, *September 14, 1992*

The biggest surprise I ever had in my seventeen seasons playing in the big leagues came on August 31, 1992. We were playing a home game at the Oakland Coliseum against the Baltimore Orioles, and at the time we had a good lead in the American League West, seven and a half games. I played right field in the top of the first inning, and then came in ready to bat in the bottom of the inning. But just as I was stepping into the on-deck circle, one of the coaches told me that the manager, Tony LaRussa, wanted to talk to me.

I figured Tony wanted to tell me something he'd noticed about the pitcher. You're always trying to identify clues about what the pitcher is going to do—a glove movement, a hand movement, anything that can help you pick up what type of pitch he's going to throw. But Tony didn't want to talk about the pitcher. When I reached him, he just stood there for a moment while I waited for him to speak.

"Jose, you've been traded," he finally told me.

It didn't register. I thought it must be some kind of bad joke, like on April Fool's Day.

So Tony repeated himself. "You've been traded."

I was in shock.

"Go upstairs and see Sandy Alderson. He'll give you the de-tails," Tony told me.

So I put my bat and helmet down and started walking up

through the tunnel. Just imagine what it was like: We were *right in the middle of the game,* only an hour or two before the deadline. I was in complete shock. None of the players said anything to me; they were too busy with the game.

Upstairs, the A's general manager, Sandy Alderson, explained that I had been traded to the Texas Rangers, in exchange for three players: Ruben Sierra, Jeff Russell, and Bobby Witt. He said I should go take a shower; there'd be a press conference afterward. That was basically it. The days and weeks that followed remain a real blur for me. It didn't really sink in, for a while, just what had happened or why. I'd been with the A's my whole career; I'd come up through the minors, and played in Oakland for eight seasons. And now this.

"I haven't even looked at myself in the mirror," I told the reporters who showed up for a press conference I gave at Yankee Stadium before my first game for the Rangers. "I feel like I'm playing in an All-Star Game, where you wear the uniform for a day and go home. Only this time you don't go home. I still can't believe all of this happened. I can't believe it happened this way. Maybe I'll never know the reason why I was traded."

I even tried to find some humor in the situation. When one reporter asked me where I had been traded, I said: "To Ethiopia. For a box of Froot Loops and a camel to be named later."

But inside I was just dumbstruck—and it seems like the whole Bay Area was as well. "Sandy Alderson never has been afraid to pull the trigger on a big trade that would help his team," Frank Blackman wrote in the *San Francisco Examiner* the next day. "But Monday night, when the A's general manager announced he had traded Jose Canseco to Texas for three players and cash, he dropped a nuclear device."

It was a weird feeling, getting on the plane to New York to

leave the West Coast and join the Rangers. Pedro Gomez sat next to me on that flight, and I told him how confusing it was to hear so many people complaining now about the trade. All I could think was, *Where were all these supporters when I came to bat at the Coliseum?* This outpouring of support was nice, but I could have used it to drown out all those boos in Oakland.

I couldn't help grousing to Pedro about it all. "I've always heard, 'Why can't he reach his potential?'" I told him as we sat up in first class, heading east. "Maybe thirty-five home runs and 100 RBIs *is* my potential. It's not a bad potential to reach. I don't think I've ever gotten credit for the things I've done. It's always been what I *haven't* done or what I *should* have done. It's not fair to me. But I guess that's one of the prices you pay for superstardom. I wouldn't change a thing if I could. I'd still go into baseball."

It wasn't only in the Bay Area that people were amazed by that trade. People all over the country were having a hard time suddenly imagining me taking the field in something other than my familiar Oakland A's uniform.

"The uniform looked so strange on him, the word TEXAS spelled across the gray shirt in blue letters," Leigh Montville wrote that week in *Sports Illustrated*. "Jose Canseco was a Texas Ranger? This could not be. Up was down, down was up and the tidy baseball universe had been altered. McDonald's sells hamburgers near Lenin's Tomb, fine. A member of the British royal family rubs suntan lotion on the bald head of an American businessman, O.K. But Jose a Ranger?"

It was true I wasn't having my best season for the A's that year. Injuries had been nagging at me for months. I had twenty-two home runs at the time of the trade, and 72 RBIs, but I was only batting .246, which was a big drop from the .307 I hit in 1988, my forty-forty year.

Still, I was only twenty-eight years old, and it was clear that I had many, many more good seasons ahead of me. When the A's traded me, that represented a huge change of course for them. I knew they needed pitching, especially after Bob Welch went down with an injury in the weeks before the trade, but they were basically pulling the plug on the powerhouse team they had built. The A's were looking for ways to cut salary and go into a kind of rebuilding mode. No one would have predicted they would do that at that time, and basically give up on being a contender, even though they still had so much talent.

As shocked as everyone was, including me, the transition turned out to be pretty easy. After a week or so with the Rangers, I felt pretty well settled in. I had known Rafael Palmeiro since we were kids growing up in Miami, and of course I was glad to be playing with another Cuban. And there were other Latino stars on the team, like Ivan "Pudge" Rodriguez and Juan Gonzalez. They made a real effort to make me feel welcome after that trade, and Raffy and I even started bashing our forearms, the way we all did out in Oakland. Eventually, I realized that this change of scenery was probably good for me.

And the whole episode did give me a little perspective on what was really going on during the time I'd spent in Oakland. Maybe I'd worn out my welcome there. Maybe I'd fallen into a trap. The shoes people put out there for me would have been very difficult for anyone to fill. And when I did manage to fill them, the shoes just kept getting bigger. It was sad, but I don't think I ever could have fulfilled the expectations people had for me out there.

I also wondered about what role the steroid issue might have played in the trade. No one in the A's organization ever came right out and said it, but by then there were a lot of rumors about me using steroids, and to this day I believe that might have been a factor in the A's decision to trade me. But that would have been just pure ignorance on their part. Using steroids made me a better ball player—and, as everyone soon found out, my expertise on steroids could make other players around me a lot better, too.

But the Texas Rangers apparently weren't worried about that. The managing general partner at that time was George W. Bush, before he was elected governor of Texas. At that time, he was very visible in the role of team owner; he used to sit right behind home plate for a lot of the games. Sometimes he'd come down to talk to the great pitcher Nolan Ryan, who had the next locker over from mine when I first joined the Rangers.

It was understood by then that teams knew all about steroids in the game. There was no question that George W. Bush knew my name was connected with steroids—the story Tom Boswell had written in 1988 wasn't the last word on the subject—but he decided to make the deal to trade for me anyway.

And then, not long after I got there, I sat down with Rafael Palmeiro, Juan Gonzalez, and Ivan Rodriguez, and educated them about steroids.

Soon I was injecting all three of them. I personally injected each of those three guys many times, until they became more familiar with how to use a needle and were able to do it themselves. Bush and Tom Grieve, the general manager, would have seen all three of those guys getting bigger before their eyes, starting within weeks after I joined the team. But they never made an issue of it, or said anything to me or to any of us about steroids.

Was I surprised that no one ever brought it up? Come on. You never really get to speak to the owners or the GM on a daily basis. They spend their days off by themselves, attending to business behind closed doors; they don't spend a lot of time mingling with the players. I never had any sort of conversation with Bush. I shook his hand and met him once, but that was about it. He was around a lot; you saw him on his way in or out, but always just briefly. We were busy practicing or playing baseball. Bush did gravitate toward Nolan Ryan a bit, probably because he was a legend, and also closer to him in age. He didn't talk to us Latinos much.

And, given how quiet he was about the subject at the time, I was pretty surprised years later when Bush actually raised the issue of steroids in his January 2004 State of the Union address. By then, it seemed to me that a lot of people, Bush included, were trying to turn this into a witch hunt—even though they themselves had played a role in helping move the steroid revolution forward, by giving a berth to me and other steroid-using players during my heyday, and benefiting from our enhanced performance.

I'm not a big fan of CNN, but that guy Paul Begala—you know, bald, with beady eyes—was actually on the money when he talked about the issue shortly after Bush gave that speech.

"In an otherwise lackluster State of the Union address, President Bush had one genuine moment of passion," Begala said on *Crossfire* on January 22, 2004. "But when he was the owner of a baseball team, Mr. Bush did nothing about steroids. Although other sports were cracking down on steroids, Mr. Bush and his fellow baseball owners refused to do a thing.

"In fact, Mr. Bush even traded for Jose Canseco, bringing him to the Texas Rangers—a man who one sports agent told the UPI was 'The Typhoid Mary of steroids.' Perhaps Mr. Bush can get some advice on the steroid crisis he's just discovered from the man he has repeatedly praised, California Governor and former steroid abuser Arnold Schwarzenegger."

I don't know about Typhoid Mary, but I don't think there's any question that when I arrived in Texas the other Rangers saw me as a useful resource. Everyone in baseball knew by then that

I was the godfather of steroids. I was the first to educate other players about how to use them, the first to experiment and pass on what I'd learned, and the first to get contacts on where to get them. I taught the other players which steroid has which effect on the body, and how to mix or "stack" certain steroids to get a desired effect.

Palmeiro, Gonzalez, and Ivan Rodriguez all started asking me a lot of questions about steroids soon after I joined the Rangers. And after I'd given them a little schooling, they told me they all wanted to get some and give them a try. So I got them each a supply through my contacts, and helped them get used to the injection process. None of them at that point wanted their wives to know about it. They would bring their steroids to the ballpark and I would inject them there, the same way I used to inject McGwire back at the Oakland Coliseum.

That was pretty typical of most players, not wanting people to know—their wives especially. So we would go into the bathroom stalls or the video room or a back room, wherever you could find a closed area, to do the injecting, and I would show them where to make the injection on the glute muscle.

Raffy, Juan, and Ivan were definitely scared the first time I injected them, but after a while it became no big deal to them, either. And throughout my time on the team, they were on a combination of growth hormone and steroids—mostly Deca and Winstrol, but with a small dose of testosterone. Combining water-based and oil-based steroids that way, they needed two separate needles, too. (They didn't take any pills. Those are probably the worst to take.)

All three of them saw some gains in size, too. Raffy, who's naturally stocky, made a reasonable gain in size and weight. Juan, on the other hand, got bigger and bigger, and didn't know when to stop. Eventually, he would grow all the way up to 255 pounds.

He was very lean when he first started playing baseball in the major leagues, so when he started getting up to that size, it was too much, especially since he was playing the outfield every day. I myself never got over 250 pounds, and I'm taller than Juan at six foot four.

Before long, other players from all around the baseball world saw what was going on with me and my buddies in Texas, how strong we all were and how our strength was helping us perform. And soon those players were coming up to me and asking me for advice about using steroids. It wasn't something you spoke about with just anybody. It wasn't like I gave daily or weekly seminars in front of the whole ball team, standing in front of them all in a white lab coat and holding up a laser pointer and telling them, "Today, we're going to learn about Deca and what it can do for you." But by then it was an open secret among players: If they wanted to know about steroids, they knew who to ask.

Of course, not everyone hunted me down for advice. Some wanted to know more, some didn't. But one thing I should make clear: No one ever gave me any grief for what we were doing with our bodies. I never saw or experienced any tension among players about steroid use. To put it another way: Even the guys who weren't doing steroids knew full well that it was something they'd consider doing, even if they might say otherwise to their wives or parents or high school gym teachers.

I can say with confidence that every single major-league player has at least given steroid use some thought, weighed the positives and negatives. How could you not? Ball players earn their living with their bodies, after all. They all want to become bigger, stronger, and faster. Of course, they'd be tempted to do anything they could to improve those bodies. If you're an editor at a newspaper, and you can get a souped-up computer that's faster, more reliable, and can do things the old one couldn't, of course, you're going to want that upgrade. It's the same thing for an athlete: Upgrading your physical capability is central to success in your chosen field. If you get bigger, stronger, and can hit more home runs, you can make a lot more money. If you saw some little middle infielder all of a sudden hitting forty homers in a season, your choice would be clear—if you can't beat 'em, join 'em.

Once I educated another player, he would usually end up learning more and more on his own, and then using his own contacts to get what he needed. That was how it went with Palmeiro, Gonzalez, and Rodriguez in Texas. After a while I assumed that they found their own sources. Steroids are everywhere. A lot of bodybuilders supplement their income by selling them. So do trainers in gyms, and sometimes the owners of the gyms themselves. I know people who have made millions and millions of dollars selling steroids. The profits can be incredible if you can get your supplies at a low rate. Pharmacists sell steroids on the side, too. Growth hormone is everywhere you look; you can see the results in every gym, in every sport, and more and more often on beaches and sidewalks wherever you live.

It's one thing to complain about steroid abuse. I agree that improper steroid use can have its dangers. But the performance enhancement that can come with responsible steroid use is nothing to be dismissed. It's an opportunity, not a danger. And those who are trying to make an issue of it are speaking from ignorance.

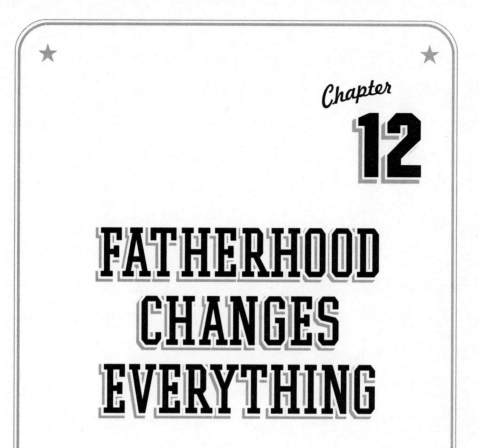

FATHERHOOD CHANGES EVERYTHING

*I look at my daughter every day
and just think, "Wow."*

JOSE CANSECO

I n May 1993, when I was playing for the Rangers, we went to Cleveland for a series against the Indians, and some friends on the team and I decided to go get something to eat. There was a Hooters restaurant near the ballpark, so we decided to go there. (The food isn't bad, actually, and if you don't like those tight orange shorts the waitresses wear, then something's wrong with you.)

When we sat down to order that day, there was one waitress I couldn't take my eyes off. The second I saw her, I knew I was going to ask her out. She was tall, blonde, beautiful, and confident, with beautiful blue eyes and a body that wouldn't quit. That was Jessica. She became my second wife.

"I remember him coming in and trying to pick me up," she says now. "He does this thing with his eyebrows where one goes up and the other doesn't. It was very cute. I didn't know who he was at all. I wasn't a sports fan. But he kept asking me to lunch, and I agreed. So the next day he took me shopping and spent, like, seven thousand dollars on me at Calvin Klein."

The next day, I was playing in the outfield when a funny thing happened. I ran back toward the wall, chasing after a ball hit by Carlos Martinez. As I went back, I lost track of the ball for just an instant, and it hit me right on the head and bounced over for a home run. That had to be the most embarrassing moment of my career, but even so, it was a fluke—the kind of thing that could happen to anyone. But because I was Jose Canseco, they turned it into a huge sensation; they'll probably be replaying that sequence long after I'm dead. It became like Madonna— one of those subjects that people always ask me about when they meet me for the first time.

Three days later, I finally got to do something I'd always wanted to do. My whole time with the A's, I was always telling them I could pitch; I'd thrown 90-mile-an-hour fastballs, too. But there was never an opportunity to give me a shot—until that May, when we were getting blown away by the Red Sox, and the Rangers' manager, Kevin Kennedy, decided to let me pitch.

It was harder than it looks, I'll tell you. I retired the side the one inning I pitched, but I also gave up three walks, two singles, and three runs. Even now, if you look up my statistics, before it says anything about my home runs, it lists my pitching stats: I have a major-league career earned-run average of 27.00, based on that one inning.

Later in the season, my right elbow started giving me trouble, ending that season early and forcing me to have ligament-replacement surgery in my elbow. The know-it-alls in the press always said I'd messed up my elbow while pitching that one inning, and for all I know they're right. The point is: They really don't know. They're just guessing. And for the rest of my life I get to say that I pitched in a major-league game, something none of them can say. And Jessica was there to see it, too.

"He flew me to Boston that weekend," Jessica said. "Within six or seven days, I was head over heels in love with him. My friends warned me about him, saying they'd heard stories about him and he was a bad seed, but I didn't care.

" 'I'm going to marry this man!'—That's what I told my friends within a week. He liked animals, and I grew up on a farm and I'm an animal lover. I always liked his sense of humor, and he liked mine, so we always laughed a lot together. Plus, I liked his exciting lifestyle."

Jessica and I had a stormy relationship, breaking up and getting back together more times than I'd like to remember. Two years after that amazing first meeting, we were thinking about separating when Jessica said she had something to tell me. I didn't know what to expect. Had she met someone else?

That wasn't it.

"I'm pregnant," she told me.

I was so happy, I couldn't believe it. Here I thought we were just heading for another of our disagreements; instead, here was this great news she had for me. Suddenly everything made perfect sense. I'd never really wanted to break up with her, and this seemed to give us the fresh start we needed—even though neither of us had been thinking much about becoming parents.

"I was shocked to find out I was pregnant," Jessica says now. "I really hadn't planned on that."

Our wedding wasn't what you would call storybook. My back had gone out on me again so we had to hold the ceremony flat on our backs in bed. That was fine with me; I like to hang out in bed. I actually conduct a lot of my business from the phone by my bed. But to Jessica, that ceremony in Florida in August 1996 left a little something to be desired. "It wasn't much of a wedding," she says. I tried to make it up to her in other ways.

Just a few months later, that November, our baby girl Josie was born. I'll never forget that night. Jessica is so strong that once she went into her contractions, that was pretty much that. She's one of those genetic freaks: Once the doctor said "Push!" it was all over but the shouting.

When Josie's head popped out, she was so dark I couldn't believe it. You know how, when babies don't have any oxygen in their bloodstream yet, their heads are a kind of purple color? Josie was a *very* dark purple.

"Hmmm," I was thinking. "Why is this baby so dark?"

They held up the umbilical cord, and I cut it. As soon as the nurse slapped her on the butt and she started crying, you could see the oxygen turn her from a dark purple to pink, pink, pink, and right away you could see her blue eyes. It was amazing. That moment blew away everything I had experienced in my life. You never know what it's all about, being a father, until you experience it for yourself.

"My life changed from then on," Jessica says. "I had her to think about, as well as myself, and it was challenging. I think both Jose and I had to do a lot of growing up after Josie was born. She brought us closer together and made us a family."

Nothing compares to the feeling of being a father. Very often, I'd be looking at Josie and I'd turn to look at Jessica. "We created her!" I'd say, "Look at her, a beautiful little girl, blonde hair, green eyes, tons of personality. *We created this.*"

The first couple of months, it seemed like we spent every waking moment just looking at her. All a baby does is sleep, poop, and eat; that's basically it for a few months. As a father, you've got to be very careful. You don't want to bounce her too hard, or hold her too tight, out of a fear that she's going to break. Those first months, she spent so much time with her mother, breast-feeding and what not; then, even when I'd try to hold her, I heard, "Be *careful!*" or "Watch out for her head!" or "You have to keep her neck straight!" so often that more than once I felt like giving up and letting the professional—her mom—do the holding.

Josie was a quiet baby. She didn't cry much. After a little time passed, though, her personality started showing itself, and her features started coming out. The life of a baseball player can take a lot out of you, with all the travel and 162 games per season in the regular season alone. But in the off-season you get to do whatever you want—and what I wanted to do was stay home and sit there watching Josie. I didn't even care what she was doing, I just loved keeping an eye on my little girl.

It took me a while to admit it, but you start to look at your life differently when you have someone dependent on you. I always had this bad-boy public image, but most of the trouble I got into was just because I was goofing off. Back when I was a kid, my dad was so serious all the time, and put so much pressure on Ozzie and me, that we never had much of a chance to feel like carefree kids. Looking back, I guess once I got into baseball I was just making up for a lot of lost time.

But after Josie was born, I developed a new sense of responsibility. I thought more about the consequences of my actions. I started thinking things through carefully and calmly before I acted. My earlier reckless days started to feel like a very distant chapter of my life. So did my free-spending ways of years before. I definitely started being more careful with my money. I put together a complete portfolio of stocks and bonds, and educated myself about how to make the most of my investments. I knew I wouldn't be earning a big-league salary forever. I had to plan for the future, not only for myself, but also for Josie.

That was another kind of education for me—an education in assuming responsibility. That was a set of lessons I was overdue in learning. And I'm grateful to my family for teaching me.

THE
STRIKE

*This year the players and owners have managed to do
what an earthquake, two world wars, a missile crisis
and a depression could not do, and that was cancel the
World Series.*

LIANE HANSEN,
Weekend Edition, *National Public Radio*

One thing the 1994 baseball season convinced me was that the Major League Baseball Players Association, led by Donald Fehr, always had one goal and one goal only: Becoming the mightiest union in the world. The union wanted power, and apparently the one way they felt they could amass that power was to make as much money for the players as possible—no matter what the long-term ramifications were for the players or the game itself.

That was the way the union handled the steroid issue, too. The Players Association was as complicit as the owners in the explosion of steroids in the game. They knew as much about it as anyone, because they dealt with the players all the time. To those of us on the inside, there was no mystery over why the union took such a hard line against steroid testing, for example. Their concern was always making money for the players, and if the players were remaking their bodies using steroids to do so, the MBPA never lifted a finger to stop it.

I believe that plenty of people within the Players Association must have known exactly which players were on steroids. And they did not care. If all you care about is jacking up players' salaries, why would you try to stop the steroid groundswell? Don't rock the boat.

Think about it this way: If Don Fehr really believed that his players *weren't* doing steroids, wouldn't he have said: *Okay, let a true drug-testing program begin?* Nothing like the joke we had during the 2004 season, for example.

But Fehr had to know the truth. He must have foreseen—Oh my god!—that if he let a real drug-testing program be implemented, too many of his top players would get caught . . . and everything Fehr had built would be at risk. So instead he just stalled, and it worked.

I'll say one thing for Donald Fehr, though. It took a strong leader to pull off what he did. You've got to give him that. He's quite a character; he's highly intelligent, has a real presence, and knows how to work the system to get the players behind him 100 percent. I think he actually attained his goal of becoming one of the most powerful union leaders ever, by developing this extremely powerful players' organization.

But the result was the strike of 1994, which was just crazy, if you ask me. You've got to be kidding: Grown men involved in a billion-dollar industry couldn't solve their own issues internally? Both sides should be ashamed of themselves for pushing things as far as they did that year. Not only was there a strike— the whole World Series was cancelled. Some of the owners may be perfectly smart people, but nobody involved in that could have had a whit of practical intelligence. They don't understand anything beyond what their lawyers told them. In the end, it came down to the nerds against the athletes, just like it was back in high school—and just like in high school, everyone lost.

That strike never should have happened, and it never would have happened if the owners had approached things intelligently. All they needed to do was find half a dozen influential players without guaranteed contracts who were willing to distance themselves from the stance of the Players Association. Those players each could have brought other players along to their way of thinking. These players would have collectively re-cruited more players, and more players, and so on, until the union was really in trouble. If the owners had approached me in the right way, I could have done it for them myself.

The owners could have broken the union that way, but they were never smart enough to think it through. They were always inclined to think in terms of brute force, to force our will. But negotiation doesn't work that way. You have to be shrewd and look for weaknesses in your opponent—and, in the case of the Players Association, there was plenty of that to go around. The Association had pissed off a lot of players, especially minority players; they were always thinking more about the whole than the individual, always thinking about profits, not the well-being of the players.

So why didn't they try something like that? For one thing, they didn't know who to go to. They had no player on the inside. When it comes right down to it, baseball owners aren't the smartest people in the world, either. People think that rich guys are always smart, or they wouldn't be able to make so much money, but often intelligence has nothing to do with it. The owners never approached it the right way, so we struck and they cancelled the World Series.

That was a dark period for baseball. Suddenly America had a new national pastime—asking: *Can baseball survive this? Will it ever be the same again? Are football and basketball going to take over now that baseball has ruined everything?*

One of the amazing things about the strike was how much you heard about it hurting the economy. The entire network of concessionaires, parking facilities, and other businesses lo-cated around stadiums, which relied on the income they generated during the baseball season, was affected. It was a real demonstration of how economically strong baseball was, that it affected so many people and so many smaller institutions. On a personal level, it was incredible for me to realize that what I did for a living touched so many people, directly or indirectly.

The timing of the strike was bad for me personally, too. I'd really been enjoying playing that season, and I was putting up good numbers. Back in Oakland, I hadn't always seen eye to eye with Tony LaRussa, who tried to play too many mind games for my taste. But in Texas I was playing for Kevin Kennedy, who was easily my favorite manager.

What made him stand out so much? Simple: He always showed me trust and respect. Kevin approached me first of all as a person, instead of treating me as just a ballplayer or a cog in the wheel. It may not sound like much, but to me it was important that Kevin treated me like a human being, with a family and emotions, ups and downs. Because of that, I trusted him completely.

And in return, I believe, he got the best out of me. I was at the ballpark on time every day, busting my ass for him day in and day out. If you look at the stats I put up for him when I was healthy, they were incredible. Kevin just made it very easy to play for him. All he asked was that you show up on time, play hard, and hang in there for nine innings. He had the good sense to keep it simple: He knew you were a grown man, and he trusted you to be a professional.

Kevin was definitely a players' manager. He made the Rangers a happy, cohesive atmosphere, and helped us to maintain good chemistry at the ballpark. If you had a problem, he wanted you to go to him, and he believed that any problem could be fixed in private. He didn't want to involve the media, because he knew the media tended to blow things out of proportion, which always had a way of turning into a huge distraction for the organization. He took good care of his team, and if you look back you'll see that he got the best years out of a lot of his players.

So it turned out that the trade from Oakland to Texas was a good thing for me. It gave me the motivation to work hard and get back to where I'd been a few seasons earlier, before my injuries started to get in the way. In my first three seasons with the A's, I'd had six hundred at-bats or more every year, and I finished all three of those seasons with at least thirty home runs and at least 110 RBIs. But after that, I had several seasons where I missed a lot of games because of injuries. I had worked really hard to get going again in 1994, and that work paid off for me.

I finished that season with thirty-one homers and 90 RBIs; that may not sound like much, but it was enough to lead the team in both categories. Juan Gonzalez had 85 RBIs, making him second on the team, but no one else on the team even hit twenty homers that year, let alone thirty. If the season hadn't been cut short, I might have had one of the best years of my career.

As it turned out, though, the Rangers played only 114 games that season, forty-eight short of the normal total of 162. If you do the math, I was on pace to finish the year with forty-four home runs—which would have tied my career high at that point—and 127 RBIs, which would have been the best total of my career. Also, even with a 52-62 record, the Rangers were in first place in the American League West at the time of the strike. We'd finished fourth during my first season in Texas, and second in 1993, and I would have liked to see what that 1994 Rangers team could have done in the postseason.

We had a lot of fun together on that team. Less than two weeks before the strike, for example, left-hander Kenny Rogers was pitching a great game against the California Angels at home. During the game, a couple of the other players, Chris James and Gary Redus, decided they had to perform a special ceremony to help bring Kenny good luck. Based on the way he was throwing, we all knew he might be on his way to a memorable performance.

All season long, I'd been getting flak about my shoes. They were scuffed up pretty bad, and the guys kept complaining that they smelled. So James and Redus got an idea, and they swiped them from me. Then in the fifth inning, after I had hit home runs my first two times up in the game, those two guys soaked my shoes in alcohol and put a match to them, right there in the dugout. It was meant as an offering to the baseball gods; and some of the guys even danced around the little fire, as if it was a bonfire or something.

They must have been on to something, too: Kenny Rogers never made a mistake, that whole game, and he finished with the first perfect game in baseball in four years, and only the fourteenth perfect game ever thrown. Too bad they couldn't have come up with some kind of crazy ceremony to try to save baseball that year.

The fans had to wait for fourteen months to see another World Series.

Chapter 14

THE MEN IN BLACK

Umps have a tough job to do, and you don't mess with them. In this league, you respect the umps or you don't stay around.

FORMER OAKLAND A'S MANAGER TONY LARUSSA

John Hirschbeck was always one of my favorite umpires. He and his brother Mark were approachable, open guys who were popular with players. John and I had a good relationship. John had to face a personal tragedy in 1993 when his eight-year-old son, John Drew, died from a rare degenerative nerve disease known as adrenoleukodystrophy (ALD). After that, both brothers put a lot of work into the John Drew Hirschbeck Foundation, a charity that raised money to fight the disease. John asked me to sign baseballs and make appearances for that foundation, and I was glad to take part in his fund-raisers, because I knew it was for a good cause and John and I had a good rapport.

"John, if I can help out, just let me know," I told him.

After I left the Texas Rangers, he took me up on that in an unusual way. In 1995, I was at spring training in Fort Myers, Florida, before a game against the Rangers. We were all just sitting around when one of the clubhouse attendants brought me a note.

"Jose, we're picketing outside of the stadium today, and we'd like you to come join us."

That was the first I'd heard about the umpires picketing, but since I liked John and I was all for helping the umpires get a settlement, I figured, "Why not?" So I walked out there and joined the umpires picketing in front of the surprised Florida fans; I even hung a sign around my neck.

Before I got out there, no one was paying much attention to the picket line. But soon there were a lot of people—and some reporters, too. The picketers had signs saying things like SCABS GO HOME and MAJOR LEAGUE UMPIRES LOCKED OUT. We handed out informational materials to anyone who wanted them, explaining how much umpires love the game of baseball.

"You saw what the game was like without the real players," I told the reporters that day. "It's going to be the same thing without the real umpires."

I think John appreciated what I did, backing him up that day. He and I continued to have a good relationship until the next year, when Hirschbeck became a lot more famous than he ever wanted to be. He was having a tough time, losing one son and finding out that another son was sick with the same disease. He and Roberto Alomar had a notorious confrontation at home plate after John made a call that Robby didn't like. They had words, and Robby spit in his face. That generated a huge controversy; all around the country, people were sounding off about it all. I'll just say this: There was a lot more to that confrontation than people know.

But after that September, John was totally different. He must have been so traumatized by the incident with Robby that I think he started going a little berserk during games; from then on, he took it out on all position players, myself included. He was constantly irate with us all, and there was nothing you could do to calm him down. It became a running joke among us players that if you were batting when John was behind the plate, you were going to strike out. He was capable of calling strikes on pitches a foot outside, or eight inches high, or eight inches low. You just walked back to the dugout shaking your head. That was all you could do. Up until that time, Hirschbeck was one of the better-liked umpires around, but things happen and people change. That's just the way it is.

There are all kinds of examples of umpires being on power trips. One time, during my rookie year, Steve Palermo was the home plate umpire and he missed a call. The pitch was down and away, but he called it a strike, and I gave him an earful, because it wasn't even close. Later in that same series, when Palermo was at second base, he told our second baseman, Mike Gallego, that I'd made a big mistake talking back to him like that.

Gallego told me that Palermo was furious. "Who the hell does this rookie think he is?" he asked Gallego. I knew from that moment that he was going to have it in for me for the rest of my career.

I still have a videotape of the time I was with the A's and Ted Hendry called a strike on a ball that was a foot outside and level to the ground. I just let him have it. You'd have to bleep out most of what I said. The next time I was up, I stood there in the on-deck circle and screamed at him some more.

"I can't believe you made that call!" I yelled. "It was terrible!"

I threw in a few cuss words, but he still wouldn't throw me out, so I went up to the plate and just kept shouting till he finally tossed me. He was one of the nicest umpires around. I always got along with him great, but in this case, it seemed obvious he was making that bad call because a week or two earlier I had questioned a call of Richie Garcia's. That's how it works—even though Garcia was in a completely separate crew, there's still a code among umpires that they will back each other up and make sure you pay.

Garcia was one weird dude. He was Latino, but it was well known in baseball that he was especially hard on Latinos. How messed up is that? I have no idea what was going on with Garcia.

Sometimes a guy just doesn't like the way you look, or the way you come across in the media. I think a lot of these umpires take it personally if you get to be a big star. Garcia had a serious attitude problem, and we players felt the brunt of it.

One of the things fans always wonder about is what players and umpires talk about during a game. I can see why; sometimes, when I catch a few minutes of a game on TV and I see a player jawing with an umpire, I try to read their lips to see what they're saying. Often it's easy to tell, but sometimes the players get a little more creative. It's a kind of art form, knowing how far to push an umpire without sending him over the edge. Some managers are really good at saying just enough, and doing it casually. Sometimes they'll even come out to the mound to talk with a pitcher, just so they can call something out to the umpire on their way back to the dugout. My own approach was to keep it simple, unless I was really losing my temper—because when that happened, forget about it.

I remember one time in the late 1980s when I was with the A's and we were facing the Detroit Tigers. Frank Tanana was pitching. He'd already been in the league fifteen years or so; he was on his way to two hundred career wins, and had the respect of everyone. You knew he was going to get a lot of calls, but he had that big old curve ball, and if they were giving him a few extra inches, you were going to have a really tough time.

So Drew Coble was behind the plate that day, and Tanana let loose with one of those big sweeping breaking balls, and it went completely around the plate. Never touched it. But Coble called it a strike! I couldn't believe it.

"Drew, wasn't that pitch outside?" I asked him.

He paused a minute and looked at me like I should have known better than to ask.

"Son," he said. "That's a Hall of Fame pitch. *A Hall of Fame pitch.*"

In other words, he was telling me that Frank Tanana was going to the Hall of Fame, and he was going to get calls like that every time, no matter how obvious it was that I was right. When Coble said that, I just laughed. He was a funny guy—maybe not the best umpire in the league, but he tried his best, which was all you could ask, and he was a great communicator. He was always making jokes, and some of them really busted you up. That made it a lot easier to take when he made calls that drove you crazy.

Every player has been on the wrong end of an umpire's revenge. They're a tight-knit group; they demand respect, and they can make or break you on the field, the same way the media can with the public. Generally I've gotten along with the umpires, but there were definitely times in my career when they had it out for me.

Moises Alou got so frustrated during the 2004 season that he broke one of the cardinal rules of baseball and complained in public that the umpires were out to get him. Everyone ripped him for that, and talked about how stupid it was for him to vent his frustration. But it's not like he was just being paranoid. I'm sure they *were* out to get him. I've seen it happen too many times.

Believe me, umpires are the most vengeful people you'll ever meet, and if you ever make the mistake of getting on their bad side, they will make your life miserable. I have no doubt that Moises had a legitimate complaint, but I'm also sure that he'll never live this down with the umpires. Whenever any umpire anywhere gets a chance to make a call against him, he will. He could be playing in the Northern League or Single-A and they'll still stick it to him on general principle. That's how umpires think.

It's really the same in all sports, and people should expect no less. The owners collude with each other in every sport, including baseball, and the umpires or referees collude with each other in their own way. This is nothing surprising. It's just basic human nature that if you have power, the temptation will be strong to abuse that power.

Fans would be amazed just how far some players—especially pitchers, even the best of them—will go to try to stay on the good side of umpires. Roger Clemens, who's a lock for the Hall of Fame, was always very conscientious about taking care of umpiring crews. One thing he would do was use his pull to get them on the best golf courses. I know, because Roger and I used to play golf together a lot of the time when we were teammates with the Red Sox, so I was out there with him. He always made sure the umps got a good starting time at courses like Blue Hill Country Club in Canton, Massachusetts.

I'm sure that if you look at these pitchers who consistently get wide strike zones, you'd see that they're generally the same guys who take care of the umpires off the field. They're the ones who do them little favors—get them into exclusive golf courses, reservations at the best restaurants. Some players are constantly signing bats and balls for them, taking pictures with their kids—even sending them Christmas gifts, like sporting equipment ordered directly from whichever company they have an endorsement deal with.

None of that is supposed to be done, but to those of us on the inside it's obvious when players are angling for favorable treatment. I remember one umpire who used to have these charity events where a lot of players would come and sign for free. People found he was pocketing a lot of the money, but what could you do? Believe me, if as an athlete, you don't do charity events for umpires, they start opening up the strike zone on you as a hitter. So the more favors you can do for them, the more breaks you'll get.

I remember one time in Texas I had a big run-in with Joe Brinkman, who was one of the toughest, most unfair umpires out there. He was always mad, just bristling with anger, and you couldn't approach him at all. He had to be the biggest hardass I've ever met in my life, and finally in this one game we got into a huge fracas and he just ripped into me, attacking me personally.

"Nobody out here likes you anyway," he screamed at me.

Then after the game—that very same game—he asked me to sign some autographs for his family. Incredible. I signed a couple baseballs and a picture or two for him, and chalked it up to experience.

The nicest, and most widely respected, umpire I ever met was Dave Phillips. Dave was present at some of baseball's biggest controversies over the years—he was there for Disco Demolition Night at Comiskey Park, and Gaylord Perry's ejection for throwing a spitball, and the whole pine tar thing with George Brett—but he was always level-headed and professional and called a very good game. Of all the umpires, he was the one I thought most highly of, and I think most players felt the same. He understood that baseball was a very emotional game and players were going to make mistakes every once in a while and question a call in the heat of passion. But he never let emotion get in the way of his calls, and he never held it against the players.

If I were going to offer umpires any advice, the first thing I'd mention would be: The most important factor to understand is the pressure players are under. Anything can happen in the heat of a moment, and whatever you say, umpires need to know that you probably don't mean it. Still, if you say something to the media about an umpire, they're going to remember it for a long, long time. I wish we could all try to leave grudges out of it. You can't intentionally make a bad call against a player because you don't like his race or you don't like him, but believe me, that happens every day during the baseball season.

On this front, I think the major leagues could take a lesson from the minors. I never had one problem with an umpire in the minor leagues. Those umps were very consistent. Why was that? Simple: They were trying to do the best job they could, because they all wanted to advance to the major leagues. If you're inconsistent in the minor leagues, you won't move up, so they try to do the best job possible. Once an ump's promoted to the big leagues, on the other hand, there's nowhere else to go; he loses the incentive to be the best he can, and starts doing whatever he wants. Thanks to the umpires union, an ump has a job until he dies, no matter how bad he might be. No player gets that kind of security; why should an umpire?

So through the years, when it's been the right thing to do, I've stood with the umpires. But now that there's an effort emerging to reevaluate major-league umpires, I support that, too. You can't just let them run amok. There's got to be a way to keep things honest.

GIAMBI, THE MOST OBVIOUS JUICER IN THE GAME

Steroid use is a topic of conversation daily among players. A lot of guys who don't do it are frustrated.

CURT SCHILLING,
June 2002

If not for the strike, I'm sure that the 1994 Texas Rangers would have finished strong, and with me as their offensive leader, they would have come back in 1995 ready to take one more step toward trying to win a World Series. Instead, after that chance was ripped out of our hands in 1994, the Rangers decided to go in another direction and traded me to Boston, where I had a couple of good seasons—which would have been a lot better if not for a series of annoying injuries. Over those two seasons, I played in fewer than 200 games; the fifty-two homers and 163 RBIs I clocked were good for the number of at-bats I had, but far from satisfying to me.

By that stage of my career, all the sportswriters thought they had me figured as a classic example of a player who would have been great if not for all the steroids I'd taken, and the injuries that they believed the steroids caused. In fact, they had it exactly backward. I would never have *been* a major-league caliber player without the steroids. I wouldn't have been capable of playing softball in a beer league—not with my health being what it was. Over the years I've been diagnosed by my doctors with arthritis, scoliosis, degenerative disc disease, you name it. I truly believe I would be in a wheelchair today if steroids hadn't been available to me. I needed steroids and growth hormone just to live. The only reason I was able to play baseball for so many years was that the steroids and growth hormone allowed me to build the right muscle structure to hold up my frame, and to recuperate fast enough after my injuries. I knew all along that it was about more than just gaining weight and being bigger, stronger, faster. It was about building a more potent body.

Before the 1997 season, the Oakland A's decided to take another chance on me, and made a trade with Boston to bring me back to the Bay Area and reunite me with Mark McGwire. The A's were going through another down period in those years, and they were hoping that news of the Bash Brothers playing together again might generate some fan interest. It did, too. As soon as fans heard about my return to the Bay Area, off-season ticket sales jumped to their highest level in three years. There was some speculation that Mark would feel weird about having me back, since I had a way of grabbing all the attention for myself, but actually he seemed glad to have me on the team again if it meant he would get more decent pitches to hit.

"Life hasn't been easy for him," Mark said of me at the time. "His child has made him a better person. I think it's going to be great this time around."

But that year I witnessed what was almost the definitive case study in the difference between the careful, controlled use of steroids I've always advocated and sheer recklessness. I'm talking, of course, about Jason Giambi, who became my teammate that year. As surely as he went overboard with partying and chasing women, Giambi went overboard with steroids. He became the single most vocal, outright juicer in the game, and nobody cared. He was a fun-loving guy, a party animal, and people loved him, especially since he was hitting and helping the team. The man could party like you wouldn't believe, but he got the job done at the ballpark.

Giambi had the most obvious steroid physique I've ever seen in my life. He was so bloated, it was unbelievable. There was no definition to his body at all. You could see the retention of liquids, especially in his neck and face; to those in the know, that was a sure sign of steroid overload, plus drinking a lot and having a bad diet. Combine that, and you end up with that chubby, thick, bloated look. You could literally put your finger on his skin and see the water under there as it indented and then filled in. That's not muscle! More dead giveaways: the color of his skin, and the reddish pimples.

It was clear to me from watching him that Giambi got turned on to steroids while he was under Mark McGwire's wing. In 1996, the previous year and Giambi's rookie season, those two had become inseparable, spending a lot of time together away from the ballpark. McGwire was like Giambi's big brother; he took him under his wing and taught him everything he knew about baseball, which was a lot. Giambi looked up to Mark. He would do anything Mark would do. At times, he would actually mimic him. Mark taught him the finer points of the game, about how to conduct yourself on the field and off. And given how much I'd been spreading the word about steroids, it was no surprise when I saw Giambi start to bulk up, too.

As soon as I rejoined the team for the 1997 season, I was amazed to see how open and casual those two were about steroids. Sometimes, the three of us would go into the bathrooms stalls together to shoot up steroids or growth hormone. I would inject myself, and Giambi and McGwire would be one stall over, injecting each other. Other times, I preferred to inject myself at home, but those two always did it at the ballpark, because it was easier that way and they knew they had nothing to worry about. Plus, they were having all kinds of fun injecting.

The three of us talked about steroids all the time that year, right in front of everybody. "My God, your veins are incredible—

what are you using?" Giambi might ask me, right out on the field during stretching or batting practice.

"Same stuff you're using," I'd say. "Deca and Winstrol."

"Wow, you've got the biggest arms," Giambi would say.

"Look at McGwire," I'd point out. "He's got the biggest arms here! Look at them! They're enormous!"

Or we might ask each other practical questions—especially Giambi, who was getting an education in steroids from McGwire and me that year.

"What dosage do you take?" he'd ask, just before taking his swings in the batting cage. "Are you due for a shot?" he might ask.

A lot of times, he wasn't really curious about the answer, he was just enjoying talking and thinking about steroids, about what they could do for his physique and his numbers. This was light conversation, and we never bothered to stop unless a reporter was around. By 1997, in front of anyone but the media, it was completely accepted that we would talk openly about steroids.

Before too long, it seemed like everybody was doing it. The bathroom stalls were the laboratory, and players would inject themselves right there. Everyone knew why you were going in there; they'd see two guys going into a stall together, and make cracks.

"What are you guys, fags?" they would joke.

But they knew we were going in to inject each other. It was as commonly accepted as getting a cup of coffee or a drink of water.

I remember instances where a guy had his syringe and a bottle of steroids in his coat pocket because we were going to travel that day. When the guy put on his coat, a needle and a vial would all fall out, and it was no big deal.

"Who does this belong to?" someone would ask.

It wasn't as if the player had to hide what he was doing.

"Oh, yeah, it's mine," he would say, and get it back, and that would be that.

The things guys would say during a game were another telltale sign. A pitcher might put the ball right in on your hands and break your bat, but you were so strong, you'd still take a powerful enough swing to send the ball sailing into shallow center field for a single. "How can we compete against this?" a pitcher would yell out from the mound, adding in a few swear words, and everyone from the base coaches to the other players to the umpires would know just what he meant by "this."

A lot of guys would carry their steroids around with them in a little black shaving bag. A complete kit would include clean syringes, vials of the different types of steroids and growth hormone they were injecting, and cotton swabs and alcohol, because we were always very careful about using proper technique. If you swabbed with alcohol every single time you injected and never used the same needle twice, there was no reason to expect any problem with infection.

Giambi was one guy who just tossed his little black shaving bag into his suitcase and brought all his steroid paraphernalia on the road with him.

Holy shit! I said when I saw how casual he and the other guys were about traveling with their steroids. I never brought steroids with me on the road, unless they were in pill form, which were easy to hide anywhere. But Giambi and some of the other guys would bring them in their suitcases—needles, vials, and all. I was thinking, "What if they inspect our bags?" But we always had charter flights, and we would go straight from the ballpark to the charter, fly to the next city, and then from the charter straight to the hotel. They loaded the bags right onto the team bus, no questions asked.

The world of baseball is like a closed society, with its own rules and structures and rituals, not really that different from one of those strange secret fraternities like Skull and Bones at Yale, the one that included both George W. Bush and John Kerry as members. One of the fundamental rules of baseball is that certain players were untouchables—and over time those players learned to use that power to the advantage of other players, too.

Mark McGwire was still one of the chosen ones, so that meant that Jason Giambi was protected, too. Everybody in the game knew that Giambi had been molded by McGwire, and whatever McGwire wants, he gets. With McGwire at his back, Giambi was as good as gold—from the owners to the media. Did you ever open the newspaper and see a headline like, GIAMBI SEEN IN NIGHTCLUB WITH 3 OR 4 GIRLS? No, because the media wouldn't touch him. (At least, not back then.)

It's impossible to measure how much steroids can help you, since each individual is different and steroids can have varying effects on different body types. But it's clear that steroids and growth hormone turned Jason Giambi into a completely different ballplayer. When he was starting out, it seemed to me that he was an average player with average ability. Look at his brother, Jeremy: He was a below-average player with below-average ability. Then all of a sudden Jason bolted out of the gate.

Giambi was a doubles hitter when he first came up. Then, as he got so much bigger, he started hitting a lot more home runs. But he paid for that transformation. Over the months and years, you could see that he was overdoing testosterone, which is a retaining agent. He didn't seem to realize that a baseball player should only be taking a low dosage of testosterone, and balance it with a ripping agent, like Winstrol or Deca or Equipoise. So instead of looking like a baseball player, he looked more like a professional wrestler.

To players who watched Jason Giambi up close, he was always an amazing character. Before he got engaged, he was an astonishing ladies' man, in a whole different league from most ballplayers. But he was always a real nice guy, happy-go-lucky, and as long as he got to the ballpark on time and performed, nobody seemed to care what he did with his night life.

Today, though, times have changed. I used to be the poster boy for steroids in baseball, but today I'd have to say the new poster boy is Jason Giambi. Before you know it, there may be a new sacrificial lamb, a new flavor of the month.

Today, these players may seem like pariahs. But don't be too surprised if some day we look back on some of them as pioneers.

BASEBALL ECONOMICS 101

*It's no secret what's going on in baseball. At least half
the guys are [on steroids].*

KEN CAMINITI

In that same 1997 season, Miguel Tejada made his major-league debut with the A's. As I got to know him a little bit, I started giving him advice about steroids, and he seemed interested in what I was saying. Tejada and I had a secret weapon: We could speak in Spanish, which made it easier to talk about whatever he wanted, even if reporters were around. I met him in spring training, but I injured myself in August right around the time he was called up from Double-A to make his major-league debut, so we never had a chance to talk as much as I would have liked. But it was obvious to me why he was so interested in steroids: Basic economics.

Back when I was starting out in baseball, I played with and against some older players who used to spend their off-seasons working in warehouses, as security guards, or in other odd jobs. Baseball didn't pay them enough back then even to take the winter off. That had changed by the time I came along, but not as dramatically as you might think.

In my rookie year, 1986, I made $60,000. The next year I made $180,000. My third year it was $325,000. I had hit thirty home runs for three straight years; I'd even been a Rookie of the Year. Nowadays, if they came across that kind of talent, they would probably be happy to hand someone a ten-year, $100 million contract. But I didn't start earning really serious money until after I was the unanimous choice for the American League most valuable player in 1988, my 40-40 breakthrough year. The A's knew they would have to come through, and in June 1990 I signed a five-year deal with Oakland for a total of $23.5 million—at the time, the biggest contract ever for a baseball player. (Up to that point, the largest such contract had been for four years, $12 million.)

If you compare the baseball player of today with the players of twenty years ago, you'll find that now they are bigger, faster, and stronger. The reason for that is simple: Competition is fierce, the money is unbelievable, and a majority of the players have been using steroids. Today, you can get $5 million out of college. Organizations are willing to lock you up for five years after your first good year or two. Back then, you had to prove yourself, go through arbitration and free agency, just to make it at all.

Young players coming up today are looking at a completely different economic picture. Let's say you're a talented young player from an impoverished area of Puerto Rico or the Dominican Republic. And let's say you realize that, if you can put together back-to-back good seasons with strong home-run totals, you can realistically set up your family and yourself for the rest of your life with a $40 or $50 million contract.

There's only one catch: To score that big paycheck, to set up your family and become one of the richest people in your country or on your island, you're going to need to guarantee that performance—and the only way to ensure that is to make the most of the opportunity presented by steroids and growth hormone. Put it that way, and I don't see any young kid turning it down. Would you? Would you really?

We know so much more about steroids now than we did even a decade ago. Today is nothing like the 1970s, when those scientists in East Germany were experimenting on women swimmers and other athletes with huge doses of steroids, having no idea what they were doing or what would happen to the women. Many of those East German swimmers have been left with major health problems, including giving birth to children with club feet and other defects. Worse yet, those women were never given a choice.

We've come a long way since then. We know enough now to be experts on the many ways of doing steroids properly, and supervising steroid use to make sure you're doing it safely. We have removed most of the question marks, and substituted reliable information about what to do and what not to do to achieve the result you want. I can't emphasize this enough: If you are going to use steroids, you have to use them properly. You can only use them under close supervision. You need to make sure you know what you're doing. This is nothing to mess around with: Steroids can hurt you, and I am the first one to say so. If you abuse steroids, they can be very harmful. That's why using them only in a careful, controlled way is so important. It takes education, personal discipline, and common sense. But if you've got all those things going for you, you never have to turn out like a Jason Giambi, or worse.

There are a lot of positive things about steroids and growth hormones that most people don't know. They were invented to help people with muscle growth and strength. There is obviously an advantage to athletes using steroids, especially in football, because football is a sport that emphasizes weight, mass, and speed, whereas in baseball, you need hand-eye coordination and quick-muscle-twitch fiber, depth perception, and so forth.

If you can incorporate all of that with mass and speed, then you have a winning combination. Despite the lingering fear of steroids, I believe that the era we are now entering, when developments like cloning and gene therapy are becoming a reality, will also see steroids be declassified from the same category as damaging drugs like cocaine.

If you do steroids properly for long enough and know what you're doing, the powers you gain can feel almost superhuman. Besides the boost to your strength and confidence level, you start running faster. Your hand-eye coordination and muscle-twitch fibers get faster. Your bat speed increases. You feel more powerful, and you can use a heavier bat without sacrificing any bat speed, which is the most important thing.

Bat speed is obviously the key to baseball. You never want to lose bat speed, but you also want to use as big a bat as you can. As you get stronger, you can use a bat with more ounces, and that's devastating for pitchers, because when you have a larger mass hitting a smaller mass, the larger mass always wins.

But the added strength isn't even the most important benefit for a baseball player. No, what makes even more of a difference in terms of performance is the added stamina it gives you all year round. On the last day of the season, you have the same strength and feel as strong as you did the first day of spring training. That's all-important over the course of the six weeks of spring training and then the long line of regular-season games that follow. Players who aren't using steroids inevitably get tired and lose strength from month to month. It gets harder and harder to maintain your level of performance as the season goes on.

Baseball players have an advantage over a lot of other athletes when it comes to steroids, because they're not trying to get to 300 or 350 pounds, the way some wrestlers or football players do. Most baseball players use steroids the way they are supposed to be used.

It's pretty simple, really. You need more steroids to gain more weight, so you inject more. But before you know it, you need to inject even more steroids to gain more weight. That's how it works. After a while, the effect is nullified. Your receptors can handle only so much testosterone, for instance, over a given period of time. Anything beyond that is wasted, and worse, it can endanger your liver, which needs enough time to filter all these chemicals out of your body.

Think of steroids like alcohol: One or two drinks a day is fine, but if you sit there and knock down twenty drinks a day, your liver's going to turn on you. Your filtration system can only cleanse so many liters of blood within a given period of time. So when you're constantly poisoning your body, your liver loses its ability to function efficiently, and you end up with liver failure.

But that only happens with steroids when you are dealing with unsupervised amounts. Every body is different. If you're going to use steroids, it's critical that you go to a doctor and get a total physical, to find out exactly what physical shape you are in and how your body functions. You must have them analyze your enzymes and your blood to make sure you don't have diabetes, any heart blockage, heart palpitations, or heart murmurs.

If you're in great physical condition to begin with, steroids are going to help you. But if you've got physical problems, you have to be careful. Using steroids could help you, but then again, they could activate some dormant problem in your system and hurt you. I don't believe steroids, or growth hormones, are for everyone. But they can benefit many people if used properly. And, for baseball players, there are very strong economic incentives to getting that kind of a boost for your strength, power, endurance, and ability to come back from injuries.

If you can maintain your peak stamina and strength over the course of an entire season, that can easily mean a gain of twenty or thirty home runs—which in turn can mean a $40 million difference in your contract. For that matter, it could mean the difference between having a job and not having a job. It does make a huge difference. How many young players would pass up a chance to make that much more money?

Let's get back to the example of Tejada, my former teammate in Oakland. I can't say for sure whether he went on to do steroids after we talked about it. But in the years that followed he obviously pushed himself to an amazing performance record. And what did he get in return? He signed a huge contract with the Baltimore Orioles before the 2004 season, for something like $72 million over six years. It was the biggest contract in the history of that franchise. Those same economic realities that have changed Miguel Tejada's life are what drive so many other players toward using steroids today. And—testing or no testing—many will continue to use them so long as the financial payoff is so dramatic.

Today, Tejada has turned into one of the best players in the game. But when I played with him, he was as raw as they come. Keep in mind, this was a kid who might as well have been born on a different planet. His parents lived in a little shantytown called Bani in the Dominican Republic, forty miles outside of the capital of Santo Domingo. Tejada's mother couldn't afford to see a doctor while she was pregnant with him; she couldn't even afford to take a break from her job until just before he was born. He was the eighth kid in his family, and soon enough, like all the others, Tejada was working to help the family survive. He would shine shoes or move concrete blocks or any other odd jobs he could find.

Do you want to tell me that a kid like that, growing up in such a poverty-stricken family, wouldn't jump at a chance to help them all out? For all I know, Miguel Tejada did it in the old fashioned way. But could you blame a guy for taking steroids instead?

Steroids used to be mysterious to most people, but those days have passed. The simple truth is, it's not that hard to tell when someone is using steroids. You just have to trust your eyes. If someone adds a huge amount of muscle and does it quickly, you know he's using steroids. There's just no other way to do it.

This might shock some people, but I have been amazed by some young players who chose *not* to use steroids. They are the exceptions. Take another young player from that 1997 Oakland A's team: Ben Grieve, son of former Texas Rangers executive Tom Grieve. Let me tell you, Ben Grieve was a kid who needed to take steroids. He had a slow bat, slow feet, and average ability. The A's actually drafted him in the first round in 1994, but that was seen by many of us as a matter of politics, a favor to his father.

Ben always seemed physically weak to me—and you know, when you're a physically weak player competing against a lot of big, strong guys, that has to play havoc with your mind, your confidence, and your performance. Just look at Grieve's stats: He hit .264 in 2001, playing for Tampa Bay. The next season he finished with a batting average of .251. The next year it was .230. And have you seen him play the outfield? He has a slow bat, no hand speed, no power, nothing. He's taking up a roster spot some kid could definitely use.

So I don't believe Ben Grieve had the ability to play at the major league level. But after he was given that opportunity, I could have taken Grieve and turned him into a stud. He would have been the perfect kid to benefit from the combination of steroids and growth hormone. If I'd had the chance to work with him for four months, I could have turned him into a power hitting machine. You work on the quick muscle-twitch fiber. You work on putting on weight in the right areas. You work on his strength. If I'd gotten to him early, worked on him physically, and put him on the right diet, you would have seen a 50 percent improvement from him.

Tejada always had talent, and he had a good throwing arm from the first time I saw him at spring training in 1997. But his numbers tell a story, too. That first year, when we were teammates, he was only with the A's long enough to play in twenty-six games—which tells you something right there. He hit all of .202 in those ninety-nine at-bats that year. The next year he played in more than 100 games and hit .233. Now look ahead a few years to 2002, the season he ended up as American League MVP. That was the first season he hit better than .275. It took him that long.

Tejada finished with good numbers, batting .308, good power numbers, thirty-four homers, and 131 runs batted in. He wasn't a unanimous pick for MVP, the way I'd been, but it was pretty close. Tejada had to wait out one more year in Oakland where the owner, Steve Schott, came right out and said he was too cheap to pay him enough to keep him with the A's, and then he got his big payday.

It's amazing to me to look at Tejada now, because I remember seeing him when he was a skinny rookie. A few years later, he pumped up like a balloon. I remember one year he came in really big after the off-season and I was almost laughing the first time I got a look at him.

"What the hell is that?" I said.

It looked kind of funny, but when you're already talented, the way he was, why not add to the package? He gained some strength, some more power, and all of a sudden his numbers were way up there. His new pumped-up body helped him move up to become one of the top three shortstops in the major leagues, along with Alex Rodriguez and Nomar Garciaparra, before Alex changed positions when he was traded to the New York Yankees. I don't put Derek Jeter in that top group, but I'm impressed by how he became such a first-rate player without using steroids. And if he'd used steroids he'd be even better.

Tejada set himself up—himself and his family back home in the Dominican Republic. All he had to do was make himself bigger and stronger, and for Tejada that paid off. Some people, like me, have done so by using steroids. That might sound like some kind of pact with the devil. But I'd call that a good business decision, and a good life decision.

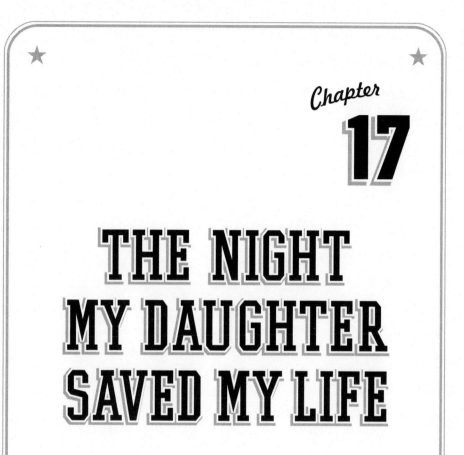

THE NIGHT MY DAUGHTER SAVED MY LIFE

If anything, I have more of a temper than Jose. He just walks away from the situation if we're arguing. I think his first wife knows that and I know that, but everybody else believes what they want to believe.

JESSICA CANSECO,
Sports Illustrated, *1999*

essica and I had our share of disagreements, as I've said. Like me, she's a strong personality, and when you put two strong personalities together, chances are good that some sparks are going to fly. For that matter, I haven't always handled myself well. Back in November 1997, after I spent that one season back with the A's, Jessica and I started arguing while we were in a friend's car. She was in the passenger seat, I was in the back, and when I couldn't get her attention any other way, I pulled her hair. The whole thing got out of hand from there, and by the time we got back to her place we were having a serious argument.

Just to scare me, Jessica locked the security gates at her house so I couldn't get out, and then called the police. That started a whole legal process. But that was an isolated incident, and I don't think it was fair to label me a wife-beater, the way the media did, because of one incident. I've actually heard people chant that at games: *Wife beater! Wife beater!* Maybe those fans assumed that because I was a big, muscular guy, I was some kind of robot, but I'm not—and it hurt. The same thing goes for the media, which wrote some pretty awful, and unfair, things about me after that incident with Jessica.

Around that time, we decided to separate. Nothing was ever very clear, but eventually, after talking about it a few times, we said, "*Yeah, let's try to spend some time apart and see how it goes.*"

I agreed to it, even though I think we still loved each other, and I was sure we would end up back together.

Throughout that time, though, we still talked a lot. One day I was trying to reach her on the phone, but I couldn't. That seemed odd, so I had a friend of mine who works for one of the airlines look into it for me. He gave me a call at my house in Weston, Florida, and he seemed worried about coming right out and giving me the news.

"Where is she?" I asked him.

"Jose, you're not going to like this." he said.

"Where is she?" I asked again.

"Kansas City," he said.

"Kansas City?!" I said.

"Kansas City," he said.

I knew what that meant. She'd flown to Kansas City to be with Tony Gonzalez, the Kansas City Chiefs' tight end. Tony was a great athlete, and played both football and basketball back in college. I had a lot of respect for him. But I couldn't believe this was happening. This was the first time I'd ever gone through something like this, and it had me in total shock. I couldn't think of anything to do but keep trying to reach Jessica on her cell phone.

Finally, she answered.

"Where are you?" I asked her.

She didn't say anything.

"Jessica, where are you?"

"Well . . ." she started to say, but then stopped.

"I know where you are," I told her. "I tracked you to Kansas City. I know you're with Tony."

For a while, she didn't seem to know what to say.

"That's right," she said finally. "I am with Tony."

I held the phone in my hand, but I couldn't have formed words if I'd wanted to. Finally, I just put the phone down and started walking toward my closet. I'll never forget that night. It felt like someone had just ripped my heart out. It was such a strange feeling.

You know, when you're in a period of separation, you suspect things. But you can go a long time without ever getting confirmation. Sure, maybe a hint here or there—but not the kind that's sitting there in front of you, staring at you: *Yes, it is what it is. Now live with it.* Then, when that confirmation finally comes, you feel the worst kind of sinking feeling: You're in love with a woman, and all of a sudden she's with another man. Or, in my case, another athlete.

There's no description for that kind of pain. It hits you all at once and overwhelms you. It feels impossible that one man could endure that much pain. It doesn't help to ask yourself questions, but you do anyway: *What happened here? What could explain this? What should I have done differently?*

To make matters worse, this came at a time when I was already depressed about baseball. No matter what I did in the game, no matter what I accomplished or how I played, it seemed I could never fill the shoes that had been laid out for me. I could never live up to the expectations the fans had built up for me. I would never get them to like me.

All I ever wanted to hear were those words:

Jose Canseco, the All-American boy. Jose, the national icon.

Let's be honest: That's what everybody wants, isn't it? Doesn't everybody dream of being a household name, known by everyone, respected by all? Doesn't everyone think about being recognized wherever you go, watching people tap each other on the shoulder to say, "Look, isn't that him?!"

I was famous enough to be all over the place in the media: on magazine covers, in episodes of *The Simpsons*. But I don't feel I was ever truly accepted. They always depicted me as the outsider, the outlaw, the villain. I was never ushered into that special club of all-American sports stars, which is reserved for guys like Mark McGwire or Jason Giambi or Cal Ripken Jr.

After all, I was dark. I was born in Cuba. I would never be allowed to feel I really belonged. I saw this from the beginning with the way they pitted McGwire and me against each other during my first run with the A's, but after I returned to the team in 1997 and saw the special treatment he was getting by then, it really hit home for me. I realized for the first time that I would never, ever become the all-American sports hero.

It was over before it even began: That was the thing I came to realize. No matter what I did—the MVP, the 40-40—it didn't matter. I could never make the fans happy enough for them to view me the way I wanted to be viewed.

Who wouldn't be depressed, facing up to that?

And then, on top of it all, I found out about Jessica and Tony.

I didn't even want to think about it or analyze it. I just knew what I had to do. I walked over to my closet in the bedroom of that big house in Weston and pulled out a gun.

This wasn't just any gun, it was something called a Street Sweeper, which is a type of a machine gun. I don't have it any more, obviously. It's actually a barrel with twelve shotgun shells in it; the back of it pulls out, like a machine gun. Whatever it hits, it's going to destroy. All it takes is one shot. I used to use that thing when we would go deep-sea fishing; if we caught a shark, I'd shoot the hell out of it with the Street Sweeper.

But that night I wasn't thinking about shooting any sharks. I pulled the gun out of the closet, and carried it with me in one hand back toward the bed. The next step would be to lie down there and shoot myself. It was all happening spontaneously. I didn't give a second's thought to writing a note, or to the consequences of such an act. I just felt I had only one choice left.

But before I could get that far, something very strange happened.

From somewhere indistinct nearby, I heard my daughter make a kind of strange sound, a little squeal, a quiet cry. Whatever I heard, or thought I heard, it snapped me out of a trance; it distracted me from what I was doing. I put the gun down and walked through the hall to go to my daughter's room to see if she was all right.

What happened? I was wondering: *Why would she make that strange noise?*

But here's the eerie thing: That house in Weston was enormous, roughly 22,000 square feet. The main part of the house alone was 13,000. You could shout, and it wouldn't even travel halfway across the house. The master bedroom was at one corner; my daughter's room was way down at the far corner of the house. And her door was shut. So there was no way on this earth that I could have heard my daughter make that sound. It was just not humanly possible.

Something had decided that it wasn't my time yet.

When I looked into her room, of course, she was fast asleep. She was just a baby, still not a year old. I lifted her up on my chest, and she stayed asleep the whole time. We walked down that long, long hallway together; then I got into bed and put her right on top of my chest. I could hear her heart beating, slow and regular. I knew she was sleeping deeply and peacefully. And it was as if I absorbed some of that sense of peace from her that day. I knew I could never leave her. That was the night my daughter saved my life.

Before the night ended, the phone rang a few times. It was Jessica, trying to reach me. But eventually I just took the phone off the hook, and lay there with Josie on my chest, letting my mind go. But my thoughts were about my daughter, not about the situation. Finally, after a long time, I fell asleep.

The next day I spoke with Jessica, and she said she was coming back. She wanted us to get back together. She kept telling me she couldn't believe she had gone up to Kansas City to see Tony. It was one of those things: They had met and talked a few times, and she'd decided to fly up to see him. Jessica and I were separated, but only recently, and I never thought she would all of a sudden take up with an athlete. Today I'm no longer bothered by the whole thing, but back then it was a new and fresh shock for me.

Tony and I talked that day, too—just a brief conversation, no hostility, no anger. I never get like that. I have absolute respect for all athletes. Hell, it wasn't Tony's fault. A beautiful girl like Jessica? What guy wouldn't jump at a chance with her? Plus, I had to admit, Jessica and I weren't really together. But in my mind and my heart we still were.

Jessica and I tried to make it work again after that, but we've never been able to. We've been back and forth so many times, I can't even count. But the thing that never changes is we always have Josie in common, and nothing is as important to me as my daughter. That's a strong bond.

Playing baseball takes a lot of time, but especially in the off season, you can spend a lot of time with your daughter, and I was always around. Jessica and I experienced so many amazing moments together with Josie—like when she first started talking. People always talk about a kid's first words, as if there were one magical moment. But it's never a word, it's more like a series of sounds that transcend into something else—a little bit of baby music, and suddenly she's spitting out a word.

Unlike me, Josie has always had a ton of personality. You can tell if kids are going to be dominating or bashful, and I was a very shy kid. Not my daughter. She's a rascal now, boy. She loves the camera, and people, and being out front and taking over. For a grown-up shy kid like me, it's amazing to watch. The older she gets, the more she develops her own personality, especially now, at the age of eight. I like just sitting there watching her. I can spend hours with her, watching her facial expressions; she's so smart, always trying to trick Dad into giving her an extra candy, or playing video games with her a little longer. Kids are so smart; they learn so fast, it's just incredible. All you can do is watch closely. If she does something wrong, you want to be firm with her and teach her the right way, but at the same time, in the back of your mind, you're thinking, "Wow, she's so smart. Man, look how cute she is!"

But you can't just go gaga on them all the time—because they'll spot your weakness every time. You can't let them see you're really smiling, because then they know: *Okay, I got Daddy now.* She definitely has me in the palm of her hand. I take her to the movies, to the arcade; she's very athletic, so I take her golfing and bowling. We play softball together. She's old enough for tennis now, so I want to start getting her into tennis.

A little while back, Jessica had a casting call for Target, which was looking for a model for a national TV commercial. But she didn't have a babysitter lined up for that day, so she took Josie along with her. For a few years, people had been telling Jessica and me that Josie should be a model; we'd even been approached by talent scouts for modeling agencies. "Wow, you have a beautiful daughter," they would say. "Is she interested in modeling?" We always said no, figuring that Josie was too young for that.

But last summer, Jessica and I had begun talking more seriously about letting Josie try a little modeling, since we knew she would enjoy it. Then, a few weeks after that, the Target casting came up. Jessica brought Josie along with her, and guess who got the national commercial for Target?

My daughter's got beautiful green eyes, curly blonde hair—and the personality to go with it. And—no surprise—that day she got her first modeling job as well.

STEROID SUMMER, THE McGWIRE-SOSA SHOW, AND THE FAKE CONTROVERSY OVER ANDRO?

Ownership is looking the other way, even though there are obvious users people constantly point to. When something happens, there are going to be huge liability suits.

REGGIE JACKSON

That next season, I signed with the Toronto Blue Jays as a free agent, and for the first time since the 1991 season I stayed healthy enough to play in 150 games. I finished with 107 RBIs and a career-high of forty-six home runs. But, believe me, no one was paying any attention at all to what I was doing. That was the summer when everyone was hitting home runs, and forty-six only ranked me third in the American League. Over in the National League, Mark McGwire and Sammy Sosa were the biggest thing to hit baseball in years. They traded home runs all summer long, battling it out to see who would take Roger Maris's single-season record.

McGwire and Sosa brought the game of baseball back to life that summer, pure and simple. They generated so much excitement, so much interest, that the cloud that had been hanging over baseball since the 1994 strike was finally lifted. People were as excited about baseball as they had ever been, even going back to the heyday of Babe Ruth and those guys.

And why? Because the owners had been smart enough not to chase steroid use out of the game, allowing guys like McGwire to make the most of steroids and growth hormone, turning themselves into larger than life heroes in more ways than one.

The owners' attitude? As far as I could tell, *Go ahead and do it.*

And why not? The steroid spectacle was making money for them. It brought the game back to life. Eventually they were going to have to find a way to deal with steroids, but back then they weren't worried about it. They weren't even testing. Instead, they gave players every reason to get bigger and stronger. If the athlete did his part, jabbed himself in the butt with the steroid needle, and grew stronger and tougher and better, the owners did their part and wrote out the checks—which just kept getting bigger all the time. Everybody was profiting, and they never even had to answer difficult questions, since no one wanted to ask them. There's a name for that kind of thing: Good business.

Baseball had been in really serious trouble since the 1994 strike, and absolutely everyone knew it, from fans to players to sportswriters to owners. The sport was on a downhill slide, and had no idea how to right itself. People thought it needed a shot in the arm. In the end, though, what it took was a shot somewhere else.

That was the point in the history of the game when the steroid revolution really exploded.

If the owners were asking themselves, *How could we bring baseball back?*, it seemed as though they finally hit on the simple answer: home runs. So how could you pump up the sport and get an exciting home run race going? The players knew the answer to that: steroids. I believe that the leadership of baseball made a tacit decision not only to tolerate steroid use, but actually to pretend it didn't exist among baseball players, even as it was making the sport more popular with the public. They obviously knew what they were doing, too. Baseball has been on a roll ever since.

If the owners want to evade responsibility for their part in the steroid revolution now, let them try. I'm not going to name any actual owners; I don't want anyone picking up a phone and sending a hit man after me. But let's put it this way: I know what they were thinking about players juicing up the game. They're good businessmen, and they made a business decision, pure and simple.

To see how successful their laissez-faire attitude toward steroids was, just look at the summer of 1998 and how interest in the game exploded. You heard it all the time that year: This was just what baseball needed, the excitement of Mark McGwire and Sammy Sosa both going after Maris's record in the same year. The McGwire-Sosa contest was great for ratings, great for attendance, and great for the viability of the game. That summer was everything the owners were hoping for.

McGwire had been a pretty big player back in Oakland, but by the summer of 1998 he was huge—up around 280 pounds. Balls that would have been fly-ball outs earlier in his career now sailed over the fence for home runs. He hit forty-nine as a rookie, so there was never any doubt that he was a natural slugger—one of the greatest ever, if you ask me.

But it took a lot of injections to get him past Roger Maris that summer.

I don't know Sammy Sosa personally, so I can't say for a fact that he ever took steroids. But I remember thinking that his transformation looked even more dramatic than Mark's. It looked like he was trying to make up for lost time by bulking up faster than McGwire ever had. He gained thirty pounds, just like that, and got up to 260 so fast, you could see the bloating in his face and neck. It seemed so obvious, it was a joke.

And the results ended up in the record books. Sammy had always been a big swinger, and when he connected, he could hit the ball a long way. But through his first nine seasons in the major leagues, only once did he hit forty homers in a season. Then he started bulking up, and with his new body hit sixty-six homers in 1998, sixty-three the next season, fifty the year after that, and then sixty-four in 2001.

The summer of 1998, though, was the high-water mark for steroids in baseball. At the time, I joked that so many guys went rushing to hide their vials in the locker room when the media showed up that it was like watching roaches scurrying for cover after the lights go on.

By now, the players had grown bolder than ever talking about their dosages among themselves. They would trade little details constantly—from injection angles to how to dump your syringes after using them. This was no small thing: It's a felony to carry a needle. Most players just slipped them back into their bags until they'd saved up six or eight of them, and then got rid of them all at once.

I think the players knew better than to dump syringes where they lived. We'd find strategic ways to dispose of them somehow—in Dumpsters or out-of-the-way trash bins. I'm not sure about the other players, but I was always very careful to wipe my fingerprints off the syringes, just in case there was a reporter nosing around, pulling out syringes and wondering, "Hey, who does this belong to?"

Sometimes, you just gave your used syringes to the clubhouse attendants, who would put them all in a bag and toss them out with the regular garbage. That's how easy it was—like throwing away the big, greasy bag after a visit to Burger King. You didn't want someone to spot you out near a Dumpster, even driving by in your car, because especially someone like me, six foot four, 250, is going to tend to be recognized: "Hey, there's Jose Canseco! What's he doing over there next to that Dumpster?"

That constant awareness of reporters coming in to the clubhouse, and the need to put away your stash, was what made it so laughable in 1998, when this so-called controversy erupted over McGwire and androstenedione. A lot of people assumed that because Mark McGwire was always shy and awkward talking to people—especially to reporters and other media types—he was kind of dumb. But just because Mark is quiet doesn't mean he's not smart . . . and to my mind the whole androstenedione controversy showed just how clever he is.

Try to think about the question for a minute without jumping to conclusions, the way everyone did back then. Mark had been suspected of using steroids for a long, long time. Nobody ever came out and said it in the media, the way that they had about me, because Mark was a white golden boy. Given all that, Mark must have been worried about when his luck would run out and his protected status would change. He couldn't have helped wondering whether the roof would come down on him, and everyone would know how much steroids had to do with his success in baseball. He was a very private person to start with; the idea of being unmasked must have eaten away at him.

Think what it must have been like for him. The summer of 1998 was like a movie starring Mark and Sammy, and I'm sure Mark wanted to protect himself in case anyone decided to try to go public with what every player in baseball knew: that McGwire was juiced. So here's what I think he did: He left a bottle of andro in his locker, where he knew a reporter would see it, and write about it. That's just what happened, and it was a big distraction. You even had politicians in Washington, D.C., like Arizona Senator John McCain, calling for andro to be controlled.

But this is where you need to stop and think. Androstenedione is a temporary testosterone booster. It boosts your own testosterone level for about an hour, and then the effect goes away. Use it right before a workout, and it may give you a little pick-me-up. It may make your workout a little more intense.

But an hour later, the effect is gone. Steroids, on the other hand, stay in your system for six to eight months at a time.

Mark was an experienced steroid user, as I know firsthand. His physique speaks for itself. And he knows as well as I do that if you're taking steroids, you don't need androstenedione. McGwire using andro would have been like a hospital patient on morphine asking for an aspirin. It just doesn't make any sense.

The andro story may have been a ploy, but if so it sure was clever. There were two big advantages for Mark in having his name associated with andro. One, it was a distraction from the real issue, which was steroids: "Oh, he's taking this other thing, and he got it over the counter. No wonder he's so strong." That was enough to keep the media occupied that season, when he hit seventy homers. Two, if he'd ever been required to take a steroid test, and he failed, it would have been easy for him to say: *That was just the andro. I didn't do anything illegal.*

Here's what I think: I don't believe Mark McGwire was even taking andro. Why would he? That bottle of andro was just sitting in his locker; that doesn't mean he actually used it. To me, it seems more likely that the whole thing was an illusion. I'm virtually certain that Mark created the andro controversy as a distraction.

The one surprising thing was how well the setup worked.

THE GODFATHER OF STEROIDS

Jose Canseco was the Typhoid Mary of steroids.

AN ANONYMOUS AGENT

The owners are going to be criticized for their complicity in the steroid revolution, but should they be? It all depends how you look at it. They knew they needed to take strong measures if they were going to re-ignite interest in their dying multimillion-dollar industry. And they may not have been aware of every last injection each of their players made.

But the owners knew something was afoot. They could see it in the long list of shattered records, and in the long parade of ripped-and-cut athletes they employed. Plenty of trainers knew much, much more—I know that because I told them myself. And the Major League Players Association knew what was going on, there's no doubt in my mind. But up to that point steroid use had been common without necessarily being widespread. It was only after the strike that you saw everything starting to blow way out of proportion.

And it didn't take an expert to recognize what was happening.

Here's one case everyone was puzzling over: Brady Anderson hit thirteen home runs over the course of the whole 1993 season. The next year he finished with twelve; the year after that he was up to sixteen. Over the course of three seasons, he squeaked out a mere forty-one homers; it was clear to everyone what kind of hitter he was—a leadoff guy with a little bit of pop, not much more than that.

Then what happened? In 1996, he came back and hit an even fifty home runs.

Was he using steroids? I never saw him inject himself, but he and I discussed steroids many times. And consider this: How else could someone go from hitting a total of forty-one home runs over three seasons to cranking out fifty in one, without a major boost from steroids? The following year, Brady was back down to eighteen homers for the season; the year after that, he finished with the same number. Was it a fluke? Or, as Jim Palmer has suggested, was Anderson's '96 season influenced by steroid use? You be the judge.

(And while we're at it, let me put to rest is this whole notion that the huge increase in home runs we've seen in recent years can be explained by higher compression baseballs. I think we all know that it's the players who were juiced, not the balls. Sure, there were other factors besides steroids—Major League Baseball now uses better bats, made of stronger wood, than it used to, and I'm sure that has made a contribution to the home-run totals. But mostly it had to do with having stronger, more consistent hitters, with quicker reflexes, who were able to maintain that strength throughout an entire season.)

You can ask Brady Anderson about the advice I gave him. For that matter, you can ask plenty of players the same question—and if you find one who's willing to be honest, they'll confirm it for you. I was the player who made it acceptable for others to do steroids—because after a while it was clear the owners were leaving the door open for me to educate them, no questions asked.

I never minded helping others get bigger and stronger, even though I knew that someday I might be competing with some of these same guys for a spot on a team. I enjoyed helping them tap their own potential to try to become better players.

You may wonder why I would share my secret weapon so openly.

Looking back, I don't think it was entirely selfless: The truth is that I never really had the greatest self-confidence, and I think I was always trying to help people, in a quest to win their approval. Even after I reached the big leagues, after all, I was still a pretty quiet and shy guy. Of course, that wasn't always the picture you got from the media. When you come into some money as a famous athlete, it's easy for people to develop an attitude about you, and there are an awful lot of reporters out there who called me arrogant. And yet I think most people who met me and talked to me came away saying, "Oh, he's just a big teddy bear."

The steroid strategy worked great for baseball, at least for a few years. But then what happened? The owners became victims of their own success. They brought baseball back, but the new excitement over the game had the inevitable effect. Salaries climbed up and up and up, to monstrous new levels. With it came the constant threat that the players' open secret about steroids would be exposed. And that was when they decided to change tactics.

That was when they told me, in effect: Go away and be quiet. We don't want you.

The owners realized that they needed to put the kibosh on steroid use, or at least pretend to. So they decided to send a loud message to all players, by getting rid of the player most closely identified with steroids: Jose Canseco. I was only thirty-eight home runs short of five hundred for my career, but at thirty-seven years old, I was out of the game. I could have been the worst player in the world and still hit those last thirty-eight home runs before my time was up. But they took that chance away from me, because they wanted to send the world a message that steroids had gotten out of control. They made an example of me. The players all knew it. And when I confronted Donald Fehr with my problem, he did nothing about it.

The baseball industry needed to cover its tracks, and that meant shutting me up. I knew way too much about the inner workings of the steroid era. I knew it had gotten to the point where a number of team trainers, weight-lifting coaches, and other on-field medical personnel were able to recommend specific steroid programs to major-league players. I was friends with some of these personnel, and we'd discussed a variety of issues concerning steroids and what using steroids can do for an athlete. I explained to them how their players could benefit, especially players who were on the disabled list.

The disabled list, or DL, was the key to the whole thing. Obviously it costs an organization money when a player is on the disabled list, especially if he's a great athlete who earns what great athletes earn. As salaries have exploded, many teams have had to carry ever-higher costs to pay their star players to sit out with injuries. So it has become a major concern for teams: How do you get them off the DL more quickly?

It's the trainers' job to get these players healthy and back in the lineup as fast as possible. I spoke about that challenge with more than a few of them, in detail, and they agreed that what I said made a lot of sense.

"Listen, what happens if all these players say they want to do steroids?" I asked them. "What are you going to do about it?"

"We don't really know," they said.

Did any of these trainers ever discuss what they were doing with the owners? I don't know. But as the years went on the word spread, and the owners and the union both fought hard to keep testing out of baseball. The message seemed clear: If the players were finding ways to pump up their bodies, enhance their performance—and inject life into the game while they were at it—nobody was going to lift a finger to complain.

As soon as the trainers I talked to started getting involved, the steroid floodgates burst. The players started doing them right there in the locker room, so openly that absolutely everybody knew what was happening. It was so open, the trainers would jokingly call the steroid injections "B_{12} shots," and soon the players had picked up on that little code name, too. You'd hear them saying it out loud in front of each other: "I need to go in and get a B_{12} shot," a player would say, and everyone would laugh. (Of course, that was the kind of joke you really only made around other steroid users, because obviously they were in the same boat as you. What were they going to do, tell on you? Not hardly.)

They weren't talking about vitamins or supplements, of course, but about a combination of steroids—in most cases Deca and some form of testosterone. I never used the term myself, because I was mixing up my own stuff and didn't need any trainer's help. That would have been like a master chef walking into McDonald's and ordering a Big Mac to taste the special sauce. The funny part is, there might have been a few players who didn't even know what was in the shots they were getting. I never pulled any of them aside and asked, "Did you know he's injecting you with steroids?" I just assumed they all knew, but looking back, I'm not so sure. There may have been a few who were so out of it that they weren't even aware of what was going on. You'd have to ask them about that yourself.

It was the pitchers who really kept that "B_{12}" joke going. For example, I've never seen Roger Clemens do steroids, and he never told me that he did. But we've talked about what steroids could do for you, in which combinations, and I've heard him use the phrase "B_{12} shot" with respect to others.

A lot of pitchers did steroids to keep up with hitters. If everyone else was getting stronger and faster, then you wanted to get stronger and faster, too. If you were a pitcher, and the hitters were all getting stronger, that made your job that much more difficult. Roger used to talk about that a lot.

"You hitters are so darn strong from steroids," he'd say.

"Yeah, but you pitchers are taking it, too. You're just taking different types," I'd respond.

And sometimes Roger would vent his frustration over the hits even the lesser players were starting to get off of good pitchers. "Damn, that little guy hit it off the end of the bat and almost drove it to the wall," he would say. He would complain about guys who were hitting fifty homers when they had no business hitting thirty. It was becoming more difficult for pitchers all the time, he would complain.

What could I tell him? All's fair in love and steroids.

I can't give chapter and verse on Roger's training regimen. But I'll tell you what I was thinking at the time:

One of the classic signs of steroid use is when a player's basic performance actually improves later in his career. One of the benefits of steroids is that they're especially helpful in countering the effects of aging. So in Roger's case, around the time he was leaving the Boston Red Sox—and Dan Duquette, the general manager there, was saying he was "past his prime"—Roger decided to make some changes. He started working out harder. And whatever else he may have been doing to get stronger, he saw results. His fastball improved by a few miles per hour. He was a great pitcher long before then; it wasn't his late-career surge that made him great. But he certainly stayed great far longer than most athletes could expect. There's no question about that.

The media were clueless, for the most part, about steroids. It was all happening behind closed doors, and they weren't privy to what happened in the privacy of the clubhouse. They didn't know that steroid use was so open that nobody really cared—that it had become integrated into the physical therapy regimen, so you didn't ever have to hide. It was as casual as taking a greenie—that is, amphetamines. It was simple: "Oh, I need to jack up my program. Who's got something in his locker?"

"Here's a needle. Go and inject yourself."

Or you just asked a trainer: "Do you know anybody who can get me a new supply?"

"Yeah, here, call this guy."

By the time the owners decided to crack down, it seemed like every player was holding steroids in his locker. If the guys in the media had ever gone into a locker and looked in a shoebox, they'd have found a stash: a couple of vials containing a week's supply of steroids, and a needle. If I had to guess, I'd say eight out of every ten players had kits in their lockers filled with growth hormones, steroids, supplements—you name it. A lot of the guys even set up informal little cliques to inject each other, the way you'd go out drinking with a bunch of guys after work. For that matter, if someone had done a thorough search of the clubhouses back then, oh my God, the shit they would have found in there: greenies, steroids, little black books, vibrators, sex toys, women's underwear, and more. There was no telling what you might find.

None of us ever really never worried much about getting caught, though, or about the media reporting on what was going on. We didn't see it as a big deal. We didn't see using steroids as being in the same category as cocaine, marijuana, crack, or ecstasy. As a matter of fact, I still don't believe they should be cat-egorized the same way as those drugs. According to the Con-trolled Substances Act of 1970, anabolic steroids are a Schedule

III substance, characterized by a "moderately high" abuse liability, which is only one category removed from Schedule II substances like cocaine and amphetamine, which are characterized by a "high" abuse liability.

People are always saying that steroids make you break down, and shorten your career. But with my back problems, they only lengthened mine. I've had back pain ever since I could remember; once, when I was in high school, I was at home when my back just went out and left me paralyzed, flat on my back on the floor, for twenty minutes. That experience was incredibly scary, even after the effect wore off and I could stand up again. There's always been a part of me that feared I'd one day be sidelined permanently by back trouble.

In 1996, while Jessica and I were married, I developed a disc problem that was so severe that I actually had to have back surgery. Three years later, in July 1999, I had a second back surgery to repair a herniated disc; that operation caused me to miss the All-Star Game, even though I was leading the American League with thirty-one homers going into the break.

Those two back surgeries were well publicized. But I actually had a third back surgery—and went to great lengths to keep it secret, because I knew that if it became public the owners might decide I was damaged goods and not give me another look. Until the publication of this book, no one in Major League Baseball has never known that I had that operation. I didn't think I had any choice but to hush it up.

Back surgery is nothing to mess around with. It's serious business. To some people, it might seem crazy even to try coming back to baseball after three back operations. After all, I can think of some guys who decided they were done with the game after just one.

Even I was surprised at how quickly I was able to come back after that third back surgery. I was on steroids and growth hormone at the time, so I guess they accelerated the natural healing process. Two weeks after the surgery, my back felt great. The key was my workout regimen: I'd been working out for a long time prior to the surgery, and I was in tremendous shape. Then, as soon as I could after the operation, I started lifting right away. I recovered so quickly, it was as if I'd never had the surgery—and that made it a lot easier to keep my secret.

Not long after that, in February 2000, I went to Las Vegas for the Big League Challenge home-run hitting contest at Cashman Field. I had figured there was no way I could make it to Vegas for this contest that soon after back surgery, even though they'd offered me $100,000 just to show up and $600,000 if I won. But my quick recovery meant I could go. I showed up at Cashman Field, went in to the locker room to change, and took off my shirt.

Barry Bonds was nearby, and when he saw me, he just stood there and stared. I weighed about 255 at that point, and I was just shredded with veins. Barry couldn't believe what he was seeing.

"What the hell have you been doing?" he asked me, slowly and dramatically, for everybody to hear.

Then we had the home-run hitting contest, and I showed everyone that I wasn't just big—I was more powerful than ever. I went against Mike Piazza in the first round. He hit nine homers; not bad, but I hit eleven. Barry went up against Shawn Green and hit nine homers, just like Piazza, but Green hit twelve and Barry was eliminated. Next I went up against Mark McGwire; that was close, but I got the better of him. Then, against Chipper Jones, it went down to the end.

"I'm too old for this," I joked to Chipper. "I'm about to have a heart attack."

The last two left were me and my old friend from Miami, Rafael Palmeiro. Raffy put on a real show, but I was fortunate enough to get on a roll, and hit some real moon shots. One of them flew completely out of the stadium and landed on Washington Avenue, maybe 550 or 600 feet from home plate. I wound up winning the whole contest—and, believe me, that made an impression on the other players there. It just went to show that I still had a lot to offer as a player.

So what did Barry Bonds do that next off-season? He showed up in spring 2001 with forty pounds of added muscle. As soon as he set foot on a field in Scottsdale that spring, he was all anyone could talk about.

"My God, look at how big he is," everyone was saying. "He's monstrous. Look at him."

Barry added all that raw muscle, and then he went out that season and hit seventy-three home runs and destroyed the home-run record. But if you look at his numbers, he had never hit more than forty-nine home runs over fifteen seasons in the major leagues before that. Suddenly he's hitting seventy-three?

In late 2004, the *San Francisco Chronicle* reported that Bonds had told a grand jury he used a cream form of steroid. So everyone finally knew for sure what was obvious all along— even if Bonds did the smart thing and insisted he never knew the cream was steroids. Maybe he didn't know, or he wasn't sure. But the simple fact is that Barry Bonds was definitely using steroids.

And it's no scandal, or at least it shouldn't be. People take medications for all sorts of things. The big drug companies spend huge amounts of money on television commercials telling you that your kid needs one drug because he can't sit still in school, or you need another because you've been feeling a little unhappy. But when it comes to accepting the simple fact that steroids and growth hormone can reshape the body in amazing ways, people seem to have this childlike need to cling to ignorance and fear. The future is here, so why fight it?

CLEAN LIVING

Heavily muscled bodies like Canseco's have now become so common that they no longer invite scorn. Players even find dark humor in steroid use. One American League outfielder, for instance, was known to be taking a steroid typically given by veterinarians to injured, ill or overworked horses and readily available in Latin America. An opposing player pointed to him and remarked, "He takes so much of that horse stuff that one day we're going to look out in the outfield and he's going to be grazing."

TOM VERDUCCI,
Sports Illustrated, *June 3, 2002*

People insist on thinking of steroid use in negative terms, as though it's a sickness, when in fact most people who use steroids properly end up a lot more healthy than when they started. Here is something to think about: When I first came into the league, major league baseball players partied a whole lot more than they do now. Back then, in the late 1980s, a lot of guys were doing recreational drugs, and of course drinking a lot. That has changed drastically.

As the years went by, and the players got more into steroids, weight lifting, and good nutrition, for most players the other drugs went by the wayside—liquor, cocaine, marijuana. When the guys realized that steroids worked, that was all they cared about. They looked better, they were stronger, they could perform at a higher level and land that big contract everyone wanted. So if there were certain sacrifices to make—like cutting back on drinking—that was no big deal. It was just one of those things that happened naturally. There are still exceptions, like that amazing partier Jason Giambi, but for most baseball players, the steroid era meant a new focus on clean living.

There are health considerations, obviously. You don't want to put too much stress on your liver with your steroid regimen. You have to look out for dangerous combinations, because your liver can't handle being stressed in three different ways at once. If you are overusing steroids, and you're also using cocaine and liquor, you've got a big problem.

So what does the smart athlete do? He uses no cocaine, no marijuana, no ecstasy, no liquor, and only a moderate amount of steroids, administered properly—and, ka-ching, he's on his way to those million-dollar contracts. That's a smart player. He lets the liver work at its normal pace, filtering out the steroid residue, and he ends up healthy, wealthy, and wise.

The one other drug that's still hanging on in baseball is amphetamines, which have always been a big part of the game. Call them what you want—pep pills, greenies, dextroamphetamine sulfate—they've been around a long time. In Jim Bouton's famous 1980 book *Ball Four,* he was the first one to talk about greenies in public. He quoted the player named Tommy Davis, saying, "How fabulous are greenies? The answer is very," Bouton continued. "A lot of baseball players couldn't function without them."

Elsewhere in the book, Bouton describes a player who had recently received a supply of 500 greenies. "That ought to last about a month," Bouton wrote.

Greenies were everywhere when I first came into the league. I would say that at least eight out of ten players were taking greenies back then; they may have been as widespread as steroids are now. They were as acceptable as popping aspirin. Some guys would mix greenies with Excedrin or another caffeine-laced product. That's old school. It goes all the way back to the early days of baseball. Especially when they had a day game after a night game, players would need a little boost waking up. They'd take a pep pill an hour or so before the game, and by first pitch they'd have some extra spring in their step.

Greenies are still around, but now the guys who take them are the exceptions. Why the big change? Again, the number one reason is steroids. I never took a greenie. I just didn't see any point. Steroids get you going. They accelerate your heart rate to the point where you don't need a stimulant to pick you up. A few players may have used a combination of both, but that's really just a few guys who like to be incredibly wired. When steroids became widespread in baseball, I think most everybody realized that mixing them with amphetamines can have an adverse reaction on you. That's when you saw greenies start to disappear from clubhouses.

The decline in amphetamines was part of the general trend toward better fitness that came with steroid use. With salaries getting so high—and even utility players bringing in $3 million a year—the smart players realized that the better care they took of themselves, the more they kept their bodies strong with steroids and good nutrition, the more years they'd be able to play—and the more money they'd make. For a while everybody was on the fitness kick, eating right, taking steroids, getting the right amount of sleep. So you saw bigger, stronger, faster, and *healthier* athletes, instead of those raggedy, run-down, pot-bellied ball players of previous eras.

If you were to take a few contemporary major-league teams, and strip down all the players, you would find that most ballplayers have pretty good bodies. They're strong and fit, compared to thirty or forty years ago. It'll be interesting to see how that changes if more players start backing off of steroids. Even though major-league baseball hasn't done anything serious to discourage players from using steroids, there's still a lot of concern about what's going to happen in the next couple years. So there's been a movement of guys changing how they use steroids—some of them using less, some quitting altogether.

For those guys who decide not to use steroids any more, it's still possible to maintain about 80 percent of the muscle mass they have gained, if they go about it the right way. And the smart ones will consider using a low dose of steroids all year round.

Some of the players, I'm sure, are thinking of quitting just because they're afraid of being caught. But that's always been a fear, and we were always careful. One obvious precaution most of us did take was doing the majority of our injections at home—that is, not taking them on the road with us. On an especially long road trip, we might make an exception, but in general the trips were eight or ten days, so the players knew they'd be fine if they injected right before the trip started and again right after we got back.

But the average baseball player shouldn't really be ashamed of his steroid use. Because the people who really abuse steroids aren't baseball players at all. It's the bodybuilders, football players, and contenders in world's-strongest-men competitions who have pushed things too far and given steroids a bad name. They're the ones who apparently believe that more is always better—when actually more is usually too much.

Carefully controlling the amounts of steroids you take, administering them at the proper time—that's the way to make them work for you, without risking your health. Like most chemicals that can help you, steroids would be dangerous if used in too large a quantity. Just consider the example of Botox, whose popularity has now spread from Hollywood. As most people know, Botox is used to paralyze muscles to stop the aging process in the face. But Botox is also poisonous—it's a form of botulism, the poison, which can kill you. The key is knowing how to use it without taking undue risks. That's exactly the way to think of steroids: Sure, they can be deadly if used in ridiculously large amounts, the way some out-of-control weight-lifters do. But if you're smart, and careful, and know what you're doing, you can use them to reach your true potential.

"NOT REALLY HERE TO PLAY"

You could sense that everybody's stopped what they're doing just to watch him hit.

JOE MORGAN

It's a general pattern with the media. Certain people in baseball develop these huge reputations, and then all of a sudden they can do no wrong. Take Tony LaRussa, the former A's manager, for example. You have eggheads showing up from Washington so they can lurk on the infield grass during batting practice, hoping to get two minutes to stand there and listen to what the great man has to say about the art of managing. Tony's an intelligent guy. He even has a law degree. But the simple truth is that being smart can help you with only one part of the job of being a major-league manager. If you're a jerk, it doesn't matter how smart you are.

People are always talking about LaRussa making pitching changes and outthinking another manager, and that's great for reporters looking for easy angles. That's the kind of thing that's pretty easy to follow from a distance, even if you don't know much about what's actually happening with a team. But let me tell you, any story like that looks a whole lot different from the other side. As a player, you pay attention to the relationships a manager has. Do his players like him? Do they respect him? Do they want to keep him happy? Do they want him to keep his job?

LaRussa uses a lot of psychology to control his players. One thing I never liked was the way he'd jump on a player who had made a mistake—and usually do it just as he was coming back into the dugout, so he was sure all the other players would hear. A manager's criticism should always take place behind closed doors.

Tony LaRussa has won a lot of games as a manager. He has also lost a lot of clubhouses. You'd be amazed at how many of his ex-players just can't stand the guy. I'm not saying this out of spite. Tony and I had our differences, but that was a long time ago. I haven't talked to the man in years, and that's just fine with me. But he's a good example of this same pattern of big names in baseball who get a free ride in the media most of the time.

To me, the real details of what people are like are a lot more interesting than these established media storylines, which are usually tilted so far toward the purely positive or negative that they get boring fast. Managers, like superstar ball players, are human beings with ups and downs and moods, good days and bad days. They are individuals before they are media caricatures.

Here, for what they're worth, are my own insider's observations on a few of the more interesting people in baseball.

JOE TORRE

I spent only a couple of months playing for the Yankees, and that's not much time to get to know someone. But I respect Joe Torre a lot, because he was straight with me.

"Jose, you're not really going to play," he told me when I first joined the team. "I'll try to get you in, but you're not really here to play."

I was glad he told me that.

"I know," I told him. "I know why I'm here."

In 2000 the Yankees had claimed me off waivers, and picked me up from Tampa Bay, mostly to prevent both the Red Sox and the A's from doing the same thing. As an added bonus, they would have me there as insurance in case someone got hurt—and maybe to pinch-hit now and then, though I'm not much of a pinch-hitter.

The Yanks didn't want the Red Sox or A's to get me because they knew I'd hit the Yankees' left-handed pitchers really well—especially Andy Pettitte, and he was a big reason they made it through the playoffs to the World Series. I've hit so many home runs against Pettitte, it's a laugh. I remember hitting two home runs against him in one game; then, the next time I faced him, I homered again. I just destroy him. He sees me and he melts. He knows he has no chance against me. So that was the main reason why the Yankees traded for me, just to keep me from whaling on Pettitte and the other lefties. From their perspective it was a great move.

But that was the worst time I ever had in baseball, sitting and watching the Yankees those last two months of the season. I played only once in a blue moon, and I couldn't stand it. It was the first time in my career that I was completely, 100 percent healthy. I could have helped out the organization with my bat and carried the team—but I wasn't getting to play.

The few times they did get me some at-bats, the Yankees put me in the outfield, even though I hadn't played out there in I don't know how long. Those were very tough times for me in New York; I lived in the city, in this horrible small apartment that was constantly under construction. (What is it with Manhattan, anyway? It seems like nothing there ever comes easy.)

In Tampa, back before the trade, I'd had a foot injury that left me with a little heel problem. But once that healed up, I ran the forty-yard dash in 3.9 seconds. "My God, you're fast," they said, but that didn't get me into the lineup.

The media made it look like I was injured and that's why I wasn't playing for the Yankees. They wanted to present some reason besides the obvious: that the Yankees had traded for me just because they're the Yankees and they could, not because they wanted me in the lineup. Joe Torre believed in the players he already had—David Justice was hot, and Glenallen Hill was hitting pretty well, too—and there was nowhere for me to play.

It was even worse in the post-season. I wasn't eligible to play in the American League Championship Series against the Seattle Mariners, which the Yankees won in six games. Then it was on to the Subway Series, against the Mets, and even though the Yankees put me on the active roster for that series, I spent most of my time sitting on the bench doing nothing and feeling worthless.

In game six, though, I was sitting there on the Yankee bench on a cold night at Shea Stadium. Roger Clemens was sitting to my right, and Andy Pettitte to my left, and I was sure I wouldn't be asked to play. But all of a sudden, in the sixth inning, Torre called down to me.

"Canseco, you're hitting," he said.

Roger and I looked at each other, both of us totally surprised. I hadn't been in a game since the regular season; I hadn't even taken batting practice that day. I was half-asleep. If it hadn't been for the cold, I'd probably have fallen asleep altogether.

"Holy shit!" I thought. So I stood up kind of slowly, hunched over with stiffness, my back all cramped up. Roger started pretending as if he had an oil can in his hand, and he started oiling me like the Tin Man.

I played along, making a squeaky little voice.

"Oil me here," I squeaked. "And oil me here."

Pettitte started playing along, too, and soon all three of us were cracking up. But that didn't last long. I went up to the plate to pinch-hit for David Cone, and it was bad. Three strikes and you're out. I never even saw the ball. I never took a swing. I hadn't played in a week or two, so to me it was like the first day of spring training. That was the worst time in my life, being completely healthy and yet never even reaching first base.

Even when they won the playoffs, I never felt like I was part of the Yankees. When they won the World Series, I kind of hid in the room. What was I going to do, celebrate? I didn't help them win anything. I wasn't even on the roster for the divisional series, for God's sake. I felt completely out of place. I just let them celebrate.

But they did give me a World Series ring, which was generous of them. And it's a beautiful thing.

ART HOWE

Another manager I liked was Art Howe—again, because he was very honest. I played for Art when I returned to the A's in 1997, and I always felt that he was telling me the truth. His attitude was a lot like Kevin Kennedy's, in the sense that he just let the guys go out there and play the game. Players respected him a great deal. He did a lot with the organization, working with the players and letting guys be themselves. He was a very easy-going, quiet guy.

It's not always the best approach to be a nice guy, but so long as it works, why not? If the team doesn't respect you, then you have to change your approach, but the players I knew all had a lot of respect for Howe.

The media gave Howe no chance to do anything as A's manager, none at all. But in 1996, his first season managing the team, the A's finished 78-84—which meant that they had won ten more games in Howe's first year than they did in any of LaRussa's last three seasons.

But it soon became clear in 1997 that the A's owners, Steve Schott and Ken Hofmann, weren't really interested in winning. I found that out the hard way, and I'll always be thankful to Art Howe for being straight with me. I went on the disabled list that August with back spasms. When I came off the disabled list and was healthy again, Howe gave me a heads-up.

"Listen, Jose, I'm probably not going to play you, because the organization doesn't want you to get your at-bats," he told me. I had a clause in my contract that if I reached a certain number of at-bats for the season my salary automatically kicked in for the following season at $5 million plus. But the A's were eager to avoid that if they could. So even though I could have helped the team win more games if I'd been in the lineup, they decided they'd rather save money than win more ball games. If you look at my stats for that year, I finished with 388 at-bats, compared to 600 or more during each of my first three seasons with the A's—yet I still had 74 RBIs and twenty-three home runs.

Once they'd given me the word that I wasn't going to play, I realized there was no changing their mind. "Well if you're going to sit me, then just send me home," I told the A's. "Don't have me here not playing."

So that's what happened—I went back to Florida. Only the organization couldn't let fans know what was really going on. Instead, they had to make it look like I was injured. For example, one of the trainers told reporters I was still having back trouble. "He's seeing a physical therapist," the trainer said. "I talk to him almost every day."

Yeah, right. Even now it makes me mad just to think about that, because it helped cement another myth about me—that I was injured all the time. Again, beware the difference between perception and reality. Probably 30 to 40 percent of the time I was reported as "injured," I wasn't really—it was just that I belonged to an organization that didn't want to play me, either for money reasons or because they'd only acquired me in the first place to stop me from going to another team.

It happens all the time in baseball that teams ask a player to be on the DL, even if the player doesn't have an injury. Usually it's because they need to open up a spot on the roster for another player. But they don't mind lying to the public about what they're actually doing. There are an awful lot of hypocrites out there in baseball. When the A's had traded for me, they'd been talking about wanting to win. When it came down to it, though, Schott and Hofmann were so worried about money that they kept me out of the lineup.

I don't know if that made them hypocrites or just stupid, but either way it sure didn't sit well with me.

DUSTY BAKER

I've never played for Dusty Baker, but we were teammates in Oakland right at the end of his career. My rookie year, 1986, was his last year as a player, and as a young, inexperienced kid I remember being amazed by him. I mean, that dude could party. The one time he asked me to go out with him, I told him no thanks: the alcohol-poisoning escapades of my minor-league days were still fresh in my mind, and I knew enough not to risk temptation.

It's funny for me to come across guys like Dusty, who could really party, and then a few years go by and all of a sudden they're wearing glasses and becoming managers and leading organizations to division titles. But I can see how Dusty would be a great manager, because he was a good player and he understands the player's life on and off the field. He has a real knack for protecting a player and getting the best out of him. I would have liked to have had a chance to play for him.

RICKEY HENDERSON

Rickey Henderson was a genetic freak, a man with such incredible legs and arms that even past his fortieth birthday he looked like a mini-bodybuilder. To me, he was one of the best players in the game, and maybe the greatest leadoff hitter of all time. He was a good teammate to have, too. He just played the game, worked hard, and busted his ass every day.

DENNIS ECKERSLEY

To me, Dennis Eckersley was one of the pretty boys of baseball. He could go out there and pitch in a three-piece suit, and he'd be fine. With his long hair, and trimmed-up mustache, he was one of the entertainers of the game. With his long hair flapping in the wind, he always looked good. He had always been out tanning, and he was manicured, too.

Dennis was one of those finicky athletes, though. He wasn't a guy who was going to overpower you. He was more about finesse and putting some movement on the ball. Plus, he was from the old school. He got up for every outing. Dennis did a good job for us on those A's teams, but I have to say that later on, when we weren't on the same team anymore, I never minded batting against him. Todd Stottlemyre and Dennis Eckersley: Among all the pitchers I ever faced in my major league career, they were the two I was always happy to see.

BRET SABERHAGEN

The one pitcher I truly hated to face, on the other hand, would have to be Bret Saberhagen. Some pitchers just throw so well you can't hit them, and that's how it was with Saberhagen, more than any other pitcher from my era. Everything he threw moved, and with extreme velocity.

Our major-league careers ran parallel in a lot of ways; for a while we even had the same agent, Dennis Gilbert. Saberhagen's first season in the big leagues was 1984, the year before I made my move up to the A's; his best seasons were in the late 1980s, when he was having all those great years for the Kansas City Royals. Later, in 1998, we were both up for American League Comeback Player of the Year, along with Eric Davis. As *Sports Illustrated* put it, I deserved credit for "resurrecting" myself "from the cartoon-superhero junk heap."

The only other pitcher I remember really giving me a lot of trouble was Duane Ward, the Toronto Blue Jays' big setup man and then closer, starting in the early 1990s. Ward was a big guy, six foot four, and an All-Star in 1993—and, with that heavy sinker he had, and that slider from hell, I hated batting against him.

Then again, I'm not sure any of those pitchers really liked seeing me coming, either.

NICE GUYS FINISH LAST

Many people are not aware of Jose's activities in charity work. He was active in Make-a-Wish Foundation. He was involved in many charity golf tournaments. He was involved in his own foundation. He was involved in distributing thousands of dollars in gifts at Guantánamo Bay and visited refugees there.

JOSE CANSECO, SR.,
My father

P eople believe what they want to believe. If you have a reputation as the bad boy of baseball, you must be a bad guy, right? Most people just don't spend much time thinking much harder than that about it—at least most people in the media. I was never into politicking for myself or putting across some bogus image, and because I didn't play the PR game, they made sure I would pay. If I did something contrary to the image of the reckless, dangerous star, they just ignored it, or treated it like some strange curiosity that proved all their assumptions anyway.

In October 1994, the year of the strike, I flew back to Cuba for the first time since my parents put Ozzie, my sister Teresa, and me on a plane in Varadero when I was just a small boy. While I was there, I made sure to pay a visit to the refugees at the Guantánamo Bay military base, renting a plane with Alex Rodriguez and dropping off food and toys for the kids there. I didn't ask for anyone to pat me on the back for that visit to Guantánamo, and I'm not asking for that now, either. But just in case anyone reading this is interested in more than a two-dimensional picture of me, maybe a glimpse of my charity work might help shed some light on the little bit of good I've tried to do in the world.

I'm just a man, with all the insecurities and weaknesses of any other man, but I'm not a cartoon character and I've always done my best to treat people right, whether it's signing autographs even when I'm tired and have already signed fifty, or smiling at someone and posing for a picture. Even long after I stopped playing baseball, people still approach me wherever I go, just wanting to talk to me for a minute, and I try not to be fake with them. I try to treat them normally, like people, and to meet their requests whenever I can.

That was my approach going down to Guantánamo, too, trying to bring a little happiness to the kids down there and all the other refugees. I've donated millions of dollars to charity in my lifetime, and I'm sure I'll donate millions more. I don't like to publicize the charities, because then it makes it look like it's all for show, and the important part isn't writing out the check, it's giving a part of yourself.

We used to talk a lot, Alex and I. "I love Jose," he told the *Seattle Post-Intelligencer.* "Jose is a great friend of mine. He has taught me an awful lot about life and about baseball. People don't realize what a great person he is and what a big heart he has. People ask how can you learn from someone who has made so many mistakes. Sometimes those are the best guys to learn from. They're able to teach you through their wisdom and their experiences."

The scene down at Guantánamo was pretty grim, I have to tell you. We had done a lot of work to make that visit a success, and before I flew down there we collected ten tons of toys with a telethon in Miami, so we could hand them out to the kids at Camp Romeo. As a Latino, I was raised believing that men aren't supposed to cry, especially not in public, but seeing all those kids gathering around me and singing for me, that almost busted me up.

I remember one girl in particular. I gave her a stuffed animal that was a long way from new, but to her it couldn't have looked better.

"Look how pretty!" she said, holding it to her chest and smiling.

That visit was so sad, but in a way it gave me hope, too. This was during the Clinton presidency, and that August the president had thrown a real curve at the *balseros* who had left Cuba hoping to make a new life in the United States of America, changing the rules and closing the door on the refugees. The new rules only allowed you to gain entry to the United States if you first returned to Cuba, so you actually had people swimming two miles from the tip of the peninsula where Guantánamo sits, across the bay itself, so they could be back on Cuban territory and be eligible under the new rules. It was a farce.

On that visit I also had a chance to meet with about twenty hunger strikers, who were hoping to force the Clinton administration to change its policy. They gathered at Camp Juliet under a tree they decided to call the "Tree of Hope."

"Maintain your strength," I told them in Spanish. "You'll get out of here. Everyone in Miami is thinking of you."

They cheered wildly.

"We're here making our statement!" one yelled back at me. "But we thank you. Having you here means everything."

At Camp Kilo, they worked through the night picking the rocks from a field to set up a crude baseball diamond. I held a bat in my hand for the first time since the strike two months earlier, and they threw me softballs. I hit some line drives into the makeshift tents they called home, and then launched a couple of long ones over the concertina wire separating the camp from the next one over. The men went crazy. They hoisted me up on their shoulders, all two hundred and forty pounds of me, and they all joined together to chant loudly.

"*Libertad! Libertad!*" they chanted.

And that turned into "Canseco! Canseco!"

That was one of the most intense moments in my life. Compared to what I heard that day, the emotion that comes from sports fans can seem hollow and superficial. This was reality. This was life.

"They're ripping their hearts out for him," Alex said that day. "And he's doing it for them, too."

I hadn't been in Cuba since 1965, when Ozzie and I were babies, but Cuba is a big part of who I am. I have always told everyone that I'm Cuban. I'm very proud of that, and always will be.

"Cubans love Canseco because he has not forgotten us," one refugee at Camp Kilo told the *Dallas Morning News* that day. "We all want to be like Canseco. Not to be a baseball player, but to get out of here and get to the USA and start a better life."

"Cubans are known in the United States because of baseball," said another man at Camp Kilo. "Today is the happiest day we've had since we've been here. It's almost like we had a taste of freedom."

One of the people I met that day was another player, named Euclides Rojas. Cuba's all-time leader in saves, Rojas was known as the Cuban Dennis Eckersley, even though he was a left-hander. But eventually he had enough; tired of living in a country that was not free, he decided to take a huge chance and take his wife Marta and his little son, Euclides Jr., and join some other people trying to escape from Cuba on a little raft.

I liked Rojas right away. He's a very smart man, with a calm dignity about him, and that day at Guantánamo, even in his flip-flops—the only shoes he had—he had a presence that made him stand out even among the other proud men at Camp Tango. He told me about how he had been floating at sea for days, and how his group had run out of drinking water. It looked like they might die out there. But then they ran into another boat full of people trying to escape from Castro, and traded food for water. Then the U.S. Coast Guard picked them up and brought them to Guantánamo.

Rojas hoped one day to pitch in the major leagues, but he had no way of knowing if he would ever be allowed to go to America, much less pitch.

"It's impossible to think of that when I am here," Rojas said that day. "These are very bad conditions."

All I kept thinking, talking to Euky, was, "That could have been me."

He and I are almost the same age. It's all just a matter of timing. If the Cuban government had not decided to let my father leave the country in 1965, we might never have been able to leave. If things had been different it could have been me in that camp, rather than Euclides Rojas.

I kept thinking, "I'm very lucky."

I didn't hear about Rojas again for a while, but he and his family finally made it to the United States after six months at Guantánamo, and the next season, he pitched for Palm Springs in the independent Western League. The Florida Marlins drafted him in the thirtieth round of that year's amateur draft, and he worked his way up to Triple-A Charlotte, but he'd ruined his elbow pitching too many innings for the Cuban National Team. That injury finally ended his career.

Instead, he turned to coaching. On the very same day his playing career ended, he started working as a pitching coach in the Marlins' system and impressed them so much, he even filled in for the Marlins as bullpen coach for two weeks during the 1999 season. Later, he worked in the Pirates' organization. Then before the 2003 season, the Boston Red Sox hired him as bullpen coach.

You've probably never heard the name, but if you watched the Red Sox in the playoffs or the World Series, you probably saw him out there, exerting a calming influence on that bullpen. So you know the rest of the story: Euclides Rojas, the same proud, brave man who I met as a refugee at Guantánamo, wearing flip-flops, now has a World Series ring, and will always be part of baseball history for helping the Red Sox win the World Series for the first time since 1918. They'll always remember that in Cuba, too, and especially in Miami. I guarantee it.

AN EDUCATION MONEY CAN'T BUY

*If you're a baseball purist like me, you know
the season doesn't really begin until Jose Canseco
gets arrested.*

DAVID LETTERMAN

The low point of my life was definitely the three months I spent in jail in the summer of 2003. And it was all for nothing.

I was arrested in June of that year for supposedly failing a drug test while on probation. To me, it was obvious that someone had switched the urine sample I gave; I know for a fact that I'd stopped taking steroids prior to the start of to my probation, so there was no other way the test could have come up positive. We later acquired a detailed breakdown of the urine sample they tested, and from that it was obvious that sample could never have come from me.

I'll never forget the feeling of stepping into the small jail cell in Florida, knowing I could end up spending five years in there. Anyone who goes through that experience knows how terrible it is. I remember the nights I spent trying to sleep on the little bed they give you, dreaming of seeing my daughter, Josie, or just being outside, feeling my freedom. Then I would wake up and be back in jail. It was devastating to realize where I was.

But to understand how I got there, you need to reach way back in my life, to the place where all my legal troubles started—on a Florida highway in the early 1990s, and a stupid argument between two young people in love.

It was late, around three in the morning, and Esther and I were having an argument, which I guess is nothing unusual for a married couple. What was unusual was the setting: I was in a 930 Porsche, she was in a white BMW, and we were driving side-by-side on the road in Florida, screaming at each other. Somewhere along the way, the cars accidentally collided. No surprise; it's hard to watch what you're doing when you're driving and fighting at the same time. But it wasn't intentional.

Someone at a gas station saw us go by and called the police. We pulled over a little later and started talking more calmly, but then the police arrived and arrested me. And, right there on the spot, they decided to cite me for domestic violence.

I couldn't believe it—and Esther couldn't either.

"What are you doing?" she asked the cops.

When you hear the phrase *domestic violence,* you think of a husband beating his wife. But this was just a total accident, and yet there I was, already tarred with the domestic violence brush.

A lot of issues extended from those original domestic-violence charges filed against me by the state of Florida. One of the prosecutors wanted Esther to testify against me, even though Esther didn't want to do that—to say I'd struck Esther's car on purpose, that I was trying to hurt her or even to kill her with the car. Esther was afraid that if she wouldn't testify against me, she might be arrested. She didn't, but in the end I went to jail anyway.

I know I'm no angel. But I truly believe that, ever since that incident with Esther, I've been tagged unfairly by the media as a violent person. As anyone who really knows me can tell you, I've never started a fight, not once in my whole life. I've never instigated a fight verbally, and I've walked away from a lot of potential fights.

But because of who I am, and the success that I've had, it's been very easy for the media to turn a couple of marital spats and bar fights into a supposed reputation for aggression and violence toward women.

In this society, once you're labeled as a person who is aggressive, that's it. If you're known as someone who goes out and gets into fights, people look for you because you're an easy target. I could be standing at a bar, get knocked out by a guy out of nowhere, end up in the hospital, and this is what would you read in the paper the next morning: CANSECO GETS INTO ANOTHER BAR FIGHT.

Which brings me to what happened in 2001.

The whole horrible experience began when my brother, Ozzie, and I went out one night in Miami. Ozzie was with his fiancée, and I was with a date, a lovely young woman named Amber. It was Halloween, and three of us were dressed up as vampires; Amber was dressed as an Indian squaw. At one point Amber left the group to go to the bathroom with some other girls, and this guy I'd never seen before reached down, lifted up her skirt, and grabbed her ass. So Amber got into an argument with him—and Ozzie and I walked over to see what was happening. When the guy saw me coming, he made what looked like an aggressive move toward me. I didn't want to get into it with him, but he had a bottle or something in his hand, so I put my hand up to stop his advance.

"Get away from me," I told him.

When one of his buddies stepped forward, my brother intercepted him and started pushing him back to the bar area. There were lots of people there, and I lost track of who was doing what, but I know that I was acting in self-defense. Eventually, the guy I was dealing with went to help his buddy, who was scuffling with my brother. My brother knows martial arts; he was able to take care of them pretty easily. The bouncers came and escorted us out, but at the time it seemed like no big deal. When the cops showed up, no one seemed interested in pressing charges, and we all went home.

Thirteen days later, though, the police called and asked me and Ozzie to come down to the station to give our side of what happened—and when we showed up they arrested us on the spot. They said they had talked to witnesses who said they saw me grab both guys by the throat and punch them. That was a complete lie, but it didn't matter.

I even took a polygraph test—a professional, serious polygraph test, administered by one of the leading polygraph examiners in the country and the same examiner used by the State of Florida in its criminal cases—and passed it perfectly. I challenged the other side to take a polygraph, and even offered to pay for it. They said no. (You can guess why.)

So then it went to a jury trial, and that couldn't have come at a worse time for me. I was going through custody proceedings with Jessica as part of our divorce, and my attorneys convinced me to plead out the charge. "Jose, if you get convicted, you're going to lose your daughter," they told me. "You might have to go to jail for fifteen years, and your daughter will hardly know you when you're finally released." That was enough to scare me into taking the deal—and accepting the probation terms that have dogged me for the past several years.

The next blow came when I was in California to see Josie and attend a charity golf tournament, and through a misunderstanding on my part I missed a probation date. I got a call from my attorney: "Jose, there's a warrant out for your arrest in the state of Florida," he told me.

So the following day I flew back to Florida and went before the judge. He put me in jail for a month, with no chance for bail. Then, when I came out, they gave me two years' house arrest with three years' probation. While I was under house arrest, they subjected me to a urine test, which actually came up negative for steroids but contained a minuscule metabolite remnant that could have been left over from prior use. The amount was so small that even the State's expert was later unable to identify the time of use. But when the State got the results it jumped the gun and arrested me. And who was it that nailed me with the steroid charge? The same prosecutor's office that went after me back in 1992. Same justice system, same result: Jose goes to jail.

I had a terrible time adjusting to jail. I had a cell to myself, but it was only about eight feet long by five feet wide. There was a regular door with a Plexiglas screen on it; the bed was a slab of metal, with a thin layer of cushion over the top. It was terrible. You ended up getting sores all over your body, no matter how much you tried to squirm to find a comfortable position.

The food was awful. It sure made me appreciate those fine meals I'd been eating for years, both in restaurants and at home with Jessica, who is one hell of a cook. In jail, you would get whatever cold slop they wanted to give you. You could order extra commissary, but that was basically garbage—chips and candy bars, pure junk food. I would rather go hungry than put that kind of stuff in my body, and I did. I lost forty pounds in jail.

Before the arrest, Jessica and I had been talking about getting back together again. She was already my ex-wife at that point, but we were talking about reconciling—mostly because of Josie, so we could both be there for her. Then one day I was talking to Jessica on the phone from prison, and in the background I heard a man's voice.

"I'm in love with somebody else," she told me. "I want to be with this man. Nobody knows how long you're going to be in jail."

Even before I was in jail, Jessica explained later, she thought it was over between us. We had been separated for three years at that point, and she says now that by the time I went to jail she was ready to move on.

But on that day, when Jessica told me she was in love with somebody else, I had a nervous breakdown in jail.

I'm not using the term *nervous breakdown* lightly. I've gone through bad periods before, but I have never experienced anything like that, and I hope I never will again. It all became too much for me. It felt like something inside me was being crushed. Everything hit me all at once, and I completely lost it. They called the medical help line there in jail, but they never showed up. That's how it is in jail: You're a number. You have no rights whatsoever. It can get very tough to handle.

Only a year or two earlier, I'd been as happy as I had ever been. My second wife, Jessica, had given birth to our baby girl. Then, all of a sudden, I was in jail, and Josie wasn't allowed to visit. I went through a long period when I didn't see my daughter at all. And that just about killed me.

The whole thing was a complete nightmare, and it's still going on. Every month I have to fly back to Florida from southern California, where I live now, just to see my probation officer. We talk for five minutes, and then I leave until the next month.

And now, just to add insult to injury, the guys from that barroom brawl are suing me now for millions of dollars. They admitted in a police report that the one guy grabbed the girl's ass, which started the whole thing (though the guy later denied that he'd done so). Yet still *they're* suing *me*. This world is completely bizarre to me.

It took me a long time—not until I'd spent three months in jail—for me to realize just how willing the media was to bury me, how few people there were actually willing to stand by me when things got tough. It was a real eye-opener, let me tell you. My time behind bars probably taught me more about society and about people than I had learned in my entire life to that point.

As profound a learning experience as it was, though, I wouldn't recommend it to anyone. Jail doesn't make you better, it makes you worse.

Before jail, any of my friends will tell you, I was the nicest guy in the world. I'd give anything to my friends, or even just to people off the street. I'd try to help all kinds of different people, even bums off the street. I was the biggest sucker.

Now I'm completely the opposite. I'm a total businessman. Nobody can run anything by me and get away with it. Before, I was such a nice guy. I would put myself in harm's way for everybody. But what my time in jail taught me is that nice guys do finish last. I've had my education. I'll always associate being a nice guy with being set up, having no one come to my defense, and ending up in jail. And that's not for me, not anymore.

Shortly after my breakdown, though, the case was dismissed and I was released from jail. Why? Because the evidence was dubious and it also turned out that the chain of custody on my blood test was full of holes. I was put in jail for no reason—for three months.

When Judge Leonard Glick, of the Miami-Dade Circuit Court, gave the word that they were releasing me, he added: "Good luck to you." As he was speaking, I reflected that I had lost my daughter, I had $130,000 due in attorney's fees, I'd lost endorsements. And there he was, wishing me good luck.

We are now suing the laboratory that turned in the questionable results.

I can't prove it, but I can't help feeling that, behind the scenes, some people in Major League Baseball were working to help bury me—to keep me in jail as long as possible. I've heard as much from people who were in a position to know, and I believe them, even if I'll never be able to convince the world of what was actually going on.

Think about it: When I was arrested after that bar fight, it was because I was *defending* a woman. But now we're going to a civil trial, and the case against me is based on their claim that steroids have made me aggressive. They're trying to make it out that I go to nightclubs all the time, beating up men and women alike.

The only people who really stood by me when I was in prison were my brother, Ozzie, my dad and my sister, and my nephews and niece. Everyone else disappeared. That taught me a lot.

And because of it all, except for my probation visits, I will never again set foot in the state of Florida.

Chapter

24

DID HE OR DIDN'T HE?

At first I felt like a cheater. But I looked around, and everybody was doing it.

KEN CAMINITI

f all the bad information that's been spread about steroids, one of the worst misconceptions is the idea that everyone who takes steroids loses their mind and turns into a nutcase. People who know me will tell you that I'm a very calm, even-tempered individual. It's very difficult to piss me off. I've had times when I've gotten angry, sure—but who hasn't? That has nothing to do with steroids. I mean, seriously, if a person is taking steroids, he's not ever allowed to get angry? And if he does, then it's got to be "'roid rage"? To me, that's just ridiculous.

Even people close to me have wondered whether steroids would eventually change my behavior. My second wife, Jessica, used to ask me all the time whether she should expect to see the steroids producing any side effects. I told her not to worry about it, and gave her a primer course on the nature of steroids and how they work.

I've never seen any sign of this so-called 'roid rage in any other baseball players, and I've never felt anything like that affecting me. Does using steroids ever alter your moods? I'm sure in some ways it can, yes. Any chemical, if used incorrectly, can alter your mood. Then again, a lot of things can do that. Spending too much time in traffic can do that. Or eating too much of one food. But people love their stereotypes, and the steroid-crazed athlete is one that's been spread by the media for years.

The anti-steroid crowd has gone to some lengths to convince the public of the emotional dangers of steroids. But there's always a specialist in a white coat out there somewhere to verify such a claim. Do such specialists really know more than I do, after personally experimenting with steroids for twenty years? No way. They may know what the books say, but have they felt it in their system? I know what works and what doesn't, through experience. I've never had mood swings, and I've never been afraid I would get them from steroids, either. I'm just not that kind of guy.

It's all about knowing your dosage. Baseball players don't need to take steroids in amounts so large that the chemicals themselves begin to change. Baseball players—at least those who know what they're doing—are shooting more for stamina and strength than for sheer bulk. It's when you see a guy gaining 100 pounds in a year that you have to worry—and, yes, there have been a few guys who have gone a little overboard.

I was very sad when the news came in October 2004 that Ken Caminiti had died, in New York, under questionable circumstances. I couldn't believe it, and like most people, at first I didn't know what to think. But I knew Ken had been having a lot of problems with drugs. Cocaine will kill you faster than anything. It's just so sad to see a fellow baseball player pass away so young.

Ken was just a year older than me, and broke into the big leagues only a couple of years after I did, but he spent his whole career in the National League and I spent mine in the American League, so I never really knew him. He was a big, powerful, good-looking guy, and always kind of quiet.

I remember being surprised when he told *Sports Illustrated* that he had used steroids. The timing seemed strange, and I wondered why he did it. I just couldn't understand; he didn't seem to have anything to gain by revealing his usage. Later, after he died, you heard all kinds of talk that his death was somehow related to steroids, even though no one had a shred of proof. To me, Ken Caminiti's death was a real tragedy—someone so full of life dying so young—but if people want to link his problems to his experimentation with steroids, they're barking up the wrong tree.

People always mention Lyle Alzado, who died tragically of a brain tumor, as another supposed steroid tragedy. But how do they know that? Scientists have done a lot of research, and up to this time they've never really tied steroids with cancerous tumors. Any time an athlete gets sick, it's easy for the media to point to steroids. But they're never doing more than guessing, because there is no scientific proof.

Even after everything I've explained in this book, I understand that some people are going to act like those hear-no-evil, see-no-evil, speak-no-evil monkeys, holding their hands over their ears or their eyes or their mouths. But are steroids really evil? No, they aren't. What *is* evil, the way I see it, is willful ignorance, or even worse—and even more widespread—the behavior of those who knew just what was going on with steroids in baseball but pretended they didn't know. They pretended they weren't involved, even though, as we all know now, nearly everyone was complicit. To me, the real question is how long people persisted in sweeping the truth under the rug, instead of facing the public directly with the facts.

I'm not talking about any one person here. No one person is ever in charge of anything, not even the United States of America. A president needs Congress if he wants to get any laws passed. He needs to deal with the Supreme Court and the judicial system. Presidents share power in other ways, too, the way George W. Bush has with Dick Cheney and Donald Rumsfeld.

It's no different with Bud Selig, the commissioner of baseball. The real power in baseball is dispersed among a whole host of owners—many of whom apparently weren't inclined to challenge the players on their steroid use, which was pumping up their bodies and their home run totals. And then later, as it became more of a public controversy, they decided together that they would deal with the potential scandal by denying everything and stalling for more time.

This book will make it much more difficult for them to deny it all much longer—at least it will if people start thinking for themselves, especially the sportswriters and broadcasters out there who knew all along that this was going on, but never found a way to report on it.

I don't have any videotape footage of me poking Mark McGwire in the butt with a needle. But this is my challenge: I'll take a lie detector test on the subject in a minute, and I'll pass with a perfect score. To you media types out there who want to attack me, the way the media has always attacked me, I say: Bring it on. Take your best shot. Try to change the subject and turn this into a debate about Jose Canseco, the big Cuban flake. If that's the only way you can distract people from the fact that for years you've pretended not to notice the steroid revolution, so be it.

But if you think I'm a bad guy because I used steroids and spread the word about them, then what does that say about all of you? How many of you have tracked down Mark McGwire, since his retirement, and asked him direct and straightforward questions? Who has taken a look at him and how much weight he's lost since he was a player? Pretty hard to figure *that* one out, eh? Once protected, always protected.

So other than McGwire, and Juan Gonzalez, Ivan Rodriguez, and Rafael Palmeiro in Texas, what more can I tell you
about players and steroids?

WILSON ALVAREZ

Later in my career, when I was playing in Tampa Bay, I educated the left-handed pitcher Wilson Alvarez on steroids and
growth hormone, and from time to time I would inject him,
usually in some isolated nook in the stadium. He had a problem with his weight, and he asked me to help him do something about that. So I tried to inform him on getting growth
hormones, which can cut fat, and I put him on a lean cycle of
steroids. He actually did pretty well on that regimen and lost
some weight—in contrast to players like Giambi, who bulked
up absurdly.

DAVE MARTINEZ

Another teammate of mine in Tampa Bay was Dave Martinez,
born in New York City, who was originally drafted by the
Chicago Cubs. Dave has also played for the Montreal Expos, the
Cincinnati Reds, the San Francisco Giants, and a bunch of other
teams, including the Devil Rays. People who assume that only
sluggers take steroids ought to look at some pictures of Dave,
who was only five foot ten and 175 pounds. He played most of
his career in the outfield.

Like so many others, Dave approached me about steroids.
He's a nice guy, and I was glad to help him out. I injected him
the first few times, just to ease him into it, since he was a little
jumpy getting an injection like that. Nobody wants a needle

stuck in them, but other than Dave, they were all pretty good about it. I'm a good injector.

I taught Dave enough that he could continue on his own, but I don't really know whether he maintained the program or not; we weren't teammates for that long, and I didn't get a chance to monitor him over a period of time, the way I did some guys. But Dave Martinez is a good example of how even a player no one would ever suspect of using steroids did just that—maybe not seriously, maybe not for a long time, but more than once and purely of his own volition.

BRET BOONE

I remember one day during 2001 spring training, when I was with the Anaheim Angels in a game against the Seattle Mariners, Bret Boone's new team. I hit a double, and when I got out there to second base I got a good look at Boone. I couldn't believe my eyes. He was enormous.

"Oh my God," I said to him. "What have you been doing?"

"Shhh," he said. "Don't tell anybody."

Whispers like that were a sign that you were part of the club—the bond of a secret code or handshake. You were united by this shared knowledge, and the experience of unlocking so much more of your body's natural potential. Still, though, sometimes you just had to laugh—and it was that way with Bret Boone. Sure enough, Bret used his hulking new body to go crazy that season. He practically doubled a lot of his numbers. He went from nineteen homers to thirty-seven that year, and from eighteen doubles the previous season to thirty-seven that year. He had 141 RBIs, after nine years in which he'd never broken ninety-five in a season. That alone should have been enough to tell you what was going on, but the reporters covering Bret might as well have been sitting up in the pressbox with their hands over their eyes.

A *Seattle Post-Intelligencer* columnist named David Andriesen actually wrote in May 2002: "Speculation was quiet and infrequent, though, and we never asked Boone last year whether his performance was steroid-fueled. Aside from the numbers, there was no reason for suspicion, and we never saw a hint of tough-to-hide side effects commonly seen in steroid users."

A little knowledge can be a dangerous thing. Like a lot of reporters with very little knowledge about steroids, and no practical experience whatsoever, this guy got caught up in the whole side-effects distraction. In fact, if you use them properly, as I've mentioned, the side effects usually aren't a problem.

The amazing thing was how obvious it was: All they had to do was open their eyes and take a look at this little guy, with his small frame and his huge arms—arms that were bigger than mine! His great season that year just goes to show you how a new set of muscles can help an athlete. And those financial rewards weren't far behind: Based on his performance in 2001, Boone went from making $3.25 million to pulling down $8 million a year.

Who wouldn't want a $4.75 million raise? Who wouldn't be willing to take some small risks for that kind of cash?

If I told you I'd pay you that kind of money to swim across a lake filled with crocodiles, chances are probably even or better that you'd take the chance. But what's riskier? Steroids or the damn crocodiles?

The crocodiles, if you ask me. By a mile.

TONY SAUNDERS

One truly sad case was Tony Saunders, a left-handed pitcher who was my teammate in Tampa Bay during the 1999 season. I tried to talk to him. I really did. He was about six foot two, but when he got going with steroids he just kept getting bigger and bigger, until he looked like a bodybuilder.

"Listen, you've got to dose that stuff down," I told him; as a pitcher he needed a leaner, sleeker physique. And he agreed. He complained to me that the growth hormone and other chemicals he'd been taking had made his body too big, too tight.

But he didn't change his program—and a terrible thing happened. That May, he was pitching in a game against the Texas Rangers, and his arm just snapped. It was awful. He broke the humerus bone, from the elbow to the shoulder, and that ended his career. It's impossible to know whether steroids were responsible for compromising his bone density—it may be that he just didn't know his own strength.

When I see things like that, I just shake my head in sadness. Some people just don't understand the power they're working with. They get so carried away wanting to get bigger—but baseball's not about bigger. Baseball is about flexibility and longevity. It's about recuperation time, maintaining a psychological edge, and stamina. If anything gives you stamina, it's the proper mix of steroids done the proper way—not heavy steroids, which can bulk you up, slow you down . . . or stop you altogether.

If people want to think of using steroids as cheating—even with the whole baseball industry in on it—that's fine with me. But if that's how people are going to talk about steroids, they should at least keep in mind that baseball players, like anyone involved in a highly competitive activity, have always looked for ways to gain an advantage. They have always pushed the boundaries of what is fair and unfair, what is cheating and what is just being clever.

Remember Gaylord Perry's mean old spitball? That extended his career for years.

Or how about corked bats? There have always been players willing to use a bat that's been filled with cork to give it a little more spring. I remember talking once with Albert Belle about corked bats. Belle was a strong man, and it was all natural; he was one of the very few superstars of that era who never used steroids, as far as I know. But sometimes he did like to swing a corked bat in a game.

"Albert, man, you've got to hide bats like that," I told him. "You know, you're going to get caught if you don't."

He gave me one of those fierce Albert looks that people were always misunderstanding. "But everybody's using them," he said. "I might as well use one."

But I think Albert was exaggerating. A lot of us never used corked bats, and never wanted to. For me, they never worked because my bats were so darn heavy—thirty-five or thirty-six ounces. (The one time I swung a corked bat—just for fun, in batting practice—I cracked the head of it.) McGwire never even swung a corked bat, I guarantee it. He had corked biceps. Why would he need a corked bat?

There are plenty of little secrets like that in baseball, things that most fans don't even know about—until someone gets caught, the way Sammy Sosa did for using a corked bat in June 2003. When Sammy's bat broke during a game, home-plate umpire Tim McClelland decided to make an issue of finding a little cork among the pieces.

To me, though, the corked-bat controversy was just another instance of what I've been saying all along: If that had been a different player, I guarantee that the umpire would have covered it up. Umps cover that stuff up all the time if they like the player.

If it had been an untouchable, a McGwire or a Ripken, then for-get about it—there's no way any ump would have made an issue of it. But it was Sammy Sosa. And the whole thing got blown out of proportion, until it became international news.

Sammy didn't deserve that.

Chapter

25

THE FUTURE
OF THE GAME

*I love playing baseball, but sometimes I feel like the
gorilla in the zoo. People watch the gorilla, stare at it,
point at it, trying to figure out why it's doing what
it's doing.*

JOSE CANSECO,
October 2, 1989

One thing that always puzzled me was when people used to claim that somehow I didn't love baseball enough, or didn't respect the game enough. That's the kind of thing I heard every so often from outsiders and media people—but never from other players.

Baseball is the best game in the world.

Believe me, I care about the game; I busted my ass for it. I played through three back surgeries. I played through elbow surgery. If you play a power game, the way I did, you're going to have some injuries; that's only natural. But I always tried to play to the best of my abilities. I always worked to honor the game.

I never sat out with a minor injury or anything like that. That's another thing people don't really recognize. They don't know what it's like to have to go out and stand up straight so you can hit more home runs after three back surgeries. That's what I did—not just for my career, but for the fans, and for the game.

No game in the world can match baseball, in its pure form. But as a sport, organized baseball has its problems. Sure, the owners turned a blind eye to the steroid revolution because they felt they had to do something to save the game. And, sure, I can't stand their hypocrisy in claiming ignorance. But steroids are not the problem with baseball. No, the real problem is: Baseball doesn't know how to sell itself to people. The people involved don't seem to care about giving the fans what they want.

Even to this day, I have a big following among fans. They remember the excitement I generated back when I was MVP—the forty-forty man who dated Madonna and kept the headlines coming. There was always a buzz of interest around me. Whether it was during batting practice or during the game, I created a stir wherever I was.

I know all this sounds immodest, but I'm not trying to blow my own horn here. My point isn't that I was the world's best player. The point is that I was an *entertainer,* I knew it, and I never had a problem with it. I've always considered myself that way; I've always told the media: We're all entertainers, or should be, anyway.

Besides Bo Jackson, who came along the year after I did, there were no athletes my size that could perform the way I could. That just wasn't how baseball players were built. There was no one who could run as fast as I could run. I remember racing Rickey Henderson and beating him constantly. "I'm not going to race you any more," he told me. "I'm embarrassed to let a guy your size beat me." Rickey was one of the fastest guys in baseball—yet despite a forty- or fifty-pound weight difference, I was actually faster than he was. Besides Bo Jackson, I was hands down the biggest, fastest guy in baseball. The fans knew it, and they loved it. It brought more excitement to the game.

I could be entertaining even when I was controversial—or maybe I should say *especially* when I was controversial. That's why, when those fans in Boston started chanting "Steroids, steroids," I just turned and flexed my muscles at them. I knew they'd go nuts, and they did. They didn't have a problem with me being on steroids. They just wanted to have some fun at the ballpark. And I gave it to them.

I truly believe that most of those fans would look at me and say: *We came out here today, and Jose gave us our money's worth—whether he hit a few home runs, or struck out, or flexed for us.* They liked seeing me walk out on the field looking good—six foot four, 250 pounds, tall, dark, and handsome. They liked watching me move, watching the way I ran. And they loved it when I did something out of the ordinary to get their attention.

The fans were entertained by watching guys like me, or Bo Jackson, or even Ken Griffey Jr., though he wasn't flashy. Randy Johnson, with his stature, was an entertainer; so was Roger Clemens. Those were people who made it worthwhile for fans to come out and pay for their tickets and parking and hot dogs and sodas. They're the people who made the fans feel: *Today, I got my money's worth.*

Back in the 1980s, the Oakland A's were a team that delivered, game after game. Mark McGwire and I were the most intimidating duo in baseball—not to mention the biggest. People still tell me today: *Jose, when you came up to bat, no matter what you did, we just sat still and didn't move.* Nobody got up to get food, or go to the bathroom, because they didn't want to miss something extraordinary, like a ball being hit 550 feet.

That team was like a juggernaut. And believe me, we made the most of it—on and off the field. Our theory was to go into cities and have our way. We went out in groups, and the women were everywhere, ready to jump into our limousines and go with us. On the team bus after the game, we'd watch them as they chased us in their cars, flashing their boobs or throwing their underwear at us. Sometimes they'd be sitting in their cars naked. It was crazy. We were like rock stars.

We had a presence, those teams. Whether we were going to a nightclub or out to dinner, people knew we were there. It was a team of characters: Mark McGwire, Jose Canseco, Rickey Henderson, Dennis Eckersley, Dave Stewart, and on and on. We had all the show guys in baseball, each one of them with a different character and an interesting background.

I think that's what the game is missing now. I think baseball is struggling again, and it'll keep struggling if some major steps aren't taken to stop the erosion. Baseball needs leadership, and it needs imagination. It needs to remember that this is a game about individual athletes, not just money and ballparks and stats. It needs to encourage its players to turn themselves into entertainers, and look for new players who are born that way. And the teams have to learn how to market their players that way—the same way pro wrestling does.

Of course, there are limits to the approach. As in any other industry, including basketball or movie making, not everyone is going to be marketable. Barry Bonds is marketable. Alex Rodriguez is marketable. Those kind of players have extraordinary talent. But baseball needs to do a lot more to bring out those personalities. The only way to do that is to hire a completely different marketing entity, outside of the Major League Baseball power structure, and market the stars of baseball in a fun, clever, unpredictable way that really gets people going.

The strategy of relying on steroids for bigger numbers and bigger players worked—at least for a while. It gave baseball energy and excitement when that's what it needed. I'm sure steroids will always be part of the game. But steroids alone aren't enough to keep the game afloat, and it's clear that the powers that be have realized that.

They blackballed me from the game because I was the Chemist—the godfather of steroids in baseball. They looked up and realized that the players' salaries had gotten too high, and the players themselves had gotten too big and strong—all because I started things off by educating a handful of influential players on steroids, and showed them how to use them properly. All kinds of records were being broken, and the old-timers were complaining about how the new records were tainted. The horses were already out of the barn, but they sent me packing anyway.

Now, I'm sure they're wondering how to get steroids out of the game—how to herd those horses back into the barn. Their first step was to cut off the individual who brought it in—the stud, the buck, whatever you want to call him. By doing that, they hoped to send a signal to everybody: *Canseco's out. Better clean up your act, or you'll be next.*

As always, though, the real reason they want to stop the steroid revolution is that these more powerful players were costing them too much money. Not that they're going broke: The owners may say they're losing money every year, but if the fans understood how many billions there are in TV money—if they realized that teams would be making thirty or forty or fifty million dollars a year even if they never sold a live ticket to a game—they would be amazed. Tickets and concessions? That's just icing on the cake.

But that doesn't stop the owners from crying poverty. The truth is that some teams are making an astronomical amount of money, while other teams are only making a lot of money. And *everybody* wants to get into the astronomical club. The Milwaukee Brewers want to make as much money as the New York Yankees, even though the Brewers are fielding a brutal, horseshit team. It's beyond me. Every team comes in at the beginning of the year and declares that they've put together the best team in the league. But the players know what a load of bullshit that is. Just look at the players they're spending their money on, and you can see that many of them aren't even *trying* to win—never mind putting together a world-class team. They're trying to save money. They don't really care about giving the fans what they want.

Baseball needs to change, but I don't know if it will. I would never buy a baseball team, because I probably wouldn't agree with most of the things the other owners were doing. I could never agree to blackballing players, the way they blackballed me, or colluding against players.

The owners are constantly being caught out in their dirty little tricks. Last year, after they were caught colluding again, I received a check from Major League Baseball for $290,000 as part of the settlement of a long-standing salary-fixing case. People blame the commissioner, Bud Selig, for this kind of problem. But I don't really think he has that much authority in the first place. No one individual ever really controls a big organization completely, and it's the same in baseball: The brotherhood steers the ship. That's why when the owners collude, they all get caught together. It's also why it's hard to believe that baseball will really change its stripes—unless there's a major shakeup.

Epilogue

FOREVER YOUNG

Genetically, I wasn't dealt the best hand. That's not to knock my father, or his father back in Spain, or all the generations that went before. My dad is smart, and he passed his brains on to us; in the end, that's what matters most. But when it comes to my body, I'm here to tell you one thing: Despite what we're all used to thinking, genetics is not destiny. It's a starting point, that's all.

Look at me. See me on TV, or in the newspaper, and you'll see that we do have choices in life about how we want to look and feel. If you don't mind turning forty and feeling worn down and powerless, and looking like someone on the down slope to the nursing home, that's your choice. But if you want to head into your forties feeling strong and active, and looking as good as you ever have, the way I do, you can choose that, too.

I have chemically restructured my body, giving myself one of the best physiques in the world and enabling myself to do things at forty that most twenty-year-old kids couldn't do. Best of all, I have prepared myself to maintain that body for years to come. My strength, vitality, and appearance are my best argument for what I'm saying. If I were exaggerating the effect that growth hormone and steroids can have when used properly and carefully as part of a program of weight lifting, fitness, careful nutrition, and clean living, then why would I look and feel as good as I do?

The only answer is, I'm telling the truth. So please keep that in mind as you see me out there talking about the future of baseball, and you see the sportscasters and media types who I know are already preparing to take their best shots at me, without even bothering to read this book and think about what I've said. I don't care much about the blowhards on TV; that's their job, to shout at each other in high-pitched voices and look self-satisfied.

But I do care about you out there—regular people with good sense. And all I ask is that you trust your own instincts. I think people know when they're being told the truth, and when they're hearing lies. And I'm sure that the truth in this book will shine like a bright light for anyone who isn't willfully blinding himself to it.

All I'm saying is that the lives we lead are the product of the choices we make. What I've learned is that there is a way to stop the aging process, or at least slow it down by 90 percent. If you stick with a program of good nutrition and a consistent approach to fitness, and know the right mix of steroids and growth hormone to take, you should be the same at fifty years old as you are at thirty.

For me, turning forty was a great experience. It felt like a celebration, not something to worry about. I can't emphasize it enough: If you look good, feel good, and have energy, life after forty is full of promise. I fully believe that in the future, as my ideas are accepted, more and more people will feel the same way.

We've still got a lot to learn about the power of steroids. I'm sure new chemicals will be developed in the coming years, which will open up new possibilities we can't even imagine at this point. As that happens, and other people experiment on themselves over time, I expect we'll see human beings commonly living to be a healthy 120 or 130 years old. What is aging, after all? Any of you out there who think you have all the answers on that one, go ahead and take a step forward.

The truth is: Even the top scientists really aren't sure exactly why our DNA starts breaking down after a certain huge number of cell divisions. What role can systematic use of growth hormone play in resetting our bodies' natural lifespan? Nobody knows, but it's going to be interesting to find out, that's for sure. Stem cell research and other developments in biomedicine and biotechnology will only accelerate the trend toward longer lives. If you think about it, such developments will surely bring all sorts of new challenges for the world of sports. Before too long, the sort of physical changes we've seen because of steroids and growth hormone could look like nothing. With the many millions of dollars at stake in sports, athletes will always pay for the latest edge they can find. Genetic engineering and gene therapy could push science to make bigger and stronger athletes than even now. Maybe the combination of genetics and steroids can make a superhuman athlete. It's just a question of working out the science.

One thing is for sure: Ideas like age and life span are totally relative. Having cracked a few books in my day on the subject of steroids and related areas, I know scientists believe that as recently as ten thousand years ago most people didn't live past thirty years old. Wrap your mind around that one: Back then you were lucky to see thirty. What we're seeing now is just the natural extension of a long trend toward longer and longer life spans.

Civilization started, after all, when cavemen figured out how to use tools. They learned to work with flint so they could make sharp points to put on the end of their spears, and that technological step not only enhanced their lives, but increased their time on this earth. Isn't that really just the first step toward applying technology to our own bodies? Some time later, a new group of cavemen figured out that there were useful properties associated with certain herbs they'd come across. Some herbs helped calm the stomach. Others helped bring down a fever. Those discoveries, and others like them, led to longer lifetimes.

There have been a lot of big discoveries along the way since then—right down to penicillin. The point is, at every step along the way, there have always been naysayers—people who thought the status quo would always remain, even though the lessons of history teach us otherwise.

For example, one so-called expert named Louis Dublin made an interesting prediction back in 1928. He said he was certain that life expectancy would never be more than 64.75 years. That's pretty priceless, guessing down to the .75 like that; you can just imagine how he worked it all out with a slide rule. He was wrong, of course. He was a fool to imagine he could place limits on human progress and human potential. As recently as 2002, life expectancy was 76.7 years—and only an idiot would expect it to stop there. A recent article in the magazine *Science* predicted that average life expectancy will reach 100 sometime around 2060.

For that to happen, of course, the human race will have to break certain bad habits—things that are truly harmful to the body, like smoking cigarettes. We will have to change as a culture to eliminate our addiction to high-pressure lives, and our fetish for stress. The problem with stress is that it takes its toll on your body and your body's ability to maintain itself. We'll have to find a way to get our act together and clean up the chemicals in the air and the water that bombard us all the time. Chemicals can rob us of life as surely as they can enhance our lives. You just have to know how to use them.

We're due for an open discussion about our attitudes about using chemicals to give ourselves a better quality of life, and I hope this book helps make that national discussion more honest and revealing. It took me some time to think about what I wanted to say in this book and compose these chapters, but things have a way of working out, don't they? If you're reading this as the steroid controversy is picking up in the new season, I hope it'll help you get beyond the headlines to something closer to the truth—the way we, the players, lived it.

The biggest and most important of those controversies has probably been the one in California over the lab that allegedly supplied Barry Bonds, Jason Giambi, Gary Sheffield, and a bunch of other top athletes with designer steroids. The more people learn about the nutritional supplements company known as the Bay Area Laboratory Co-Operative (BALCO), the more they understand what cutting-edge stuff we're talking about here. The important thing to know is that, according to press reports, BALCO was doing it right: They were giving blood tests to Bonds and Giambi and the others. As I've been telling people for years, that's the only way to design a cycle that's right for you—to know the details of your body, your different hormone levels, and tailor your dosage accordingly.

The *San Francisco Chronicle* has come a long way on this subject over the last fifteen or twenty years. It was the *Chronicle* that helped create the public image of me as a dangerous criminal, from that overblown 1989 headline CANSECO ARRESTED—LOADED PISTOL IN HIS JAGUAR on down. But you've got to give them credit for being one of the few papers to do any serious reporting on the rise of steroids in baseball. When they ran those two big stories in December 2004—one saying that Jason Giambi had testified to using steroids, the other reporting that Barry Bonds had told the grand jury he used steroids without knowing what they were—the reality of steroid use in baseball finally hit home, even among longtime doubters.

Ever since those two *Chronicle* stories hit the stands, people across the country have finally begun to talk about steroids as a reality, not just a dark rumor. The week after they hit, you finally saw prominent media people admitting that the presence of steroids in baseball had been swept under the rug. That was when Howard Kurtz made his point about the media on his CNN show. "But in fact, when Mark McGwire broke the home run record with seventy homers back in '98 and Bonds with seventy-three broke that record, those were great stories," he said on December 12. "Maybe nobody in the press wanted to interfere with what was a nice story for baseball."

That was a big step forward, and I hope the discussion surrounding this book will be the next one. Ultimately, it all depends on whether people are looking for answers, or just settle for pointing fingers and assuming they know more than they really do.

As for the BALCO case itself, it's hard to know which way it will turn. Usually when a legal case ends up becoming a media circus, the way this one has, nothing much pans out in terms of prosecution. That's often why these leaks start in the first place: The case isn't as strong as prosecutors would like. Barry Bonds is smart, we all know that, and if he keeps denying that he ever knowingly used steroids, he'll be in the clear. The only issue that Bonds will have to face is the question of whether he perjured himself in front of that grand jury. If he's careful, he will be fine, but if he says something that contradicts his sworn testimony, he could end up doing some time in jail. Having been there myself, I hope for his sake that doesn't happen.

No matter how this BALCO case works out, the one thing we can all agree on is there's no going back to the way it was before.

There's no more pretending. What we have to look forward to is a world where honesty about steroids is the only policy.

The challenge is going to be demonstrating to people that steroids can be a good thing.

I've never said it will be easy to educate the American public about all this, to get them to accept what biochemistry and biotechnology can do to change our lives. We're really only getting started on that national conversation, and we're in for an awkward period as the revelations about steroids start to sink in. In the short term, you can count on plenty of people urging baseball to crack down, to wipe steroids out of the game.

What I'm hoping is that some more intelligent, forward-looking voices will come out and urge baseball to embrace the potential of steroids—to fight for their place in the game, and in our lives.

As for me, I plan to enjoy the freewheeling debate this book will help unleash. I've said again and again that the reporters who covered me were blinded by their own biases and prejudices about me as a Latino, and never got to know me. They thought they understood me, but they were really just shouting in an echo chamber, reacting to an image they helped create. Those same people have been putting out the word that I've written this book out of desperation. And you know what? They can think what they want to think. I don't really care about all that anymore.

Life has taught me so much about myself, and made me appreciate what really matters. When I was in prison, I vowed that when I got out I'd make the most of every day and appreciate every minute I could spend with my daughter, Josie. A vow like that is something you never forget; our time together is the most important thing to me. She has me wrapped around her finger, but so what? She's not the first beautiful little girl with a big personality to have a daddy who loves her to death.

Do I think about the disappointments I've had in life? Not much. I still wish I'd had a chance to reach five hundred home runs in my baseball career, which would have put me into the Hall of Fame; all it would have taken was one more season, if a single organization had given me that shot. But what's done is done. I'm through looking back on all that. What matters is looking forward to the years ahead, to watching Josie grow up, and to the fresh challenges that will await me in my work life.

I've always had a lot of fans who stood by me through ups and downs, and also a lot of detractors. To both groups I'd say: Don't you worry about Jose Canseco. I've been through a lot in my life, but despite everything I'm doing just fine. I may not be a hero, but I'm not the bad guy they made me out to be, either. Accept me as I am, the way I've learned to accept myself—and you may just find you're in for a few surprises.

ACKNOWLEDGMENTS

There are many people to thank for making this book possible. I would first like to thank Major League Baseball for giving me the opportunity to play the game I love—as well as for their crazy politics that has made the content in this book necessary. Thanks to Doug Ames and Michael Wallman. Thanks to Judith Regan, Cal Morgan, Daniel Nayeri, and the entire team at Regan-Books. Thanks to Brian Saliba. Thanks to Steve Kettmann. Thanks to Bret Saxon. Thanks to my entire family, who's always been my support group: my brother, Ozzie; my father, Jose Sr., my sister, Teresa; my niece, Barbie; my nephews, Frankie and Jessie; and my dog, Zeus. And a special thanks to the love of my life, my daughter, Josie.

INDEX OF NAMES

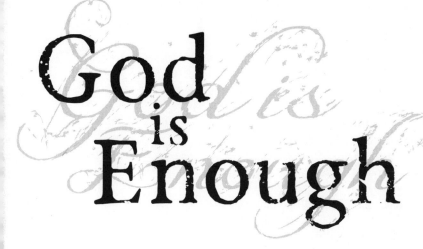

God is Enough

Refocusing your life

RAY GALEA

God is Enough
© Matthias Media 2010

Matthias Media
(St Matthias Press Ltd ACN 067 558 365)
PO Box 225
Kingsford NSW 2032
Australia
Telephone: (02) 9663 1478; international: +61-2-9663-1478
Facsimile: (02) 9663 3265; international: +61-2-9663-3265
Email: info@matthiasmedia.com.au
Internet: www.matthiasmedia.com.au

Matthias Media (USA)
Telephone: 724 964 8152; international: +1-724-964-8152
Facsimile: 724 964 8166; international: +1-724-964-8166
Email: sales@matthiasmedia.com
Internet: www.matthiasmedia.com

Scripture quotations are from The Holy Bible, English Standard Version, copyright © 2001 by Crossway Bibles, a publishing ministry of Good News Publishers. Used by permission. All rights reserved.

ISBN 978 1 921441 70 7

Cover design and typesetting by Lankshear Design Pty Ltd.

CONTENTS

*For Ray, Jenny, Shane, Amanda
and Sylvia, each of whom has
shown me by their faithfulness that
God is enough for them.*

*Thanks to Emma Thornett from
Matthias Media and my daughter,
Amy Galea, for making me look
good with their editing work.*

INTRODUCTION

I think I'm coming out of a six-year midlife crisis. I hope so, anyway.

I think the midlife crisis hits the moment you realize you're not going to achieve whatever goals you have set for yourself in life, whether consciously or not. Time is running out—or worse, time *has* run out. I am 49 years old. It is not going to happen!

Being a man, my midlife crisis is particularly connected with my job. The only problem is that I am a minister, a pastor of God's flock. I feel I should somehow be above such things. And what's really tragic is how superficial my unfulfilled goal is. I'm embarrassed to tell anyone what it is. I finally got it off my chest and told my congregation early last year, so I guess I can let you in on the secret: I want a big church. 1000 people will do nicely! But deep down, I don't think it's going to happen.

I knew I was in trouble when I caught myself reading 2 Chronicles looking for tips on how to grow a church. I had started treating God and his word as a means to an end. Somehow, over time, I had started believing the lie that I needed something other than God to feel content.

I had simply lost my way.

I can still remember when Jesus was my all in every sense. But then other things—good things, noble things—began to creep in. I was no longer centred as I had been in my younger faith. The glory of God had ceased to be my greatest joy.

I've been around long enough and spoken to enough people to know that we all lose our way. Many of us are disappointed with God. Life is turning out less like we had hoped and more like we had feared. And, unlike my superficial dream, sometimes our disappointment concerns deep matters of the heart. These matters are not inane or superficial; they cause a great deal of grief.

I know a growing number of faithful couples who long to have their own children but cannot. Consistent prayer, endless fertility diets and expensive and intrusive IVF procedures have all failed to produce a single newborn child, and now it's too late.

I think of the unmarried woman who recently celebrated her 43rd birthday alone, harbouring the nagging doubt that there must be something wrong with her. She had never imagined her future without a husband, but now it looks as if that is what her future holds.

I know a couple who privately came to the realization

that their eight-year marriage, which promised so much, has delivered very little. They are trapped by their own vows in a loveless relationship for as long as they both shall live.

I think of the 22-year-old who found himself in a wheelchair for life after a car accident en route to a Christian conference. He has had to cope with endless unhelpful comments from other Christians, as well as the subsequent losses of a fiancée whom he loved, a job at which he was very good, and the mobility he had taken for granted until the accident.

What are your disappointments in life? Perhaps, like me, you have unmet superficial desires—perhaps it is achieving that certain position in the company, or getting that high mark in a significant exam. Or maybe you are scarred by grief so profound that you can hardly talk about it. Or perhaps you're not so much disappointed as unmotivated; you have allowed the good and the not so good to hijack the best, and the passionate days of your early Christian life seem so long ago. Whatever the case may be, the issue is the same for all of us: is God enough?

We are simply not satisfied with our spiritual blessings in Christ. We end the statement, "For me to be content, I need …" with anything but "Christ alone".

As I've worked at refocusing myself, the psalms (Psalm 73 in particular) have reminded me of what I'd forgotten. In Psalm 73, the psalmist writes:

> Whom have I in heaven but you?
> And there is nothing on earth that I desire
> besides you. (Ps 73:25)

What a profound truth this is: God is enough. This is what centres me as a Christian. Being with God is all I desire. He is all I ultimately need. I just love shouting it out loud: "God is enough!"

My goal in writing this book is to keep us centred and focused. I have chosen eleven of my favourite psalms. The psalms are brilliant in the way they poetically and elegantly give us core biblical truths in the context of prayer and praise. Not surprisingly, the book of Psalms formed the songbook for Israel to worship the God who creates, sustains and rescues his people.

In my selection I have tried to reflect the variety we find among the psalms. Some are songs of praise; some are songs of lament. Some are corporate; some are individual. King David wrote most of them, although the choir leader, Asaph, wrote two and Moses wrote one. Some speak of the Messiah, others are written by the Messiah, and still others speak of life under the Messiah's rule. This may explain why the New Testament quotes the book of Psalms more than any other Old Testament book.

The book of Psalms is organized into five broad divisions, but I have cut across those divisions with reckless abandon. My configuration is more like a devotional systematic theology. It begins with the character of God (Psalm 139), followed by the nature of humanity (Psalm 8), the person and work of the Messiah (Psalms 2 and 22), sin, guilt and mercy (Psalm 51), the haunting reality of death (Psalm 90), the nature of revelation in creation and Scripture (Psalm 19), the righteous life in the presence of

God (Psalm 15), living with the tension between what we see and what we believe (Psalm 73) and, finally, the need to pass on the baton to a generation yet unborn (Psalm 78) so that in the end they, like us, will be able to say:

> Whom have I in heaven but you?
> And there is nothing on earth that I desire
> besides you. (Ps 73:25)

One final thing before we begin. Please—let me plead with you—please get out your Bible and read each psalm twice before you read the relevant chapter.

1 | THE ONE WHO KNOWS ALL

Psalm 139

The hunger of the human soul

Why do people feel the need to go to counsellors and therapists? I used to be one, so I would often ask myself this question. At one level, it's because people are in need of advice and insight—they are struggling in their marriages, they are deeply depressed, they don't know how to discipline their children …

However, in my experience, advice is not always what people want. Many end up going to a qualified stranger for one very simple reason: *to be known*. They want to share their life in a safe place and have another human being know their story and accept them. Isn't this why we desire close friendships and marriage? To be known and accepted by another? The human psyche deeply craves to be understood.

A friend of mine once scribbled a short poem on a polystyrene coffee cup and gave it to me after church. He wrote, "If I could find a world where I could understand people who understood me, then I would be happy".

Being at church among God's people fulfilled that longing for him (although only in part). That longing is also part of the reason for self-help groups such as Alcoholics Anonymous and Gamblers Anonymous: they provide a place where you can tell your story to people who have walked in your shoes and who share your struggles, knowing that they will understand and not condemn you.

We all want to be understood. You may know what it's like to have someone carefully listen to you and then thoughtfully reflect back their understanding of what you have said. Your instinctive response is to say, "That is *exactly* how I feel!" You can almost judge how well you listen to others by how often you hear that response. It shows you understand.

I think of the Samaritan woman who met Jesus at the well. When she returned to her village, she called people to "Come, see a man who told me all that I ever did" (John 4:29). Normally it would be terrifying to meet such a man, but for her it was absolutely thrilling. With five marriages behind her she finally met the man of her dreams, who just happened to be the Messiah.

We were built to be known, and in Psalm 139 we discover the mighty, wonderful counsellor God, who knows us inside out and outside in.

The great know-it-all

The beginning of Psalm 139, written by King David of Israel, introduces us to a God who is the great know-it-all.

> O LORD, you have searched me and known me!
> You know when I sit down and when I rise up;
>> you discern my thoughts from afar.
> You search out my path and my lying down
>> and are acquainted with all my ways.
> Even before a word is on my tongue,
>> behold, O LORD, you know it altogether.
> You hem me in, behind and before,
>> and lay your hand upon me.
> Such knowledge is too wonderful for me;
>> it is high; I cannot attain it. (Ps 139:1-6)

Look at the verbs David uses to describe God. God searches, knows, discerns. He is acquainted with all my ways. All of life is covered and nothing escapes his radar. If I sit or stand, if I am near or far, whether I am going out at 8pm or coming home at 3am; all my ways are known to God. As the famous Police song goes, "Every breath you take, every move you make ... I'll be watching you". Sting may have had a lover (or a stalker!) in mind, but his words capture God's moment-by-moment awareness of everyone on the face of this earth.

God knows what you are going to say before you say it. Some of the garbage that leaves our mouths may come as a surprise to us, but it does not surprise God. It may horrify him, but it never surprises him. David writes,

"Even before a word is on my tongue, behold, O LORD, you know it altogether" (v. 4). None of the things you say, none of the things you think and none of the things you do is off limits to God. He is all-knowing. The technical word is 'omniscient'.

I once went to a 21st birthday party where two 14-year-old friends claimed they could read each other's mind. But they could only do it using numbers from one to ten, and they needed to be facing each other. Their 'mind-reading' abilities were fairly limited. But no matter how we communicated the number to one guy, the other would get it right every time. To this day I don't know how they did it. It was one cool trick. Even though it was only a trick and their mind-reading was limited to ten digits, it was still impressive.

If a person really did know the thoughts of another, we'd be dumbfounded—it just doesn't happen. So it is difficult for us to fully grasp the concept that God knows, in detail, every precious and private thought we have. We still think that by closing the door or whispering in someone's ear, we can shut God out—but of course we cannot. It does us good to remember that God knows when you undress another person in your mind. He listens to every piece of gossip you utter about another human being. None of your thoughts or conversations is off the record!

We live out all of life in God's presence, as Proverbs 5:21 reminds us: "For a man's ways are before the eyes of the LORD, and he ponders all his paths". This is also what

David is saying in Psalm 139. In a nutshell: God is inescapable. The idea overwhelms David: "Such knowledge is too wonderful for me; it is high; I cannot attain it" (v. 6).

Think of the effort it takes for you to know one single person well. Now consider that God is intimately involved in the life of every person on the earth—all six and a half billion of us. This is why we can all pray at the same time without worrying about whether we are going to overwhelm God. We do not need to coordinate the timing of our prayers; God's concentration is not limited. When it comes to prayer, God does not need the departed saints to assist him. And unlike my computer, God has unlimited memory. So pray directly to God, anytime, anywhere. As you do so, remember that you are trusting God, not educating him.

No place to run

Our all-knowing God is also ever-present.

> Where shall I go from your Spirit?
>> Or where shall I flee from your presence?
> If I ascend to heaven, you are there!
>> If I make my bed in Sheol, you are there!
> If I take the wings of the morning
>> and dwell in the uttermost parts of the sea,
> even there your hand shall lead me,
>> and your right hand shall hold me.
>> (Ps 139:7-10)

David tries to imagine a place where God is not, but to no avail. If David climbed up to the heavens and stood on Mount Everest, or sank down into the waters of the Mindanao trench, God would be present. If David moved to the far side of the sea (which for an Israelite was the end of the earth), still God would be there. God is present in the place of the dead, even hell itself! Hell is not a place where people will be in fellowship with God, but they will feel his justice, as they exist in utter darkness for all eternity.

There is no place to run—the prophet Jonah certainly found this out. There is no godforsaken place on the face of the earth. Distance is irrelevant to God. There is no place where God is not. The technical word is 'omnipresent'. In fact, God is all-knowing *because* he is all-present.

Darkness, which can hide us from each other, is a meaningless category for God:

> If I say, "Surely the darkness shall cover me,
>   and the light about me be night,"
> even the darkness is not dark to you;
>   the night is bright as the day,
>   for darkness is as light with you.
>   (Ps 139:11-12)

It's as though God has a pair of those military night-binoculars. He can see in the dark. We often use darkness to stop people from watching us do things we are ashamed of. That is why they are called 'deeds of darkness'. But darkness is an ineffective barrier for God, whose eyes pierce the jet blackness of the night. The distinction between private and public, which we modern Westerners so carefully guard, simply does not exist when we stand before God. Everything is public!

However, the thrust of this psalm is to comfort, not to condemn. You may know the feeling of being completely alone as you lie in bed with tears streaming down your cheeks. You may feel equally alone lying next to a husband or wife who doesn't know you, or doesn't want to know you. This leaves you feeling profoundly unloved and disrespected, each memory as painful as the next. But in this psalm, God is saying to you, "I know your pain. I understand and I am with you." You need never feel alone. What a comfort!

From the womb

God is everywhere and he knows everything; he knows us even in the womb.

> For you formed my inward parts;
>> you knitted me together in my mother's
>> womb.
> I praise you, for I am fearfully and wonderfully
>> made.
> Wonderful are your works;
>> my soul knows it very well.
> My frame was not hidden from you,
> when I was being made in secret,
>> intricately woven in the depths of the
>> earth.

Your eyes saw my unformed substance;
in your book were written, every one of them,
    the days that were formed for me,
    when as yet there was none of them.

How precious to me are your thoughts, O God!
    How vast is the sum of them!
If I would count them, they are more than the
    sand.
    I awake, and I am still with you.
        (Ps 139:13-18)

The all-knowing ever-present God knew David personally before he was born. Likewise, when you were at your
most fragile, God fashioned you in the womb. He knew
you before you were able to know yourself; even before
your parents knew you. When you were just one of 30
possible names, only a tiny foetus, God was intimately
involved with you.

Whether your conception was the result of a one-night
stand or a loving, committed marriage, it was God who
ultimately fashioned you in the womb. Even if your
parents did not plan to have you, God certainly planned
to make you. This is why abortion is so tragic; it denies
God's creative purposes in the life of the unborn.

This personal God has made an astonishing humanity,
inspiring David's praise: "I praise you, for I am fearfully
and wonderfully made. Wonderful are your works; my
soul knows it very well" (v. 14). The craftsmanship of the
human body leaves the Rolls Royce for dead. When was

the last time you looked in the mirror and congratulated God on his handiwork?

God not only created David but also planned out the days of his life: "In your book were written, every one of them, the days that were formed for me, when as yet there was none of them" (v. 16). God is not simply a fortune teller, able to read your future; he is *determining* your future. Not a day passes when God is not in control of every detail of your life. There is no such thing as fate; there is only the personal hand of God at work. You may be overlooked in the crowd, too insignificant to rate a mention on the news or in the conversations of others, but you are known by the one who ultimately counts. At one level this is terrifying, but at another level it is incredibly comforting.

All of this raises a question: will you be satisfied with God knowing you? Are you able to say, "Whom have I in heaven but you? And there is nothing on earth that I desire besides you"?

U-turn

At this point, the psalm appears to make a 180-degree turn. You would be excused for wondering what has happened to David. Has he lost it?

> Oh that you would slay the wicked, O God!
>   O men of blood, depart from me!
> They speak against you with malicious intent;
>   your enemies take your name in vain!
>   (Ps 139:19-20)

David is clearly upset with "the wicked"—those who speak of God with evil intent, thinking he will not hear them. They do not understand that God is all-knowing and ever-present. They blatantly defy this God, thinking they can take him on. David is so upset that he actually wishes God would "slay" these people. What do we make of David's change in tone? It would be easy for us to dismiss this section by putting it down to David's sin, but the language used here is not unique to Psalm 139. At the very least, David's reaction betrays a jealousy for God and his glory—a jealousy lacking in the modern Christian.

Recently, I saw the lovable Oprah Winfrey on YouTube answering a question about her spirituality.[1] She explains that around the age of 27, while attending her Baptist church one Sunday morning, she was listening to the preacher talk about how God is all-knowing and-ever present. She was happily in tune with the message until the preacher spoke about how God is jealous for his honour. Oprah did not like this, and it was a key moment in her decision to leave mainstream Christianity.

I think the passage Oprah heard was very likely Psalm 139. How ironic it is that she is not interested in a God who cares about his honour, when surely Oprah cares for her own honour. If you misrepresented Oprah, I have no doubt that she'd send her lawyers to take you to task— and rightly so! Why do we treat God so differently from how we like to be treated ourselves?

Even though it is right to be jealous for God's glory, the language of the psalm is hard to hear:

> Do I not hate those who hate you, O LORD?
>   And do I not loathe those who rise up
>   against you?
> I hate them with complete hatred;
>   I count them my enemies. (Ps 139:21-22)

You might read these verses and think to yourself, "At last, a verse that justifies my hatred for my own enemies. If it's good enough for David, it's good enough for me!"

But we need to think more consciously about how to apply the psalm. First, David speaks from a different theological time zone to us. He was a member of the old covenant. The enemies of God were the enemies of Israel, so they were the enemies of King David. But for those in the new covenant, the enemies of God are redefined. At one level, we are all the 'enemies' of God for whom Christ died (Rom 5:10). There is no 'us and them'. At another level, the enemies of God are identified as the powers of sin, the world, death and the devil. And as new covenant members, we are called to love the enemy and instead hate sin (Matt 5:44).

We also need to remember that this is King David, the Messiah, speaking. And as the definitive Messiah, Jesus is the one who on the last day will reject those who reject him and his Father. It is for Christ, not us, to hate God's enemies all the way to hell.

And on that day, when God judges his enemies, his all-knowing, ever-present character will be a source of terror, not comfort. In Revelation 6, we see this terrifying picture of God's final judgement:

Then the kings of the earth and the great ones
and the generals and the rich and the
powerful, and everyone, slave and free, hid
themselves in the caves and among the rocks
of the mountains, calling to the mountains
and rocks, "Fall on us and hide us from the
face of him who is seated on the throne, and
from the wrath of the Lamb, for the great day
of their wrath has come, and who can stand?"
(Rev 6:15-17)

On that day, it would be better for the enemies of God
to have a thousand tons of granite fall on them than to
stand in the presence of the Lamb's wrath. Meeting God
unforgiven is a nightmare that never ends. You don't know
what terror is until you stand before this holy God on the
last day and discover there is no place to run or hide.

Importantly, Psalm 139 explains why Jesus is able, on
the day of judgement, to judge the secrets of our
thoughts. It also explains why his judgements will be
just. With a God who knows all and is ever-present, his
verdicts will not rest on the human standard of 'beyond
reasonable doubt'. God has access to all the information.
Unlike our court system, there will be no doubt about
the rightness of God's judgements.

A clear conscience

Psalm 139 is not written by an enemy of God, but by one
who trusts God. It's written for those within the circle of

faith as a word of comfort. This psalm produces praise and wonder, and inspires confession:

> Search me, O God, and know my heart!
> Try me and know my thoughts!
> And see if there be any grievous way in me,
> and lead me in the way everlasting!
> (Ps 139:23-24)

It is impossible to keep any secrets from God. So David calls on his God to search him out. He does not want to pretend before a God who knows all. In the same way that I invite the spelling checker on my computer to expose my typing errors and bring them to my attention, David calls on God to bring to light any offensive way within him. Confession is not about informing God of our sin; it's about agreeing with God's verdict on our life.

Make it your aim to have a clear conscience before God. We ought to live our lives with the aim of being able to say alongside the Apostle Paul, "You are witnesses, and God also, how holy and righteous and blameless was our conduct toward you believers" (1 Thess 2:10). This should be our deathbed boast.

You may be mindful of those past sins that dog your life and line your past; sins that weigh heavily on your conscience, even though you've confessed them with repentance. Please know that God is saying to you, "I knew you would commit that sin before I made you. I chose you, knowing you would commit that sin. I was present when you committed that sin. But I want you to know: I stapled that sin to the body of my dear Son, and it is left at the cross, never to be used against you."

The good news is that now there *is* one thing that God does not know—your sin. God's great promise is that "I will remember their sin no more" (Jer 31:34).

FOR REFLECTION
- How has this psalm's description of God affected you? Does it comfort you or threaten you?
- Are you willing to invite God to search you out? If not, why not?
- Do you make it your aim to have a clear conscience?

2 | THE GLORY OF MAN

Psalm 8

What kind of animal is man?

Mark Twain once said, "Man is the only animal that blushes. Or needs to".[2]

Years ago, three teenagers came across a homeless man sleeping under the awning of a major Sydney hospital. The teenagers doused the man with petrol, then set him alight and watched him burn.

When things like this happen, you can't help but wonder: what kind of animal is man? It's ironic that when we want to identify a compassionate attitude, we call it 'humane'. Sometimes there is nothing humane about us humans.

In Psalm 8, the psalmist answers the questions, "What does it mean to be human?" and "What is our place in God's universe?" But he does so on God's terms, and he does so as a way of praising God. This psalm stops us from singing, "To man be the glory, great things he as done", and it redirects us back to the truth: "To God be the glory, great things he has done."

We praise God

> O Lᴏʀᴅ, our Lord,
>> how majestic is your name in all the earth!
> You have set your glory above the heavens.
>> (Ps 8:1)

King David opens and closes this psalm with a song of praise. It is a declaration of God's glory in all creation. Before we can honour the name of God, creation is already at it. What's more, the heavens cannot contain God's glory.

David uses the word 'Lord' in two ways in the opening sentence. The first 'Lᴏʀᴅ'—in small capital letters—refers to God's personal name ('Yahweh' or 'Jehovah'), which he revealed to Israel. The second 'Lord' is a title, pointing us to God's control and lordship over the universe.

What sets humans apart from the rest of creation is that we choose to praise the God who is Lord of the universe. David seeks to celebrate the work of God's name and character, which he sees in creation and beyond. God's fingerprints are clearly all over this universe. The heavens and the earth radiate with their maker's splendour. The creation is God's 'bling'.

However, it's not just kings who praise God, and it's not just the majesty of his creation that tells of his glory. Praise manages to fall from the lips of the smallest infant.

We are arrogant

> Out of the mouth of babies and infants,
> you have established strength because of
> your foes,
> to still the enemy and the avenger. (Ps 8:2)

As Spurgeon once wrote, "How often will children tell us of a God whom we have forgotten!"[3] Jesus knew this. While he is in the temple performing miracles, the children shout, "Hosanna to the Son of David!" (Matt 21:15). The religious head-kickers (the chief priests and the teachers of the law) hear the children shouting and are indignant. They say to Jesus, "Do you hear what these are saying?" In other words, "Shut them up—they are blaspheming!" Jesus' simple and profound response is to quote Psalm 8:2. Jesus accepts praise that is addressed to God, while the Pharisees are certified as the enemies of God, shamed by the children's insight.

The praise of the insignificant kid shuts the mouth of the arrogant: it always has and it always will! When my daughter Madeleine was five years old, she was sharing with me her love for Jesus and how he died on the cross for her sins. In a moment of fatherly pride, I said to her, "Maddy, you are smarter than 90% of all the professors in all the universities in all the world". She replied with amazement, "Really Daddy, wow!" Then she paused for a moment and asked, "But what's a professor?"

She may not have known what a professor was but Maddy knew enough to praise the God of the universe, while most of the intellectuals of our world prefer to sideline him as irrelevant.

We are special

The wonder of creation inspires awe in David, as he considers the special attention God has given to humanity:

> When I look at your heavens, the work of
>   your fingers,
>   the moon and the stars, which you have
>   set in place,
> what is man that you are mindful of him,
>   and the son of man that you care for him?
>   (Ps 8:3-4)

You can imagine David as a young shepherd boy lying on his back, gazing at the stars in a clear Middle-Eastern night sky. With the heavens being so big and us being so small, why are we so important? The more science opens up the endless solar systems, the punier we seem. Yet among the millions of planets, solar systems and galaxies he has made, God has given special honour to humanity.

Consider Jesus' view of humanity in Matthew 6:26, compared to other creatures found on earth. He says, "Look at the birds of the air: they neither sow nor reap nor gather into barns, and yet your heavenly Father feeds them". Notice he doesn't say "Are you not *as* valuable as they are?" What he says is, "Are you not of *more* value than they?"

We are kings of the world

You don't have to live in Buckingham palace to be royalty. Notice the royal language that is applied to us in Psalm 8:

> Yet you have made him a little lower than the
> heavenly beings
> and crowned him with glory and honour.
> (Ps 8:5)

We bear the honour and privilege of being made in the image of God. It's clear that Psalm 8 is a prayerful reflection on Genesis 1:26-27: "So God created man in his own image, in the image of God he created him; male and female he created them" (v. 27). Humans were made on the sixth and last day of creation as the pinnacle of God's creative work. And as his image bearers, we are called to rule God's universe on his terms.

When an ancient Near-Eastern ruler conquered a kingdom, it was customary for the king to place an image of himself in the newly acquired land. This made it clear who now ruled the land. Outside a major shopping complex in the heart of Sydney, stands a statue of Queen Victoria. Apparently, out of the kindness of their hearts, the Irish unloaded this symbol of British rule for the colony 'down under'. Queen Victoria's image remained as a constant reminder to all Australians that they were part of the British Empire. Similarly, we are made in God's image to signify God's kingship over his creation.

Any casual reading of the Bible makes it clear that God detests images and statues of himself. It is profoundly disrespectful to God to reduce him to a deaf, dumb, blind and loveless object (see Psalm 115). The only thing allowed to represent God on this earth is you!

Although we are only one small species, on one small planet, in one small solar system, God's special affection rests with us. This is a long way from the worldview of noted Australian author and atheist Philip Adams. He writes:

> I believe, I know, that we live on a minor planet in an off-Broadway solar system on the edge of the Milky Way and that, in the final analysis, we're as significant as the eight billionth grain of sand beyond the final palm tree in the most distant oasis in the Sahara ... Like the hippopotamus and the hedgehog, humans are simply an evanescent [vanishing] expression of the life force, as destined for oblivion as dodos and dinosaurs.[4]

This is not the sort of stuff that will get you up in the morning with a spring in your step. It certainly won't do much for your self-esteem. How profoundly different it is to the biblical worldview:

> You have given him dominion over the works
>   of your hands;
>   you have put all things under his feet ...
>   (Ps 8:6)

God did not create us to stand side by side with the rest of creation; he made us to rule the world under him—a world where everything is placed under our feet and in our lap.

God is denied his rightful praise whenever humans are reduced to being viewed as purely animals. Likewise, God is dishonoured when humans are elevated to the status of gods. The framework that secures God's centrality places humans in creation as part of it and at the same time as distinct image-bearers who rule under God. This is the framework David expresses in Psalm 8.

The evolutionary worldview has destroyed the concept of our uniqueness within the created order, and as a result God and humans are dishonoured.[5] It is a mindset that puts our existence solely down to the result of time and chance. It dissolves the distinction between humanity and the rest of creation, so that humans are ranked equal with every other creature. The result is that more tears are spilt over five beached whales than over the 70,000 human abortions performed in Australia each year.

Of all the creatures on this earth, God has given only his image-bearers the right to rule and manage the rest of creation:

> You have given him dominion over the works
> of your hands;
> you have put all things under his feet,
> all sheep and oxen,
> and also the beasts of the field,
> the birds of the heavens, and the fish of
> the sea,
> whatever passes along the paths of the
> seas. (Ps 8:6-8)

Our rule is quite comprehensive. The more we walk on this planet, the more we subdue it. We ride the horses—they don't ride us. We discovered penicillin and the fever was cured. We invented refrigeration, so now we enjoy fruit all year round. We placed men on the moon and robotic toys on the surface of Mars. There seems to be nothing we cannot do.

How dare you have low self-esteem? God could have made you to be a dog, or the cockroach you stepped on yesterday, instead of one of his unique image-bearers.

We are part glory, part ruin

A thousand years after David wrote this psalm, the writer of Hebrews quotes it (Heb 2:6-8) and then emphasizes the dominion of man:

> Now in putting everything in subjection to
> him, he left nothing outside his control.
> (Heb 2:8b)

The rule of man is complete; God has left *everything* subject to him. However, the writer of Hebrews then concedes what we all know:

> At present, we do not yet see everything in
> subjection to him. (Heb 2:8c)

The problem with Psalm 8 is that we know better. We know that everything is *not* subject to man. Psalm 8 is Genesis 1-2 without Genesis 3. It fails to list our failures—not least of which is our gross mismanagement of our environment. Psalm 8 carries a partial truth, not the whole truth. As Francis Schaeffer rightly put it, we are a glorious ruin—part glory and part ruin.

Our control of the world is not so complete after all. A brief encounter with a tsunami victim will make this clear. Earthquakes and floods regularly overwhelm communities, wreaking havoc on millions. Insurance companies recognize our lack of dominion, refusing to cover damage caused by what they call 'acts of God'. For every wave we ride, we get dumped by another. Sometimes we catch the fish and sometimes a white pointer takes a bite out of us.

And even if we have managed to domesticate plants and animals, we fail to tame something as small as the tongue:

> For every kind of beast and bird, of reptile and
> sea creature, can be tamed and has been tamed
> by mankind, but no human being can tame the
> tongue. It is a restless evil, full of deadly
> poison. With it we bless our Lord and Father,
> and with it we curse people who are made in
> the likeness of God. (Jas 3:7-9)

One moment we sing, "O LORD, our Lord, how majestic is your name"; the next we tell our loved ones to shut up! Rule the world? We can't even rule the words that leave our mouths and destroy our relationships.

It is so true that "at present, we do not yet see everything in subjection to him". We can't even keep ourselves alive. Sin and death mock us. As we consider the rulers we were made to be, death is the final declaration that we do *not* ultimately rule.

Jesus restores our glory

The writer of Hebrews sees the hope of Psalm 8 fulfilled specifically in Jesus:

> ... At present, we do not yet see everything in subjection to him. But we see him who for a little while was made lower than the angels, namely Jesus, crowned with glory and honour because of the suffering of death, so that by the grace of God he might taste death for everyone. (Heb 2:8-9)

Everything humans hope for is realized in Jesus. Where angels and humans failed, the one born in a manger succeeded.

You don't have to wait for the age to come to see that everything is subject to Christ. His rule was evident throughout his earthly life. When caught in a life-threatening storm, he said to the wind and waves, "Shut up!" (Mark 4:35-41). When confronted by demons who raped the soul of a man, he said, "Get out!" (Mark 5:1-13). When faced with a man who was paralysed for 38 years, he said, "Get up!" (John 5:5-9). When he met men who feared God, he said, "Follow me!" (Matt 4:18-22, 9:9). When he came to the tomb of a friend who had been dead for four days, he shouted, "Come out!" (John 11:17-44).

He could look people in the eye and ask, "Which one of you convicts me of sin?" (John 8:46). No-one could. Jesus even has authority over death: "I lay down my life that I may take it up again" (John 10:17).

Jesus' authority over everything reveals his divinity; it shows us that he is God (Matt 9:6). But it also reveals his *humanity*. Jesus is a sneak preview of our glorified selves in the new creation. He is what we were *meant* to be as God's image-bearers.

Furthermore, Jesus took on flesh and suffered death in order to deal with that which undermines our role as image-bearers:

> Since therefore the children share in flesh and blood, he himself likewise partook of the same things, that through death he might destroy the one who has the power of death, that is, the devil, and deliver all those who through fear of death were subject to lifelong slavery. (Heb 2:14-15)

Before Christ shares death *with* us, he tastes death *for* us. At its core, Christ's death on the cross is an act of liberation, enabling humans to live life without the fear of death.

My daughter Amy once asked my wife, "Mum, can you say no to dying?" It's a good question. The answer, as we all know, is "No". That is why we are described in Hebrews as being enslaved to the fear of death. We are such a long way from our high calling to be crowned with glory and honour.

This is one of the most profound paradoxes of the human condition. We have eternity placed in our hearts, and yet we walk in the valley of the shadow of death.

Our fear of death has many faces, from humour to despair. It's captured in Woody Allen's well-known joke: "I'm not afraid of dying. I just don't want to be there when it happens."[6] Noted existential philosopher Albert Camus wrote that "life is a sustained protest against death"—a bit like that moment in the movies when everything happens in slow motion just before the man drives his car into a brick wall at 100 km per hour with his foot pressed hard on the brake.[7] Our whole life is like that moment; it's about trying to stop the inevitable.

As a result, many spend their lives fearing death or denying it will ever take place. Some refuse to go to funerals or organize their own wills, while others refuse to ponder the big questions of life. Some develop health obsessions, trying to milk another five years out of life, while others try to cram ten lifetimes into one because one is all they have. Many claim at funerals that their deceased loved ones will live on in their children or in their dreams. These are all deeply unsatisfying solutions to our slavery and fear, compared to the freedom and certainty Jesus offers.

In Christ, death has been defeated in history. At the end of history, death—the last enemy—will be completely destroyed. Resurrection of the body has now been experienced by one man: the Lord Jesus. That man becomes a forerunner for all who follow him. Relationship with the living Lord means we can now take our foot off the brake. Those in Christ are no longer enslaved to the fear of death. Of course we don't look forward to the process of death; personally, I would prefer to die in my sleep rather than suffer with cancer or die in a car accident. But we embrace what is for us a doorway into the age to come. We can now begin to rule as God would have us rule.

This is why Martin Luther said so bluntly, "He who fears death or is unwilling to die is not a Christian to a sufficient degree; for those who fear death still lack faith in the resurrection, since they love this life more than they love the life to come".[8] So we who have been set free are no longer chained to our mortality, but are liberated to praise God for our renewed humanity.

I recall the last time I saw Les Vitnell. He was the senior minister of the church, and I was appointed as his assistant. Not long after I joined the church staff team, Les developed cancer. I went to visit him just before he died, sometime later. As I stood at his bedside I asked him, "Les, what is it like to know that within 24 hours you are going to be in the presence of God?" With a smile he said, "Ray, I have to tell you, I'm a little excited!" Of course he could be excited, because he knew his Saviour, who liberated him from the fear of death.

Les is very different to some Christians, who so desperately cling to the hope of healing that they will not allow anyone to talk to them about their death. They think that talk of death shows a lack of faith. I often think that as Christians, we are at our best when we die.

Les was one good example—he died so very well! He is a man who can now say with full conviction, "Whom have I in heaven but you? And there is nothing on earth that I desire besides you."

Whatever reasons King David had for thanking God, we who live after the resurrection of Jesus Christ have so many more. So let us join David and declare: "O LORD, our Lord, how majestic is your name in all the earth!"

FOR REFLECTION

- How does Psalm 8 challenge the way the world sees the place of humans within the created order?
- What implications flow out from Psalm 8 and Hebrews 2 regarding Christ?
- Why do we have more reasons to praise God than King David?
- Is praising God part of your prayer life?

3 | A KISS FOR THE KING

Psalm 2

In the days when men were men and women
were queens ...

Queen Elizabeth I ruled Great Britain over 400 years
ago. She had a habit of flirting with European royalty,
and for a brief time she considered marrying a French
Catholic, the Duke of Alençon. (Clearly she had a
preference for Mediterranean men—and who could blame
her?) But one of her Puritan subjects wrote her a letter
claiming it was inappropriate for the British monarch to
marry the French duke. Queen Elizabeth was furious. She
summoned the man and ordered her men to cut off the
hand with which he wrote the letter. His name, most
appropriately, was John Stubbs. He held up his bloody
stump and shouted to the crowd, "God save the Queen!"
before he fainted. As if chopping off his hand wasn't

punishment enough, the Queen then sent him to prison for 18 months.

Now that is what I call royalty with a kick. These days, Queen Elizabeth II cannot even prevent the paparazzi from ruining her holidays. How times have changed!

God is like Queen Elizabeth I. He has authority, and he will exercise it. Psalm 2 teaches us that those who defy God and his king have not a hope in heaven or hell of getting away with it.

Psalm 2 contains four distinct scenes. As we work through the psalm, imagine a camera focusing on four different images and locations.

Scene 1: Kings against the King

The opening scene begins with the earth's nations and rulers plotting to overthrow God and his anointed one. This is a world in open rebellion against God:

> Why do the nations rage
>   and the peoples plot in vain?
> The kings of the earth set themselves,
>   and the rulers take counsel together,
>   against the Lord and against his Anointed,
>   saying,
> "Let us burst their bonds apart
>   and cast away their cords from us."
>   (Ps 2:1-3)

The psalmist does not ask the opening question because he is confused, but because he is astonished at the sheer stupidity of such a rebellion. Such plans will always come to nothing. In every attempt to overthrow God, people come off second best and so their plotting is in vain. Yet still they rage "against the LORD and against his Anointed".

Who is this anointed one? In the Old Testament, all kinds of people and things (e.g. priests, prophets, altars, tents) were anointed with oil to mark them as set apart to serve the Lord God. But the expression "the anointed one" (or "the LORD's anointed") particularly referred to Israel's king. This is what the title 'Messiah' or 'Christ' means. The Messiah is God's anointed and God's appointed King. He is the one to whom God has given the right to rule the universe (2 Samuel 7).

And so the opening scene of Psalm 2 is the usual story of human rebellion—not kingdom versus kingdom or man versus man, but man versus God. The nations take their stand against the Lord (the God of Israel) and against his anointed one (the King of Israel). We are all familiar with the World Wide Web. Well, this is the World Wide Rebellion, which began with Adam and Eve. By the time you get to the sixth chapter of Genesis, God's verdict on man is that "every intention of the thoughts of his heart was only evil continually" (Gen 6:5). This is complete, thorough and wilful defiance.

A friend of mine told me of a woman in his church who was renting out her house as a retirement investment. She had the tenants from hell. Her mortgage repayments were high, so she needed the tenants to regularly pay the rent. But their payments were irregular, and eventually they stopped altogether. It was four months before the sheriff was able to remove the tenants. If that was not bad enough, they trashed the house before they left, costing the owner thousands of dollars in repairs. They made it even worse by leaving behind a photo of one tenant staring at the camera and sticking up her middle finger (what my kids used to call "the rude finger"). This is what we do to the God who gave us this world to live in. We deny the owner his rights.

The world has always hated God. There has never been a time when it did not. But that hatred reached its climax when God and man met face to face—when Jesus Christ came into the world. While Psalm 2 describes the treatment of King David, it also operates as a prophecy about the plot against Jesus. The Apostle Peter draws this link for us after the crucifixion. As he prays to God and reflects on those involved in the death of Jesus, he quotes Psalm 2 and then explains its connection to Jesus:

> "… for truly in this city there were gathered
> together against your holy servant Jesus, whom
> you anointed, both Herod and Pontius Pilate,
> along with the Gentiles and the peoples of
> Israel, to do whatever your hand and your plan
> had predestined to take place." (Acts 4:27-28)

Psalm 2 looks forward in time to the world's stand against God's anointed, and all those who were directly involved: Herod, who questioned Jesus and "treated him with contempt and mocked him" before sending him back to the Roman ruler Pontius Pilate (Luke 23:6-12); Pilate, who gave the final permission to execute Jesus; the people of Israel who cried out "Crucify him"; and the Roman soldiers who finally pierced and nailed the Christ to the cross.

God became a man, and man hunted God down. I once heard about a school Easter pageant in London, organized by a lady who was not a Christian. She asked a local minister to give an address at the pageant, suggesting topics such as 'Peace for our world' or 'Love in a loveless world'. But the minister informed the woman, "I will be speaking on the topic, 'Given half a chance, man's first inclination when he meets God face to face is to kill him'".

We need to remember that what they did to Jesus at the cross is what we in our sins have always been trying to do—in essence, remove God from our lives; break free, once and for all.

In their song 'When Love Comes to Town', the megaband U2 captures our personal connection with the events of the cross:

> I was there when they crucified my Lord
> I held the scabbard when the soldier drew his
>   sword
> I threw the dice when they pierced his side
> But I've seen love conquer the great divide.[9]

Scene 2: God the King

We now turn the camera to see God's reaction to the rebellion:

> He who sits in the heavens laughs;
> > the Lord holds them in derision.
>
> Then he will speak to them in his wrath,
> > and terrify them in his fury, saying,
>
> "As for me, I have set my King
> > on Zion, my holy hill." (Ps 2:4-6)

As we see God's reaction to a world tripping over itself to remove its king, we learn three things.

1. He is fully enthroned

When I was 11, we had a string of casual teachers at school. I clearly remember the way we made more than one of them leave the class in tears, never to be seen again.

But God is not at all intimidated by our rebellion. Human defiance does not tarnish his rule. The rulers and nations may take their stand against God and against Jesus, but this does not alter the fact that God rules. He is fully enthroned. When Nietzsche declares that "God is dead", and stand-up comedians make jokes at God's expense, do not think that God has lost control. He is not feeling insecure; he is not tortured with an inferiority complex. Nothing could be further from the truth.

2. He laughs

What did God do when Judas, out of greed, handed Jesus over to the priests (Matt 26:14-16)? What did God do when the priests, out of envy, handed Jesus over to Pilate (Matt 27:1-2, 18)? And what did God do when Pilate, out of fear, handed Jesus over to the soldiers who then crucified him (Matt 27:24-26)? In a nutshell, God laughed. God will always have the last laugh because he is the sovereign judge of all the earth.

But this is not the laughter of one who enjoys what is happening. It is the laughter of one who scoffs at the sheer stupidity of mankind. Rebellion is wrong, but it is also just plain dumb. It's as foolish as walking onto a freeway in front of a massive truck going at full speed, and thinking that the truck is going to come off second best. There is simply no contest.

God laughs at our futile attempts to defy him.

3. His king is installed

To his enemies, God is unequivocal: "I have set my King". God's king is installed, so be very afraid. In effect, God is saying, "Do what you like to him—he is still the King." And we know this is true because as much as they tried, God's enemies could not get rid of King David. And a thousand years later, they certainly could not remove King Jesus.

On the cross Jesus disarmed the devil, solved the problem of sin by paying its penalty, lavished his love upon us, destroyed death and satisfied God's justice. All this ensures that Jesus' kingdom will never end.

And notice where God has staked Jesus' claim to kingship: on Zion. 'Zion' is code for the city of Jerusalem, which is seen in the Bible as the centre of God's kingdom. To make Jesus' kingship clear, God made sure his enemies secured a placard above Jesus at the cross. On it was written, "This is the King of the Jews" (Luke 23:38). It was written in three languages (Latin, Greek and Hebrew) so all the world would know that God had installed his king on Zion.

The irony is that God's enemies did not realize they were declaring the truth when they labelled Jesus the King of the Jews. Their purpose was to mock him.

In fact, crucifixion itself was usually a very public symbol of defeat. About 70 years before the time of Jesus, a gladiator named Spartacus led a slave rebellion. Spartacus and his runaway slaves defeated two Roman forces in succession, overran most of southern Italy, and ultimately grew to be many thousand strong. The Roman army's wrath eventually came upon these slaves with a vengeance, and Spartacus and his men were killed in the battle. To make the point that Rome would not tolerate such rebellion, 6,000 other slaves were crucified on the Appian Way leading into Rome for all to see. Their bodies were left on the crosses for months.

In God's strange irony, he used the foolishness of the cross as the place where his Son would be publicly installed as the victorious King. A symbol of crushing defeat becomes the platform for God's greatest victory. In the words of Paul, "the word of the cross is folly to those who are perishing, but to us who are being saved it is the power of God" (1 Cor 1:18).

Scene 3: God's anointed King

Now the camera focuses on the king who has been anointed and installed. God announces his plan for this king:

> I will tell of the decree:
> The LORD said to me, "You are my Son;
> 　　today I have begotten you.
> Ask of me, and I will make the nations your
> 　　　heritage,
> 　　and the ends of the earth your possession.
> You shall break them with a rod of iron
> 　　and dash them in pieces like a potter's
> 　　　vessel." (Ps 2:7-9)

We learn two important things about the King.

1. Son of God

Firstly, this king is the Son of God. If you reject God's anointed one, you reject his one and only Son. Rebellion against Christ is deeply personal for God.

I can relate to that. One day when my daughter was at preschool, my wife found her on the ground with a group of preschool boys kicking her, while the ring leader raised his clenched fist, chanting, "Kill girl, kill girl!" Those boys were very lucky I was not around that day. She is my precious daughter and their attack was very, very personal.

Those boys only had my wife's anger to face. Imagine facing God's anger because you have killed his Son. You would only do such a thing if you didn't realize what you were doing—and this is true of the men who crucify Jesus. Jesus knows this, praying "Father, forgive them, for they know not what they do" (Luke 23:34) as he hangs on the cross.

To many, Jesus does not look like the Son of God while he suffers and hangs on the cross, but it's a different story when he rises from the dead. Jesus doesn't *become* God's Son when he rises from the dead, but his resurrection makes it obvious to everyone that he *is* the Son of God with power (Rom 1:3-4; Acts 13:32-33).

What was hidden at the cross is made public at the resurrection. Christ's resurrection is not simply a reversal of death but also a revelation of victory. It is not to a dead king that we are called to submit, but to the living Son of God. Dead people are not scary—they're just smelly; but a living Lord is awfully intimidating. And this living King has defeated for the first time our nemesis and ultimate enemy: death.

2. Heir to the universe

Secondly, God has given everything to his Son. God made the entire universe *for his Son*. Understand this, and you understand the meaning of life. The Father invites the Son to ask for the nations and the universe as an inheritance. This is why Jesus is called "the firstborn of all creation" (Col 1:15). In the Middle East, it is the firstborn son's privilege to receive the family inheritance. For Jesus, the scope of that inheritance includes the heavens and the earth; he inherits the lot with no exception. What belongs to God belongs to his Son, and this includes the nations and rulers who rebelled against them. God's Son will rule over them. There is no hint of doubt.

The authority of Jesus is so complete that if any oppose him, he will dash them to pieces like broken pottery. Or, to put it another way:

> God has highly exalted him and bestowed on
> him the name that is above every name, so that
> at the name of Jesus every knee should bow, in
> heaven and on earth and under the earth, and
> every tongue confess that Jesus Christ is Lord,
> to the glory of God the Father. (Phil 2:9-11)

Willingly or unwillingly, whether from the heights of heaven or the pits of hell, all will bow. God created this world for his Son, and he will rule it.

As Bob Dylan once wrote:

> The iron hand it ain't no match for the iron rod
> The strongest wall will crumble and fall to a
>   mighty God
> For all those who have eyes and all those who
>   have ears
> It is only he who can reduce me to tears
>
> ...

> Of every earthly plan that be known to man,
> He is unconcerned
> He's got plans of his own to set up his throne
> When he returns.[10]

On that day God's enemies will long to die, but they won't be able to. They will be begging God to kill them. Yet God does not want to dash anyone to pieces. He does not delight in the death of a rebel.

Scene 4: Kiss the King

The last section of Psalm 2 is a call to those who have rebelled—to the earth's rulers, then and now. God commands them to be wise, to be warned, and to serve the Lord; to give up and take refuge in him.

> Now therefore, O kings, be wise;
>> be warned, O rulers of the earth.
> Serve the LORD with fear,
>> and rejoice with trembling.
> Kiss the Son,
>> lest he be angry, and you perish in the way,
>> for his wrath is quickly kindled.
> Blessed are all who take refuge in him.
>> (Ps 2:10-12)

Kiss the Son—God's king—or kiss heaven goodbye! When you kiss a king, it's a sign of submission. It's a mark of surrender, showing that you will no longer wage war with God. This kind of kiss says, "I want peace with

God's king on God's terms".

In the film *The Devil's Own*,[11] Brad Pitt plays an IRA terrorist. In response to some gesture by the British towards the IRA, he says, "They say the word 'peace', but at the end of the day, all they want is surrender". God is saying that the two must go together: peace can only come if we surrender to him and to his Son.

We have a choice to make, but what choice is it when the options are so clear?

A ministry trainee at my church was once explaining the rule of Jesus to two Iranian doctors who had spent eight years studying medicine in Russia. On hearing of Jesus' authority they immediately wanted to become Christians. Surprised by their quick reaction, the trainee wisely asked them, "Are you sure? Do you want time to think about it?" They responded, "We have no choice!"

Do you see your response to Jesus with such clarity?

Accepting Jesus as Lord is motivated not just by the truth of Jesus' claims, or by the fear of punishment, but also by an extraordinary promise of blessing. Psalm 2, so clearly fulfilled in Jesus, also applies to those who submit to him. For example, to the church in Thyatira Jesus says:

> "The one who conquers and who keeps my works until the end, to him I will give authority over the nations, and he will rule them with a rod of iron, as when earthen pots are broken in pieces, even as I myself have received authority from my Father. And I will give him the morning star." (Rev 2:26-28)

And to the church in Laodicea he says:

> "The one who conquers, I will grant him to sit
> with me on my throne, as I also conquered and
> sat down with my Father on his throne."
> (Rev 3:21)

In a surprising twist, those who confess Jesus as Lord get
to share in the inheritance and rule of Christ. This is why
God allows us to call Jesus our brother and not just our
Lord (Rom 8:29; Heb 2:11). This is why we are deemed
to be co-heirs with Christ (Rom 8:16-17; Gal 4:7). This
is why we are told that the meek will inherit the earth—
not this earth, but the new heavens and the new earth
(Matt 5:5).

What is the difference between Bill Gates and the
average Christian? Apart from 60 billion dollars, it's that
Mr Gates's dreams are simply too small. Nothing he owns
can be seen from the moon. Christians are insatiable
dreamers who refuse to be satisfied with nothing less than
everything.

We rightly want it all. Jesus has it all. Kiss the Son and
we get it all. When we understand this, we will not treat
our jobs as if they were careers, our houses as if they were
palaces, and our lovers as if they were gods. Only then
will we understand the psalmist's cry: "Whom have I in
heaven but you? And there is nothing on earth that I
desire besides you."

Kiss the Son, or kiss it all goodbye.

FOR REFLECTION

- Are you denying God his rightful rule in any area of your life at the moment?
- What does it mean to "take refuge" in Jesus? From what do we need protection?
- Do you long for your heavenly inheritance? How is this longing and hope reflected in your day-to-day life?

4 | THE SUFFERING AND GLORY OF THE GOD-MAN

Psalm 22

Famous last words

What does a person think of in their dying hours? What will you be thinking about on your death bed as your life is reduced to weeks, days, hours and minutes and breaths? What goes through the minds of men and women on death row? What does a crucified man think of as he hangs there, left to die a merciless death?

A friend recently lent me a book that contains the dying words of various well-known people. Apparently some people don't think about very much at all in their final moments! The playwright George Bernard Shaw has this written on his tombstone: "I knew if I hung around long enough this would happen". Spike Milligan's tombstone says, "I told you I was sick". On his death bed,

Oscar Wilde is said to have declared, "This wall paper is appalling. One of us will have to go."

A little more sobering are the final words of the philosopher Socrates, who was arrested for corrupting the youth of Athens. He decided to take his own life before it was taken from him:

> Socrates in the prison cell in Athens, according to Plato's account, took his cup of hemlock "without trembling or changing colour or expression". He then "raised the cup to his lips, and very cheerfully and quietly drained it". When his friends burst into tears, he rebuked them for their "absurd" behaviour and urged them "to keep quiet and be brave". He died without fear, sorrow or protest.[12]

And I always thought that the 'stiff upper lip' came from the British.

Then there was Polycarp, Bishop of Smyrna in the second century AD. He could have escaped death by running away or by denying Christ, but he refused to do either. Just before he was burnt at the stake, he prayed:

> "O Father, I bless thee that thou hast counted me worthy to receive my portion among the number of the martyrs."[13]

What a way to go!

A person's dying words will often tell you a lot about them—which is why, when we turn to Jesus' last words, they are such a surprise. His last words speak more of desperation and confusion than bravery and conviction: "My God, my God, why have you forsaken me?" (Matt 27:46). His life ends with a question, a picture of fear and uncertainty.

But, as people often do, Jesus is applying words spoken by another to his own situation. The words that fall from the lips of Jesus as he dies also once fell from the lips of King David. They come from Psalm 22, written about 1000 years before Jesus came to earth. It is prophetic in nature and uncanny in its accuracy, predicting several very specific things about Jesus: his words on the cross, the casting of lots for his clothes, the taunts of those around him, and his death by crucifixion (notable especially because crucifixion was not known at the time the psalm was written). Some have rightly said that this psalm works like the fifth gospel of the crucifixion.

As Jesus suffers this crucifixion and cries the opening words of Psalm 22, he no doubt has the whole psalm in mind. So let us enter into the mind of this crucified man as he makes sense of his pain and his situation.

Abandoned

> My God, my God, why have you forsaken me?
>   Why are you so far from saving me, from
>   the words of my groaning?
> O my God, I cry by day, but you do not answer,
>   and by night, but I find no rest. (Ps 22:1-2)

As King David suffers and groans and prays, God remains silent. The situation remains unchanged as David's pleas continue. He asks God to step in, but his prayers are not answered. And it is the same for Jesus on the cross. As he cries out to God, there is no reply. This is the abject horror of the silence of God.

But notice that even though things don't get better, it never occurs to David that perhaps God does not exist, nor does he turn away from God. God's silence has not turned David into a cynic or an atheist. God is still his God: "My God, my God …"

David is facing the classic philosophical problem of suffering and evil. If God is all good and all powerful, why do the innocent suffer? (And let's not forget that no-one was more innocent than Jesus.) In the face of suffering, many conclude God is not good, or he is not powerful, or he is simply not there at all. David, however, does not look at the injustice of his situation and conclude there is no God. Even if God is silent now, he has spoken in the past. David knows God's track record is faultless.

Mindful of the past

> Yet you are holy,
>> enthroned on the praises of Israel.
> In you our fathers trusted;
>> they trusted, and you delivered them.
> To you they cried and were rescued;
>> in you they trusted and were not put to
>>> shame. (Ps 22:3-5)

David and Jesus both know that others prayed and were heard by God. Three times David notes that others trusted, and three times he notes that they were delivered, rescued, or not put to shame.

Without going into detail, David recounts the history of God's dealings with those who trusted in him. They cried out and were eventually saved. Not one ended up saying, "It wasn't worth it", or "What a waste of time". Not one experienced regret.

Israel's history is littered with God's faithfulness to his people: Abraham, Moses, Joshua, Deborah, Ruth, and now David. The one who suffers now stands where God's people stood before him; he trusts in the same God. That is why this is not blind faith.

But the psalmist's call is to trust *now* in light of what God has done *in the past*. Our world views this trust as total insanity.

Insane?

> But I am a worm and not a man,
> > scorned by mankind and despised by the
> > > people.
> All who see me mock me;
> > they make mouths at me; they wag their
> > > heads;
> "He trusts in the LORD; let him deliver him;
> > let him rescue him, for he delights in
> > > him!" (Ps 22:6-8)

These words may well have been written a millennium before Jesus' life, but they were written with him in mind. On the cross Jesus experienced exactly the same scorn, mocking and taunts:

> And those who passed by derided him, wagging their heads and saying, "You who would destroy the temple and rebuild it in three days, save yourself! If you are the Son of God, come down from the cross." So also the chief priests, with the scribes and elders, mocked him, saying, "He saved others; he cannot save himself. He is the King of Israel; let him come down now from the cross, and we will believe in him. He trusts in God; let God deliver him now, if he desires him. For he said, 'I am the Son of God.'" And the robbers who were crucified with him also reviled him in the same way. (Matt 27:39-44)

Whatever David was battling with, we certainly know what Jesus is facing.

On the cross Jesus is despised, mocked and insulted by everyone—from passers-by who throw his words back in his face, to the thieves who hang with him, to the priests who accused him. "He saved others," they say, "he cannot save himself". They do not realize that if he saves himself then he will not save others.

And through it all, God does not step in. There is no apparent answer to Jesus' prayer, "My God, my God, why have you forsaken me?" At this point, it seems totally insane for Jesus to continue to trust in the one who has abandoned him.

I recall the story of Mike Sunker, a man born into an Indian Hindu family in South Africa during the apartheid regime. One day, his sister brought a Bible home. His father threw it against the wall, declaring that he would not have white man's religion in his house. Out of curiosity Mike began to read the Bible, and over the next few years he came to trust in the Lord Jesus for his salvation.

In time, Mike and his wife had a child. That is when the trouble began. The child grew but, sadly, died at six months. Mike's Hindu relatives told him, "The reason why your child has died is because you have turned against the Hindu gods. Now they have turned against you." He was devastated, but continued to trust in the Lord Jesus.

Wonderfully, a second child was born, but six months later this child also died. Again, Mike's Hindu relatives told him it happened because he had turned against the Hindu gods and now they had turned against him.

Fortunately, a third child was born and grew to six months. Tragically, this child died at the same age as the other two.

Yet Mike still trusted God. He said, "It's not so much that I had any faith left. It was just the sheer grace of God that carried me through." And Mike has continued to trust God. But where is the logic in trusting a God who is at worst against you, and at best not there at all?

Now, Mike Sunker is the first to tell you that he is a guilty sinner who deserves to face the judgement of God. He knows he has received far less than what he deserves. But with Jesus at the cross, for the first (and only) time in history, we have someone who is truly innocent and does not deserve to face God's judgement.

And this is not just a case of an innocent person being treated unjustly. There's more to it. What is so amazing about the psalmist's continuing trust in God is that he has never before encountered God's silence. This is a new experience.

Forsaken for the first time

Yet you are he who took me from the womb;
>> you made me trust you at my mother's
>>> breasts.
On you was I cast from my birth,
>> and from my mother's womb you have
>>> been my God.
Be not far from me,
>> for trouble is near,
>> and there is none to help.

Many bulls encompass me;
>> strong bulls of Bashan surround me;
they open wide their mouths at me,
>> like a ravening and roaring lion.

I am poured out like water,
    and all my bones are out of joint;
my heart is like wax;
    it is melted within my breast;
my strength is dried up like a potsherd,
    and my tongue sticks to my jaws;
    you lay me in the dust of death.

For dogs encompass me … (Ps 22:9-16a)

The psalmist has known and trusted God for his entire life. For David, God has been his God from the womb. But the relationship between God the Father and God the Son is immeasurably deeper and more profound. Jesus' umbilical cord reaches back before his birth into eternity. He has always existed with his Father. In his prayer in John 17:24, Jesus says, "Father … you loved me before the foundation of the world."

On the cross, the only relationship that never had a beginning has come to an abrupt halt. The one who said of Jesus, "This is my beloved Son, with whom I am well pleased" (Matt 3:17) is now saying and doing nothing! There is simply silence.

And if his Father's absence is not bad enough, those around Jesus have turned on him. We see vicious animals representing Jesus' enemies, each image allowing us to feel his fear—bulls, lions and wild dogs with open mouths, all ready to tear apart the Son of God.

The situation is so frightening that the heart of Jesus melts away. His mouth is dry with fear. He may be the Son of God but he is also the son of man. Jesus' humanity is in full view; there is no bravado here, no stiff upper lip. His fear is real.

And so it is astounding to realize that, all along, Jesus knew this was coming. He knew God would forsake him, and he knew it would involve his own crucifixion:

> … a company of evildoers encircles me;
> they have pierced my hands and feet—
> I can count all my bones—
> they stare and gloat over me;
> they divide my garments among them,
>   and for my clothing they cast lots.
>   (Ps 22:16b-18)

Lucius Seneca, a Roman contemporary of Jesus, gives us some idea of the pain of crucifixion:

> Can anyone be found who would prefer wasting away in pain dying limb by limb, or letting out his life drop by drop, rather than expiring once for all? Can any man be found willing to be fastened to the accursed tree, long sickly, already deformed, swelling with ugly weals on shoulders and chest, and drawing the breath of life amid long-drawn-out agony? He would have many excuses for dying even before mounting the cross.[14]

But the real agony is not the physical horror. The real agony is the break in fellowship that takes place within

God himself between the Father and the Son. God is far away from his Son. He does not act to rescue or save or deliver. For the first time, there is a separation within the perfect relationship.

Psalm 22 gives no explanation for all this suffering or for God's silence, but elsewhere in the Bible the reason is clear:

> But he was wounded for our transgressions;
> he was crushed for our iniquities …
> (Isa 53:5a)

> For Christ also suffered once for sins, the righteous for the unrighteous, that he might bring us to God … (1 Pet 3:18a)

> For our sake he made him to be sin who knew no sin, so that in him we might become the righteousness of God. (2 Cor 5:21)

We owe a debt we cannot pay. Jesus pays a debt he does not owe. He does it so we can escape the horror of hell—the horror of being forsaken by God. There at the cross, as the darkness descends, judgement falls on the judge who has become our sin.

And through all the suffering, the psalmist clings to his God:

> But you, O Lord, do not be far off!
> O you my help, come quickly to my aid!
> Deliver my soul from the sword,
> my precious life from the power of the dog!

Save me from the mouth of the lion!
(Ps 22:19-20a)

Jesus also clings to his Father, entrusting himself to him who judges justly. We see this in the garden of Gethsemane, when Jesus knows exactly what he is about to suffer:

> And going a little farther he fell on his face and prayed, saying, "My Father, if it be possible, let this cup pass from me; nevertheless, not as I will, but as you will." (Matt 26:39)

> And being in an agony he prayed more earnestly; and his sweat became like great drops of blood falling down to the ground. (Luke 22:44)

Jesus is about to go through unbearable pain, but he keeps trusting in a God who does not seem to be listening.

Rescued

All of a sudden, the psalmist moves from lament to praise:

> You have rescued me from the horns of the
> wild oxen!

> I will tell of your name to my brothers;
> in the midst of the congregation I will
> praise you:
> You who fear the LORD, praise him!

> All you offspring of Jacob, glorify him,
>   and stand in awe of him, all you offspring
>   of Israel!
> For he has not despised or abhorred
>   the affliction of the afflicted,
> and he has not hidden his face from him,
>   but has heard, when he cried to him.
>   (Ps 22:21b-24)

His prayer has been heard. God's silence has ended.

But David's experience is different from that of Jesus, and the difference is this: David is saved *from* death and rescued from his enemies. Jesus, on the other hand, is saved *through* death. He is raised on the third day, never to die again.

> In the days of his flesh, Jesus offered up prayers and supplications, with loud cries and tears, to him who was able to save him from death, and he was heard because of his reverence. (Heb 5:7)

God answered the prayer of his righteous one, raising him to life and placing him above every name, so that at the name of Jesus every knee shall bow (Phil 2:9-11). The one scorned becomes the one we look to. We can now escape the silence of hell. This is why Psalm 22 does not end with the sufferer rejoicing alone. He calls on the congregation, God's people, to join him in praising God.

But this victory also has international implications. The whole earth is called to join Israel in turning and bowing down:

From you comes my praise in the great
       congregation;
  my vows I will perform before those who
       fear him.
The afflicted shall eat and be satisfied;
  those who seek him shall praise the LORD!
  May your hearts live forever!

All the ends of the earth shall remember
  and turn to the LORD,
and all the families of the nations
  shall worship before you.
For kingship belongs to the LORD,
  and he rules over the nations. (Ps 22:25-28)

The scope of what Jesus did at the cross is not limited to
one people, nor to one time. The psalmist announces that
future generations will proclaim this righteousness:

All the prosperous of the earth eat and
       worship;
  before him shall bow all who go down to
       the dust,
  even the one who could not keep himself
       alive.
Posterity shall serve him;
  it shall be told of the Lord to the coming
       generation;
they shall come and proclaim his righteousness
  to a people yet unborn,
  that he has done it. (Ps 22:29-31)

In fact, this psalm is being fulfilled as you read these very words, for I am proclaiming Jesus' righteousness 3000 years after it was predicted that I would.

WHAT WAS JESUS THINKING about on the cross? He was thinking of you. You, who at the time of Christ's death, were yet to be born.

What is the answer to Jesus' question, "My God, my God, why have you forsaken me?" The answer is "You". *You* are the reason Jesus was forsaken. It was his love and our sins that kept him on the cross.

Jesus final words were not "My God, my God, why have you forsaken me?" They were "It is finished" (John 19:30). This is how the last verse of Psalm 22 can be translated. It is finished; he has done it. Jesus is alive, and you're forgiven, and heaven's gates are open wide.

Famous last word

I opened this chapter with some famous last words. You are facing some even more important last words: the words that will leave the lips of God on the day of judgement. You will either hear, "Well done, good and faithful servant" (Matt 25:23) or "I never knew you; depart from me, you workers of lawlessness" (Matt 7:23). Your life is heading either into the fist of God's judgement or into the hands of a loving Father. The French philosopher Jean-Paul Sartre said, "Hell is other people", but he was wrong.[15] Hell is no people and no God. The reason Jesus was forsaken was so that we don't have to be.

I remember a woman in our church who was a single parent with two boys. She found out she had a tumour in her uterus the size of a tennis ball. She was in pain for two years until she finally died. Just before she died, she said to my wife, "With all the prayers I have prayed, and despite all the things I'm going through, I am so glad there is one prayer I will never have to pray: 'My God, my God, why have you forsaken me?'"

FOR REFLECTION

- In what way does Psalm 22 act like a fifth gospel?
- Why did Jesus say, "My God, my God, why have you forsaken me?"
- A Christian will never have to pray, "My God, my God, why have you forsaken me?" Why not?
- Is it possible that you have grown tired of hearing the word of the cross? How can you prevent this?

5 | THE MERCY OF GOD

Psalm 51: part 1

Several years ago I killed a man. That is, I killed him in a nightmare. And before you psychoanalyse me or offer a 'word of knowledge', I should explain that I tend to have bad dreams when I sleep under too many blankets.

In the dream, I was a soldier in a war zone. As the faceless enemy came towards me, he killed the soldier to my right and then the soldier to my left. I knew I was next, so I pulled out a knife and plunged it into his heart. To make sure he was dead, I turned the knife. He died at my hands.

I'm not sure you can sin in your dreams, but I was not taking any chances. I confessed that deed to God and to every person I met for the next three days. I've never felt so guilty in my life. And yet I've never felt so relieved, knowing it was only a dream.

King David discovered one day that he had adultery and murder on his hands, but it wasn't a nightmare from which he could wake up. It was real.

David's need

Many psalms don't give us the context in which they were written, but the note at the beginning of Psalm 51 tells us exactly why this prayer of confession was written:

> To the choirmaster. A psalm of David, when Nathan the prophet went to him, after he had gone in to Bathsheba.

To put it more starkly, the literal translation is "… after David had entered into Bathsheba". I won't go into all the details here—you can read the full story in 2 Samuel 11-12. For now, it is enough for us to note that up to this point, King David has lived an impeccable life. He is described by God as a man after his own heart, and with good reason. But now David finds himself in the awful situation of being an adulterer and a murderer. He needs God's mercy. How did this happen?

"In the spring of the year, the time when kings go out to battle … David remained at Jerusalem" (2 Sam 11:1). While his troops were out on the battlefield, David committed adultery with his bodyguard's wife, Bathsheba. To cover up her subsequent pregnancy, he organized the death of Bathsheba's husband. After nearly a year of thinking he had got away with it, the prophet Nathan came to David and exposed his sin, saying, "You are the man!" (2 Sam 12:7).

Can you imagine the sheer weight of guilt and the shame at that moment for this Messiah, this King of Israel? What do you do when your deeds go public? You have nowhere to run, no place to hide. You're left with endless self-recriminations—"What have I done? What have I done?" This is a nightmare from which you cannot wake up. David realizes he has only one option.

David's plea

> Have mercy on me, O God,
>   according to your steadfast love;
> according to your abundant mercy
>   blot out my transgressions.
> Wash me thoroughly from my iniquity,
>   and cleanse me from my sin! (Ps 51:1-2)

David's plea is simple: "Have mercy on me, O God". In other words, "Please do not treat me as I deserve; please don't hold my sins against me. Please give me what I have no right to be given: mercy."

Specifically, David asks God to "blot out my transgressions". A transgression involves crossing a line you know is there; you know something is wrong, yet you deliberately do it anyway. David also speaks of his "iniquity", which is an old-fashioned term for one's evil nature. The more familiar word 'sin' carries the sense of missing the mark or the target.

If the mark is to love your neighbour as yourself, David has seriously missed it. He has managed to break four of the Ten Commandments by coveting his neighbour's wife, stealing his neighbour's wife, committing adultery with his neighbour's wife, and then murdering his neighbour.

Call it what you like but at its heart, sin is rebellion against the living God. David knows it and so he pleads for forgiveness:

> Hide your face from my sins,
>   and blot out all my iniquities. (Ps 51:9)

He asks God to blot out his sins, as if each sin was a debt written down in God's ledger, needing to be cancelled. David wants his adultery gone; his murder erased; his coveting wiped out.

David also uses the language of cleansing. Sin has made him spiritually unfit to be in God's presence. He is unclean before God, so he asks God to wash his sins away:

> Purge me with hyssop, and I shall be clean;
>   wash me, and I shall be whiter than snow.
>   (Ps 51:7)

Hyssop is a herb, sprinkled with the blood of sacrifices on the Israelites to make them ceremonially clean before God. Of course it wasn't the hyssop that made the people clean; it was the blood of sacrifices, shed for sins.

The Bible is clear: without the shedding of blood, there is no forgiveness. That is why the temple was more like an abattoir than a museum or a cathedral. At the place where man approached God, much blood was spilt to remind Israel that the pay packet for sin is death. But, while the Old Testament allowed the blood of animals to atone for sin, there was no sacrificial provision for high-handed sins like David's (Lev 20:10; Num 35:31-32; cf. Num 15:27-31). There was no way of atoning for adultery or murder. You simply faced the uncompromising penalty of death.

The New Testament is also clear: the blood of animals does not bring forgiveness (Heb 10:4). For that, we need the Son of David to shed his blood once and for all at the cross. We are all able to say the sinner's prayer only because Jesus died the sinner's death. In Jesus' sacrifice, adultery and murder—along with every other sin—was dealt with decisively.

David is confident in God's power to cleanse: "wash me, and I shall be whiter than snow". He knows that if God promises something, it will happen. David clearly understands his own sin, but he also clearly understands God's promises. In effect he is saying, "If you do it, Lord, it will be done. I will be forgiven." This is justification by faith alone.

The nature of humanity is that we fuss over the outward and care little for the inward. We want clean cars, clean houses and clean skin, but we're not so concerned about being clean before God. The modern Western mind can be so profoundly superficial.

David, however, has come face to face with his sin and cannot ignore it—the prophet Nathan made sure of that. David feels the weight of his wrongdoing:

> For I know my transgressions,
> and my sin is ever before me. (Ps 51:3)

But David's guilt is not determined by the fact that others know of his sin. It's determined by the fact that David knows and God knows. That's why there is no excuse. God is right and David is wrong, so David needs God's mercy.

In fact, in verse 4 the way David expresses his need for mercy is almost offensive.

David's judge

> Against you, you only, have I sinned
> and done what is evil in your sight,
> so that you may be justified in your words
> and blameless in your judgement.
> (Ps 51:4)

I would have thought David sinned against a few more people than God alone. Let's consider who they might be: there is Bathsheba, her husband, Uriah (whom David murdered), David's own family, David's other wives (whom he betrayed), and the nation he led as king.

Imagine for a moment an arsonist who starts a fire that destroys 50 homes. Shortly afterwards, he goes to a church in the local area and confesses in an open prayer time, "God, against you, you only, have I sinned and done what is evil in your sight". He would be lucky to get out alive.

So where is David coming from?

The Bible tells us that you can sin against your own body (1 Cor 6:18) and against your neighbour (Matt 18:21). But at a more profound level, every sin is ultimately directed against God himself. This is why God's forgiveness is what matters most to David.

God is not simply one injured person among others. He is not just part of a long line of victims of David's sin. This is God's world. Each person is made in the image of God, so when we sin against another person we sin against God himself. I clearly remember the prayer of one member of our church after the September 11 attacks. He prayed, "Lord, this was not just an attack against the United States. It was an attack against you."

There is only one opinion that ultimately counts, because there is only one judge whose mercy is needed. Understand this truth and you will put the rejection of others in its place. God is the one whose judgement and forgiveness will shape your eternity.

David's rationale

On what basis does David ask God to forgive him? Notice that he *doesn't* say, "Lord, have mercy on me because I have been faithful" or "Remember, Lord, I am a man after your own heart. You said so yourself, and I have chapter and verse to prove it!" or "Have mercy on me because this is the first time I have fallen so badly. It is out of character for me, so give me a break."

David does not even mention his "blameless" past

(2 Sam 22:24). Not once does he ask God to take it into account. That's what convicted criminals do when they want leniency from the court. They appeal for mercy based on their past performance, supported by character references. They get people to highlight how 'good' they have been in the past. "Judge, I may have murdered, raped and pillaged, but I did give $50 to the Salvation Army nine years ago."

But not David, even though he had an impressive track record. For example, when no-one would fight Goliath, it was a young David who trusted God and fought the giant for God's honour. When Israel's first king, Saul, tried to hunt David down, David refused to exercise revenge on him because he was still God's appointed king. So if anyone could make an appeal based on past performance, it would be David.

But David knows his own sin and he also knows God's holiness. He has no problem with God's verdict. In confessing his sin, David agrees with the word of God and the justice of God: "... so that you may be justified in your words and blameless in your judgement" (v. 4b). Five times in three verses, David owns his sin. He speaks of "*my* transgressions", "*my* iniquity" and "*my* sin". What a contrast to the way we deal with sin today. At a time in history when everything begins with 'I' (iPod, iPhone) or 'my' (MySpace), very few people will personalize their sin.

Furthermore, David knows his sin is not just one mistake in an otherwise sinless life. His sin can be tracked all the way back to conception:

> Behold, I was brought forth in iniquity,
>   and in sin did my mother conceive me.
>   (Ps 51:5)

David's transgressions are part of a life wrapped up in sin from its very beginning. It is the same for us. We are all sinners even before we commit our first conscious sin. In fact, we sin *because* we are sinners. We sin by choice and we sin by nature.

Yet David does not use original sin to justify his behaviour or absolve himself of responsibility. Rather, he speaks of it to justify God's verdict. This is a clear reminder that avoiding murder and adultery is not in itself the answer, because individual sins are not the ultimate problem. They are merely a symptom of it. The heart of the problem is the problem of the human heart.

We work overtime to excuse our behaviour. We are desperate to give each other permission for any and every form of antisocial behaviour. The current mantra in every television sitcom seems to be "It's not your fault". We have effectively managed to eradicate the language of 'sin', and with it the reminder that there is a God whose heart we have broken. Consequently, we deny ourselves the cleansing freedom that comes in facing the truth about ourselves and accepting the forgiveness God offers.

It is worth restating the point. David does not rely on his past good behaviour to earn God's forgiveness, and he does not blame his mistakes on his sinful nature by saying, "Well, I'm only human". Ultimately, David's only hope is God's mercy. David requests forgiveness on the basis of God's abundant mercy and steadfast love—the unfailing covenantal love that forgives anyone who genuinely asks for mercy.

David's starting point

Any relationship with the true God must begin with a clean confession; no 'ifs' and no 'buts'.

The Apostle Paul openly declared he was the 'foremost of sinners' by his persecution of Christians (1 Tim 1:12-15).

The tax collector in Luke 18 went home from the temple justified because he refused to trust in his own righteousness, instead crying out, "God, be merciful to me, a sinner!" (Luke 18:13).

John Newton was also willing to come clean and confess. As a slave trader, he met the mercy of God in the Lord Jesus. He wrote of his sin and God's mercy in that most familiar of hymns: "Amazing grace, how sweet the sound that saved a wretch like me".

I can't count the times I have read the words of David from Psalm 51 to men and women who have finally admitted to a life of shame. I remember the tears of one man, ten years ago, who finally admitted to a long list of sexual encounters with other men while married to his wife. His confession was accompanied by true repentance. His tears of shame were replaced with tears of joy and relief.

Have you come clean with God? Relationship with God begins here:

Have mercy on me, O God,
according to your steadfast love …
(Ps 51:1)

FOR REFLECTION
- Do you think confession and repentance of sin takes place only at the start of the Christian life, or is it an ongoing activity?
- When was the last time you confessed your sins to God and asked for mercy?
- Are you confident in God's promise of mercy? Why or why not?

6 | A NEW CREATION

Psalm 51: part 2

A new heart

Whatever the crime, from the trivial to the serious, we love it when people are caught out on camera. We've all seen those television shows where the journalist and his cameraman walk up to confront the driver who has just parked in the disabled parking spot without a permit. And in the latest reality show incarnation, *Border Security*, we can watch customs officers catching people out as they try to smuggle all kinds of things into the country.

When we see people caught out with irrefutable evidence of their crimes, it satisfies that longing for justice we all have. But there is nothing worse than being the one who is caught out. Thanks to the prophet Nathan, King David was that man.

In Psalm 51 we have already seen this king face up to

his sin by asking God for mercy. But the psalm does not end there. Importantly, David asks not only for a pardon but also for purity:

> Behold, you delight in truth in the inward
> being,
> and you teach me wisdom in the secret
> heart. (Ps 51:6)

David is not satisfied with God's forgiveness. He also wants to possess a heart of truth—the kind of truth that was missing when he sent his bodyguard, Uriah, off to war with a note that would end Uriah's life in battle. David longs for a heart of wisdom—the kind of wisdom he did not have when he called Bathsheba to his bed. David wants to be not only a forgiven man but also a faithful man.

He is aware of his lies and attempts to cover up his sin. He knows the solution is not just to try a little harder to be obedient. With a nature that has been sinful since birth, nothing less than a new creation is required.

> Create in me a clean heart, O God,
> and renew a right spirit within me.
> (Ps 51:10)

The word 'create'[16] here is the same word used in Genesis 1:1: "In the beginning, God created the heavens and the earth". It describes God creating something out of nothing. And David wants a brand new heart.

The 'heart' refers to more than just your emotions. It is

the foundation of your choices and thinking, the centre of your being. David doesn't simply want a heart bypass; he wants a heart transplant, and with it a new spirit that will say 'No' to adultery and 'No' to murder and 'No' to coveting.

This is 'born-again' language. David wants to be what every genuine Christian is: a new creation, born of the Spirit, with a God-given ability to say 'No' to sin. The Apostle Paul describes it in the New Testament:

> For the grace of God has appeared, bringing salvation for all people, training us to renounce ungodliness and worldly passions, and to live self-controlled, upright, and godly lives in the present age, waiting for our blessed hope, the appearing of the glory of our great God and Saviour Jesus Christ … (Titus 2:11-13)

But is this possible for David? Did he go too far? Did he cross the line and commit the unforgivable sin? Let's face it: he took the life of another man. On the basis of Old Testament law, he deserves the death penalty. What will happen if God does not forgive him?

David's fear

> Cast me not away from your presence,
>   and take not your Holy Spirit from me.
>   (Ps 51:11)

Ever since I first became a Christian in 1980, there has been significant debate about whether Christians can or should pray (or sing) this line from verse 11. The issue is this: is David afraid of losing his salvation, or is he only afraid of losing his kingship?

Those who argue that he fears the loss of his salvation point to the fact that the first line in verse 11 runs in parallel with the second line. So when David says "take not your Holy Spirit from me", he means "Cast me not away from your presence". In other words, "Lord, do not reject me as your child".

Those who say that David was afraid of losing his kingship point to King Saul's experience. After King Saul failed to trust God, God's Spirit left him and came upon David to anoint him as the next king (1 Sam 15:10-16:14). David obviously remembers this. Now that David has sinned, will he lose the Spirit to another would-be king?

But God has already made the following promise to David:

> "When your days are fulfilled and you lie down
> with your fathers, I will raise up your offspring
> after you, who shall come from your body, and
> I will establish his kingdom. He shall build a
> house for my name, and I will establish the
> throne of his kingdom forever. I will be to him
> a father, and he shall be to me a son. When he
> commits iniquity, I will discipline him with the
> rod of men, with the stripes of the sons of men,

but my steadfast love will not depart from him,
as I took it from Saul, whom I put away before
you." (2 Sam 7:12-15)

God has given this unconditional promise to the Davidic line. He did not give any such promise to Saul, which may indicate an assurance in both directions.

But perhaps the issue is less complicated. Perhaps Psalm 51:11 is nothing more than the natural response of a man who is deeply aware of the seriousness of his offences. He wonders, if only for a moment, whether he went too far.

Would the fear of losing it all not be your concern if you crossed the line David crossed? I can imagine that if I committed murder and adultery, I too might say the same thing, even though I know that "… neither death nor life, nor angels nor rulers, nor things present nor things to come, nor powers, nor height nor depth, nor anything else in all creation, will be able to separate us from the love of God in Christ Jesus our Lord" (Rom 8:38-39).

Psalm 51 is a snapshot in David's life, taken at a point in time when he is living somewhere between confession and comfort.

David's problem

The book of Psalms begins by affirming the blessed state of the man "who walks not in the counsel of the wicked" (Ps 1:1). The Psalms end with a flurry of praise for God the King who is to come. This shows us that the anointed one in Psalm 2 was not fully realized in David. Even the great King David looks forward to another king, another messiah, who will be tempted in every way, but who will be without sin—the Lord Jesus, Son of David (Matt 1:1). What we get in Psalm 51 is a reminder that this messiah, David, is a man of God who knows his sin and the joy of forgiveness. Like us, David needs a saviour. He needs his son to save him.

But for now, this messiah is more in the grip of guilt than grace. We must not forget how burdened David is. He is God's appointed king for Israel, and he has committed murder and adultery. Psalm 51 is a heavy prayer of confession. David is under the weight of enormous guilt, and rightly so!

We also need to understand that David's guilt is not just psychological. It is not that he needs a quota of therapy and a self-help course to help him love himself a little more. David is actually guilty. And he does not need to forgive himself; he needs to seek *God's* forgiveness.

Nor is it just a social problem, a crime against the state. The solution is not simply to lock David up for 30 years or give him the death penalty. Such payments may satisfy his debt to society, but they will never come close to satisfying his debt to God.

And David's problem is not just religious, requiring him to offer up endless sacrifices and fasts. David is clear about this:

> For you will not delight in sacrifice, or I
>   would give it;

> you will not be pleased with a burnt
> offering. (Ps 51:16)

Religion is not going to fix up this problem—not even Old Testament religion, handed down by God himself. Sin has come between God and God's king, and atonement needs to be made so that God's wrath is turned aside. David needs to humble himself before the living God:

> The sacrifices of God are a broken spirit;
> a broken and contrite heart, O God, you
> will not despise. (Ps 51:17)

David was broken and contrite and yet, even in the depths of his shame, he was confident that God would be merciful.

God's mercy

God's grace not only saves us; it completely transforms us. And so in his prayer, David describes the results of God's mercy, as he looks forward to a time of grace.

Joy

> Let me hear joy and gladness;
> let the bones that you have broken
> rejoice …
> Restore to me the joy of your salvation,
> and uphold me with a willing spirit.
> (Ps 51:8, 12)

David wants again what he once had: the joy of salvation. Joy is the one Christian emotion that springs from a thankful heart and an experience of forgiveness. David longs for the joy of being right with God and being clean before him—a joy David once knew well. He wants to reclaim the happiness of knowing that God will not count his sins against him, grievous as they are.

Instruction

When his joy returns, David will pass onto others what he has learnt:

> Then I will teach transgressors your ways,
>> and sinners will return to you. (Ps 51:13)

This sounds a little like the reformed smoker telling everyone they should give up smoking. But for David, teaching sinners God's ways must include telling them about the mercy of God that has made him whiter than snow. It must include sharing with the fallen that he too has sinned, and he too has had his transgressions blotted out. He wants other sinners to share his joy; to turn back to God and seek forgiveness. It's only when you know forgiveness that you can call others to repent:

> Brothers, if anyone is caught in any
> transgression, you who are spiritual should
> restore him in a spirit of gentleness. (Gal 6:1)

Knowing that the ground at the foot of the cross is very flat, we make it our aim to live by the Spirit. From this vantage point we restore brothers and sisters who are caught up in sin, but we do it gently.

Praise

> Deliver me from bloodguiltiness, O God,
> > O God of my salvation,
> > and my tongue will sing aloud of your
> > > righteousness.
> O Lord, open my lips,
> > and my mouth will declare your praise.
> > > (Ps 51:14-15)

A man experiencing the joy of salvation cannot remain silent. Like a person in love, a forgiven sinner can't help telling the world of his newfound love. Praise in the psalms is about declaring who God is and what he has done, and what God has done is forgive and restore David according to his great compassion. David cannot help but sing of God's grace.

A sure thing

> The sacrifices of God are a broken spirit;
> > a broken and contrite heart, O God, you
> > > will not despise. (Ps 51:17)

This is David's hope, and ours. It is the key verse in this psalm. David knows that God will accept him if David confesses that he has sinned against the God who loves him. What is needed on David's part is confession and repentance—nothing more, nothing less.

This is not to say that David is disparaging the Levitical sacrificial system—far from it:

> Do good to Zion in your good pleasure;
>> build up the walls of Jerusalem;
> then will you delight in right sacrifices,
>> in burnt offerings and whole burnt
>>> offerings;
>> then bulls will be offered on your altar.
> (Ps 51:18-19)

David's vision reaches beyond his own forgiveness to Zion's prosperity. The restoration of the king is part of a complete restoration of Zion, the city of Jerusalem. David looks forward to a time when God's people, with broken and contrite hearts, will offer God-appointed sacrifices that will please God.

However, as we know, there will be but one sacrifice required, and it will take place just outside Jerusalem at the place of the skull. It is because this one sacrifice has now been made that God's people can approach the throne of grace—and with confidence (Heb 4:16)!

So come, and come now. Never ever tire of confessing your sins. David has been where you have been and where you will be again: guilty of transgression, racked with guilt and feeling deeply unclean. You may be guilty of adultery, murder, lust, anger, or any other form of rebellion against God. But you can be certain of this: "a

broken and contrite heart, O God, you will not despise".
That is one certain promise. So when you find yourself
ashamed, burdened and crying out for mercy, make sure
that you also listen carefully to the angels in heaven—
who, along with God, will *always* rejoice over a sinner
who repents (Luke 15).

FOR REFLECTION
- Why can we be confident that God will be merciful
  when we repent?
- Are there sins in your life of which you have not
  repented—sins that particularly weigh on your
  conscience?
- Are there sins of which you *have* repented, but for
  which you do not feel confident of God's mercy?
- How does the joy of salvation show itself in your life?

7 | TIME IS NOT ON OUR SIDE

Psalm 90

Just before the funeral service, the undertaker came up to the very elderly widow and asked, "How old was your husband?" "Ninety-eight," she replied, "two years older than me." "So you're ninety-six", the undertaker commented. She responded, "Hardly worth going home, is it?"[17]

Life in your face

People often say that Christians are dreamers and wishful thinkers who don't face up to life as it is—but in fact it's quite the opposite. The Bible confronts us with the reality of life in a very in-your-face kind of way. The Christian worldview acknowledges the beautiful and the ugly in each of us and makes no excuses. Christians can celebrate the wonder of birth and confront the reality of death. Christianity is about real life.

Nowhere is this more true than in the matter of death. Each Sunday, Christians gather to hear of death—either the death of their saviour or the reality of their own death. Psalm 90 is one of those passages that confronts us with our mortality. As one of the set passages in the Anglican funeral service, it may well be read at your funeral.

Psalm 90 is the only psalm attributed to Moses, who preceded King David by at least 300 years. Moses led God's people out of slavery in Egypt through the desert for 40 years towards the promised land. But, along with all but two of the rescued Israelites, he failed to make it into the promised land because God had numbered the days of Moses and of the Israelites (Num 14:26-30). In the book of Numbers, we read again and again of how thousands were put to death by God for their consistent rebellion. Yet throughout that time, God remained true to his promise and to his people.

A fixed address

> Lord, you have been our dwelling place
> in all generations. (Ps 90:1)

God has been the refuge for every generation of Israel. Verse 1 literally says, "Lord, you have been our hiding place, generation after generation".

Psalm 90, which speaks of the darkness of death, begins with an emphatic declaration: God has never failed to be with his people. Israel has always been engraved on the palms of God's hands (Isa 49:16). And God continues to be the refuge for every generation of his people. Jesus' parting words to his disciples as he ascended into heaven were, "I am with you always, to the end of the age" (Matt 28:20).

The "dwelling place" in Psalm 90 is not so much a location but a person. The Promised Land, the city of Jerusalem and the temple were all special to Israel because that was where God allowed his name to dwell with his people.

But this God is not just the God of Israel. He is not just one nation's God, or some minor local deity. This God is from everlasting to everlasting. He existed even before Israel was given birth.

> Before the mountains were brought forth,
>> or ever you had formed the earth and the
>> world,
> from everlasting to everlasting you are
>> God. (Ps 90:2)

God is not like the rest of us. He does not have a beginning and an end. The birth-death, womb-tomb timeline does not apply to him. Before the earth was given birth, God was there. You have heard the expression, "He is as old as the hills". Well, God is older still.

The child's question, "Who made God?" doesn't work with God. If you answer it by naming something or someone, then God by definition stops being God. What makes him God is that he is timeless. He alone is immortal. He goes back in time forever. He goes forward in time forever. You could say he is simply outside of time. There was never a time when the creator did not exist, and that cannot be said about anything or anyone else.

God's timing and ours

God is "from everlasting to everlasting", but humans have only a short stay on the stage of life. The God who makes us from dust and breathes life into us is the same God who takes that life away:

> You return man to dust
> and say, "Return, O children of man!"
> (Ps 90:3)

God limits our time on the earth, and sends us back to where we came from. The dust of the earth becomes the dust of death. There is a massive contrast between God's timing and ours:

> For a thousand years in your sight
> are but as yesterday when it is past,
> or as a watch in the night. (Ps 90:4)

This verse is not saying that the six days of creation are mathematically equal to 6000 years. Moses is not giving us information about God's digital watch. He is simply saying that what is a long time for us (1000 years) is, for God, just like a day or an afternoon nap. It's like saying, "What is a lot of money for you is but loose change for Bill Gates". When you are from everlasting to everlasting, a millennium is the equivalent of 40 winks. And while there is always something particularly tragic about the death of a child—a life cut terribly short—we need to recognize that whether a life is six years or 60 years or 600 years, it's all short in God's everlasting timescale.

But we find it impossible to comprehend such a vast scale of time. Who can comprehend eternity? Just considering the events of human history in the past 1000 years leaves you thinking, "It's taken us a long time to get where we are now". It is too easy for us to forget what a short time-span this is for God, and so we think that God has forgotten about us. Our own lack of perspective leads us astray.

The Apostle Peter picks up this very idea. To those who doubt whether Jesus is ever coming back, he says:

> But do not overlook this one fact, beloved, that with the Lord one day is as a thousand years, and a thousand years as one day. The Lord is not slow to fulfil his promise as some count slowness, but is patient toward you, not wishing that any should perish, but that all should reach repentance. (2 Pet 3:8-9)

Peter's point is clear: God's timing is not our timing, so do not be deceived into thinking that God's promises will not come true. The return of Jesus is not like those carpet stores that are forever having closing-down sales every week. He *will* return, but we need to grasp the fact that God simply marches to his own drum. So we need to be patient.

Man's brief moment in time

Our time on earth is short, and not only when compared with God's timescale. It is just short. The classic Rolling Stones' song 'Time is on my Side' got it badly wrong. Like new grass, we are here today and gone tomorrow:

> You sweep them away as with a flood; they are
> like a dream,
> like grass that is renewed in the morning:
> in the morning it flourishes and is renewed;
> in the evening it fades and withers.
> (Ps 90:5-6)

Each species has its own life span. A quick Google search tells me that the blue whale can live for up to 90 years. Humans in the West have an average life span of 70 to 80 years. The freshwater crocodile gets upwards of 50 years, and the great white shark gets between 30 to 40. The honeybee lives for up to five years, the dragonfly lives for around two years, the common butterfly gets about two to three weeks, and some types of grass live for but one day—fresh and alive in the morning but dead by sunset. We are like that one-day grass when compared with the everlasting God. Reality comes down to this: life is short!

But why is life short? Who decided to number our days? It was God, who sweeps men away "as with a flood". Death is God's decision. People don't die because the devil outsmarts God, or because the doctors can't stop the infection, or because the ambulance comes too late. People die because God turns men back to dust. We don't like to hear it, but this is as true as saying that "God is love" (1 John 4:8).

And why has God numbered our days?

> For we are brought to an end by your anger;
> by your wrath we are dismayed. (Ps 90:7)

God is angry because of our sin, and he will not allow us to rebel forever. The Bible tells us that "the wages of sin is death" (Rom 6:23). Death followed the sin of Adam and Eve into paradise. As a result, humans were evicted from God's presence and were no longer entitled to access the tree of life. Like a cut flower, the remaining glory of Adam and Eve would eventually perish. Physical death follows spiritual death (culminating in the second death; Rev 21:8).

Occasionally, someone in our world will acknowledge this truth. I once heard Denzel Washington recount his reaction to reading the script for the film *Training Day*, in which he played a corrupt and vicious policeman. He said, "I will do the film on one condition. The main character has to die." When asked why, he said, "Because the wages of sin is death".

Most people, however, do not acknowledge this. They do not think they deserve to die. In one of his songs, Bob Dylan writes that the "disease of conceit ... give[s] you the idea that you're too good to die".[18] He is right, and you see it at every funeral—each eulogy is an attempt to show that the deceased was too good to die. Of course, the coffin proves otherwise. No-one is too good to die.

So we die because God is angry. And Moses points out that God's anger is evident throughout all of life, not just at the end:

> You have set our iniquities before you,
>> our secret sins in the light of your
>>> presence.
>
> For all our days pass away under your wrath;
>> we bring our years to an end like a sigh.
> The years of our life are seventy,
>> or even by reason of strength eighty;
> yet their span is but toil and trouble;
>> they are soon gone, and we fly away.
>>> (Ps 90:8-10)

Australians borrow an expression from the sport of cricket to describe a long life: "He had a good innings". But it is only a good innings compared to that of others who are also under the wrath of God. 80 years is a good innings, but 80 years is not good enough! Time passes so quickly; how many get to the age of 80 and wonder where it all went? I'm 49 and I am wondering the same thing.

What's more, you only make 80 if you're lucky. Even for the 'lucky' ones, the last decades of life are usually marked by the reality that another year means another specialist.

Human life is littered with "toil and trouble", a constant reminder of God's anger. Yet rarely do we contemplate the strength of his anger:

> Who considers the power of your anger,
>   and your wrath according to the fear of
>   you? (Ps 90:11)

The only thing that matches the power of God's wrath is the level of fear due to him. God's wrath is as great as the injustice we have done him. And so we face the consequences of God's anger: toil, trouble, and eventually death.

The prayers of a man who fears the Lord

So how should we respond? It's not as if we can stop death. One professor recently said in an interview with Andrew Denton, "Even if we cured all diseases, we'd only extend [the] human life-span by about seven to ten years. What's killing us now is ageing ..."[19] He then suggested (with a laugh) that the war on terrorism be replaced by a war on ageing.

But the ultimate response to death is to fear the Lord, which is the beginning of wisdom (Ps 111:10). Wisdom prompts us to face the fact that our time is cut short by God.

What follows in Psalm 90 is a number of prayers from Moses, a man who faced the certainty of his own death (Deut 31:14, 16).

Teach us to number our days

The wise man knows his time is short, and lives his life accordingly:

> So teach us to number our days
>> that we may get a heart of wisdom. (Ps 90:12)

This is the key verse in the psalm. You can't measure the anger of God but you can measure out your own days. The teaching of the Jehovah's Witnesses organization forbids the celebration of birthdays, but here is a verse that teaches us to mark birthdays. We are specifically instructed to number our days, because we need to grasp that they *are* numbered. Moses calls upon us to consider our short time on this earth. We are to number our days on earth just as we carefully count our holidays. Perhaps you are like me: I am mindful of each day of my holidays and I am most careful with them because they are precious few. And don't they go by so quickly?

And we are not to count the years nor months but the days, one by one, because there are not many of them and the next 24 hours could be our last.

We have a custom in our family: when someone has a birthday, we read this psalm. In so doing we are reminded to fear the God who has numbered our days. We are mindful that each person has a different quota. So we count them: 1, 2, 3, 4, 5—gone ... 11, 12, 13, 14, 15 —gone ... 25, 26, 27, 28—gone ... 56, 57, 58, 59—gone ...

It's the nature of the young to think they will live healthily and forever. But there comes a time to grow up and put away childish thoughts. We need to ask God, in the words of Martin Luther, to "teach us that we must die"![20]

Sadly, we often do not learn from close encounters with death. My wife once saw a current affairs show on television where a woman shared how she developed cancer. Fortunately, this woman survived. But it did not make her humble and say, "I must make the Lord my dwelling place". Instead her response was, "I now know I can overcome anything!" She refused to number her days. Little did she realize that death was only postponed. It would come back to knock on her door again.

Have pity

Every human lives with the following tension: on the one hand, as Ecclesiastes says, God "has put eternity into man's heart" (Eccl 3:11). Each human has within them the desperate hunger to live forever. But on the other hand, God has also limited our days. He makes us return to the dust from which we came.

This tension can lead to deep despair. How do we find meaning in life when everything is "vanity and a striving after the wind", and there is "nothing to be gained under the sun" (Eccl 2:11)? When the writer of Ecclesiastes looks at the world and sees the meaninglessness of man's existence, he decides that he hates life (Eccl 2:17).

But Psalm 90 is not just filled with despair. It is not just a lament over our temporary and transitory nature. There is a time to laugh and time to cry (Ecclesiastes 3), and joy is found even in this age. Moses asks God to turn away his anger and show compassion:

> Return, O LORD! How long?
> Have pity on your servants! (Ps 90:13)

What makes this life bearable is the unfailing love of God.

Satisfy us with your love

> Satisfy us in the morning with your steadfast
> love,
> that we may rejoice and be glad all
> our days.
> Make us glad for as many days as you have
> afflicted us,
> and for as many years as we have seen
> evil. (Ps 90:14-15)

We find joy in the undying love of God for his people, cemented in his covenant with Israel. This is true even when our days are filled with sorrow. Moses could only see from a distance what we can see up close—that God's unfailing love reached its climax when he who handed out death died for us:

> … but God shows his love for us in that while
> we were still sinners, Christ died for us.
> (Rom 5:8)

Those in Christ live every day knowing that God gave us his best when we were at our worst. Staked in history is God's definitive expression of his love for sinners. For the last 2000 years God has been singing from the cross, "I could not love you any better". This love can satisfy us whether we live to eight years or 80 years of age.

The God who set eternity in our hearts has satisfied our desire for immortality. When Christ returns, he will usher us into a new creation where death—our final enemy—will no longer be present. Death will finally have been swallowed up in victory (1 Cor 15:50-57).

Establish our work

> Let your work be shown to your servants,
>> and your glorious power to their children.
> Let the favour of the Lord our God be upon us,
>> and establish the work of our hands
>>> upon us;
>> yes, establish the work of our hands!
>>> (Ps 90:16-17)

It is death that renders our labour meaningless, and it is resurrection that renders our labour meaningful. The Apostle Paul concludes his long discussion on the resurrection in 1 Corinthians 15 by calling believers to give themselves fully to the work of the Lord for one reason: their labour in the Lord is not in vain (1 Cor 15:58). Work in the Lord will not come to nothing!

I learnt early on as a father that if you take adult shovels to the beach, you can build the biggest sandcastles in the shortest time to impress your children and everybody else's. One afternoon I remember looking up the beach and seeing a range of sandcastles in all their glory, from the very big—like mine—to the very small. I also remember that at the end of the day, not one of those sandcastles was left standing. The relentless tide left absolutely no evidence of their presence or the efforts of those who built them.

Likewise, death washes away any trace of our labours. Within 100 years, few if any will be alive to personally remember you. But resurrection means that your life and labour will be remembered and rewarded. By defeating death, God has given eternal significance to our choices and efforts in life. Resurrection means that our work in the Lord really does echo into eternity. Don't waste your life by living as though death rules.

FOR REFLECTION

- If you knew that one year from now you would die or Jesus would return, what would you change about the way you are living?
- How can you regularly remind yourself to number your days and live with wisdom?

8 | HIS MAJESTY'S VOICE

Psalm 19

The moment you hear the claim that no-one comes to the Father except through his Son (John 14:6), the most natural question to ask is, "What about those who have never heard of Jesus?" It is a matter of justice. How can God condemn the person who has never been given the message of life? In spite of what the police officer might say to you, ignorance *is* an excuse.

I want to make several points up front. The first is that all have rebelled against God by choice, and that is why we all die. Whatever God will do with those who have never heard about Jesus, we know that they are not innocent. All have sinned and the wages of sin is death (Rom 3:23, 6:23).

The second thing to say is that we entrust those who never hear to the God who judges justly. As Abraham said in the context of possible collateral damage on a city about to be punished, "Far be it from you to do such a thing, to put the righteous to death with the wicked, so that the righteous fare as the wicked! Far be that from you! Shall not the Judge of all the earth do what is just?" (Gen18:25).

The third thing to point out is that each person is judged by what they know, never by what they do not know. That is why the more you know, the more responsible you are (Luke 10:13). God would not otherwise be just.

But Psalm 19 gives yet another answer to the question of those who have never heard.

The voice of creation

The first section of Psalm 19 announces that no part of creation is silent about the glory—let alone existence—of its maker:

> The heavens declare the glory of God,
>> and the sky above proclaims his
>>> handiwork. (Ps 19:1)

From the perspective of time and space, every single corner of the universe carries the fingerprint of God. Never has there been a moment when the universe was silent about God's splendour:

> Day to day pours out speech,
>> and night to night reveals knowledge.
>>> (Ps 19:2)

You just can't shut creation up! It communicates endlessly —literally, it "bubbles forth". Creation never stops talking about the magnificence of the one who formed it.

I know many people who ask why God does not speak personally to them. It's a real battle for them. But this psalm is crystal clear: God speaks to each one of us 24 hours a day, seven days a week, through the world he has made. You don't need the Bible to tell you that there is a God and that he is magnificent:

> Their voice goes out through all the earth,
> and their words to the end of the world.
> In them he has set a tent for the sun,
> which comes out like a bridegroom
> leaving his chamber,
> and, like a strong man, runs its course
> with joy.
> Its rising is from the end of the heavens,
> and its circuit to the end of them,
> and there is nothing hidden from its heat.
> (Ps 19:4-6)

God has revealed himself to *all* people—not just his own (this is known as 'general revelation'). No-one is exempt. The whole earth has heard, from the New York artist, to the German scientist, to the South American native. So the answer to the question, "What about those who have never heard?" is that they simply don't exist. We must acknowledge that everyone has heard His Majesty's voice.

One famous theologian, Karl Barth, said that the

cosmos is dumb.[21] But if this is not completely right, as Psalm 19 suggests, then what exactly do we know from creation?

In his letter to the Romans, the Apostle Paul elaborates on what we can learn from creation:

> For his [God's] invisible attributes, namely, his eternal power and divine nature, *have been clearly perceived*, ever since the creation of the world, in the things that have been made. So they [men] are *without excuse*. (Rom 1:20)

Creation may not say much, but what it says is crystal clear. In effect, it is saying, "Read my lips: there is a God and he is powerful and he is your creator". In the words of Francis Schaeffer, "He is there and he is not silent".[22] It is not that people don't know about God; it is that they know and are without excuse. On the day of judgement we cannot plead the Fifth Amendment and we cannot plead ignorance.

Some of us have had the torturous experience of sitting for an exam on a topic we were never taught. It still feels unfair after all these years! In 1993, in a school not far from where I used to live, the English department realized one week before the final exams that the students had been taught the wrong novel text. And when I say 'final', I mean the exams that determined university entrance for the students. But God is not guilty of this mistake. He will only judge people on the basis of what they know, and he has clearly revealed himself to them in his creation.

The psalmist likens the glory of the sunrise to the emergence of a bridegroom from his chamber, and its daily course to an athlete in full stride. The sun's inescapable heat captures the all-encompassing aspect of general revelation reaching out to every corner of the earth. God is not hiding and no-one has missed out (this may well explain why there are so few genuine atheists in the world).

God has said so much, yet the world has listened so little. There is a resistance to hearing God's voice in creation.

> There is no speech, nor are there words
> whose voice is not heard. (Ps 19:3)[23]

If creation is shouting out the glory of God, and there are no "words whose voice is not heard", then the problem is not that the message is not being received; the problem is that the message is not being received as intended.

Ever since the first man's sin, our antennas wilfully malfunction. The airwaves are full of messages but we only get a snowy picture on our radar. Why is it that I cannot get Foxtel on my television? It is simply because I refuse to install it. Our wilful nature refuses to listen—in fact, can't listen—even though the evidence is around us and in us. In the words of the Apostle Paul, we suppress the truth of God and exchange it for a lie. In doing so, we worship what is made instead of the one who made it (Rom 1:18-25). The result is that, while some of us are atheists and others are agnostics, we all make God in our own image.

Does this mean atheists are lying when they claim they do not believe in God? I don't think so. But how can one be an atheist suppressing the truth, and yet be telling the truth? The best analogy I can find is the man who drinks a bottle of whiskey a day. As a result, he has lost his wife and his job due to repeated drunken behaviour, and he is suffering cirrhosis of the liver. Yet he can look you in the eye and say, "I'm not an alcoholic!" He is telling you what he thinks to be true, and at the same time he is suppressing a vast amount of evidence. In a similar way, atheists are simply denying the divine.

The voice of the Word

Having described God's general revelation in creation to all people, the psalmist now describes God's revelation of himself in the Bible to his own people (this is called 'special revelation'). As we will see, this is a lot less ambiguous.

When the psalmist moves from the voice of creation to the voice of Scripture, the name of God changes from 'God' (*El*) to 'LORD' (YHWH)—that is, from God's general name to his personal name. My generic name is 'man' and my personal name is 'Ray'. In the same way, our Creator's general name is 'God' and his personal name is 'Yahweh', often translated as 'LORD' (using small capital letters). God revealed his personal name only to Israel (Exod 3:14-15). Psalm 19 moves from the God of all mankind to the Lord of Israel. It's a revelation now—not of God's glory but of his specific will.

> The law of the LORD is perfect,
>> reviving the soul;

the testimony of the LORD is sure,
　　making wise the simple;
the precepts of the LORD are right,
　　rejoicing the heart;
the commandment of the LORD is pure,
　　enlightening the eyes;
the fear of the LORD is clean,
　　enduring forever;
the rules of the LORD are true,
　　and righteous altogether.
More to be desired are they than gold,
　　even much fine gold;
sweeter also than honey
　　and drippings of the honeycomb.
　　　　(Ps 19:7-10)

God's word is to be obeyed

The psalmist uses six titles for God's written word.

Title	Definition
Law of the LORD	Instruction, not simply commands
Testimony of the LORD	What God bears witness to as valid
Precepts of the LORD	Precise application to the small details of life
Commandment of the LORD	An order intended for obedience
Fear of the LORD	Reverence for a God who is worthy
Rules of the LORD	The authoritative verdicts of God on our thoughts and actions

These definitions remind us that the written word of God comes with the authority of the God who speaks. It is truly God-breathed (2 Tim 3:16). It covers all facets of life and is intended for obedience. God speaks not simply to be heard and understood, but to be obeyed.

Of the six parallel titles, the odd one out is "the fear of the LORD" since it suggests more about us than God. In this context, it is clear that our attitude to God's written word is the same as our attitude to God. Isaiah 66 makes the same point:

> "But this is the one to whom I will look:
>> he who is humble and contrite in spirit
>> and trembles at my word." (Isa 66:2b)

We often struggle to fear God and tremble at his word. People ask perfectly valid questions concerning the Bible, such as:

> "Which translation of the Bible can I trust, if any?"
> "Was the Bible tampered with over the centuries?"
> "Which interpretation should I hold?"

A number of excellent books address these questions, and if they are your questions then please do seek answers.[24] But you really need only consider that the God who went to all the effort of speaking and revealing himself would be sure to guard the preservation and interpretation of his word.

It's actually hard to remain vague and uncertain when you read the Bible. If you look at the stars, it's not clear whether they are telling you to leave your wife or remain faithful to her. When you read the Bible, however, you can't dodge the specifics as easily. You can't really say, "I'm not sure what it means".

And so the problem with the Bible is not that it is ambiguous and open to many interpretations, but that it's painfully clear about issues that require us to change. As Mark Twain put it:

> Most people are bothered by those passages in Scripture which they cannot understand; but as for me, I always noticed that the passages in Scripture which trouble me most are those that I do understand.[25]

When I first began to read the Bible with an open mind as a young adult, I discovered that God and Ray Galea thought very differently on a lot of issues. One of us would have to change. I've since realized that becoming a Christian is about conceding that I am the one who needs to change or, in the words of Jesus, "repent". That is how we fear God and tremble at his word; we trust it. And Psalm 19 gives us plenty of reasons to do so.

God's word is like God

Since the Bible is God's word, it is not surprising that its qualities reflect the perfect character of the one who ultimately wrote it. As a result, it is desirable and valuable and trustworthy. Look at the way it is described in Psalm 19:

Quality	Definition
Perfect	Complete in every part
Sure	Trustworthy, completely reliable, corresponds to reality
Right	Upright and righteous
Pure	Free from contamination
Clean	Acceptable to God
Enduring forever	Timeless
True and righteous	Lines up with objective norms of truth
More desirable than gold	Precious, full of intrinsic value
Sweet	Truly enjoyable

We live in a world that, at best, can only offer an opinion on the big questions of life. At worst, it promotes half-truths driven by the latest ideology. In contrast, the Bible speaks a timeless truth that transcends culture. What it has to say is as true in Malta in the second century, Spain in the 13th century, Tanzania in the 18th century and Bolivia in the 21st century.

As you survey the qualities of God's written word, can you think of anything else in your life that you can describe in the same way? I suspect not. God's word is in a class of its own. The complete works of Shakespeare are impressive, but they fall well short of the brilliance of the Scriptures—as does everything written by man. There is certainly a massive difference between the Bible and the next four top-selling books in the world: *Quotations from*

Chairman Mao, the Qur'an, a Chinese dictionary and then *Chairman Mao's Poems*.[26] I will leave it to you to see which of the qualities listed above are apt descriptions for any of these writings.

God's word changes us

Jesus said, "You will recognize them by their fruits" (Matt 7:20). In Psalm 19 we learn that God's word deeply affects the one who meditates on it:

- it revives the soul (v. 7)
- it makes wise the simple (v. 7)
- it gives joy to the heart (v. 8)
- it gives light to the eyes (v. 8).

The word of God revives and gives true life to your soul. As Moses finished his final address to the people of God, he said: "For it is no empty word for you, but your very life …" (Deut 32:47). If you are hoping to make it to the end, then follow God's word.

One government-sponsored program in Australia urges drivers on long road trips to 'Stop, Revive, Survive'. While we don't know how long the road before us is, we need to be prepared in case it is a long one. God's word revives by afflicting the comfortable and giving comfort to the afflicted.

God's word also gives wisdom, making the simple wise and turning fools into people who live without regret. The wise man does not lean on his own understanding (Prov 3:5), but the fool trusts his own knowledge and so becomes gullible to the world's deceptions. At my church we live by this mantra: "We refuse to believe the lie that we are wiser than God and his word". The categories in the Bible are not smart versus dumb, but wise versus simple. You can be a smart businessman who skilfully works the stock market, yet still be a fool. On the other hand, you can have an IQ of 75 and work in a sheltered workshop, yet have the wisdom to hold fast that Jesus is Lord.

The word of God also gives joy to the heart. Meditating on the Bible not only affects our minds, it also educates our emotions. Joy is the one unique Christian experience that comes in response to knowing the living and loving God.

I find I am drawn to read the Bible for two simple reasons. I need to know that someone loves me with a love I cannot earn or lose. I also need to know that someone is in charge of this crazy world, because I certainly am not.

As you read God's word, it gives light to your eyes. You will know where you are going and you will have the strength to follow through. My wife and I sometimes say to each other, "Darling, have you stopped reading the Bible recently?", which is code for "You're a pain in the neck to live with at the moment!" The more we absent ourselves from God's word, the more demanding we become of each other. We lose our light and our joy; we become foolish.

The voice of the sinner praying

God's word is a double-edged sword. When you come under it, you find yourself both warned and blessed:

> Moreover, by them is your servant warned;
>> in keeping them there is great reward.
>> (Ps 19:11)

The reward involves blessing for those who trust and obey God's word; those who know that God's ways are always the best ways. With this kind of trust comes a willingness to stand with God and agree with his verdict on your life:

> Who can discern his errors?
>> Declare me innocent from hidden faults.
> Keep back your servant also from presumptuous
>> sins;
>> let them not have dominion over me!
> Then I shall be blameless,
>> and innocent of great transgression.
>> (Ps 19:12-13)

Reading the Bible is not about information but transformation. People who come under the influence of God's word develop a hunger and thirst for what is right. As Jesus said, "Blessed are those who hunger and thirst for righteousness, for they shall be satisfied" (Matt 5:6). They have a desire to please God with the words of their lips and the motives of their heart:

> Let the words of my mouth and the
>> meditation of my heart

be acceptable in your sight,
O LORD, my rock and my redeemer.
(Ps 19:14)

IF YOU HAVE BEEN A CHRISTIAN for some years, you may have found that you diagnosed yourself as spiritually anorexic as you read this chapter. With five translations of the Bible on the bookshelf, you rarely open and read it—let alone study and prayerfully meditate on it. You are slowly starving yourself to death.

As a result you are feeling unloved, uninspired and insecure. You may have noticed that you have become far more demanding of your loved ones and friends, requiring of them what in the end only God can give. You are nowhere near ready to say to God, "Whom have I in heaven but you? And there is nothing on earth that I desire besides you" (Ps 73:25).

Do you want to remain in doubt and despair and disobedience? Have you hit rock bottom yet, or do things still need to get worse? When was the last time you were convicted of a sin of which you then repented? When was the last time you rejoiced in your salvation? Can you sense God's Spirit convicting you to return to his word? If so, then come back to God, your rock and your redeemer, and delight in his word and his salvation. These words are not idle words for you. They are your life!

FOR REFLECTION

- Do you trust God when he says that all men "are without excuse" in their rejection of him (Rom 1:18-23)? Why do you think we find this so difficult to accept?
- Reflect on your attitude to God's written word. Do you think of it as a rough guide, or as something to be obeyed? Is this attitude reflected in your life? Is it more precious to you than anything else in your life?
- What does God's word offer you?

9 | WHO CAN DWELL IN THE LORD'S PRESENCE?

Psalm 15

M ost Christians only get it half right. We know we are saved by grace *apart* from good works. What we don't understand is that we are saved *to do* good works—to be like Jesus, glorifying God by our obedience. Many of us think that with our salvation assured by the death of Christ and the gift of the Spirit, we are simply waiting for Jesus to return; how we live has no significance, no effect on God. We know our sins are forgiven but we have no category for our obedience.

But we have been saved to serve. To put it simply, we have been saved to love God wholeheartedly and to love our neighbours as ourselves (Matt 22:35-39). And, as Psalm 15 makes clear, loving God and loving our neighbours cannot be separated.

The question

This brief psalm begins with a very simple question:

> O Lord, who shall sojourn in your tent?
>> Who shall dwell on your holy hill? (Ps 15:1)

The "holy hill" is Zion, the city of Jerusalem. It is viewed within the Old Testament as the city of God and, as such, the city of peace (hard to imagine today, given the constant and bloody conflict in the Middle East). The "tent" refers to the dwelling place of God, soon to be turned into a temple under King Solomon. It symbolized the presence of God amongst the Israelites.

Why would David want to live on a hill and in a temple? Temples are usually such cold and impersonal places, more like museums than homes. However, in the days before Christ, the temple is where God's name dwelt:

> One thing have I asked of the Lord,
>> that will I seek after:
> that I may dwell in the house of the Lord
>> all the days of my life,
> to gaze upon the beauty of the Lord
>> and to inquire in his temple. (Ps 27:4)

To live in the house of the Lord is to gaze at God himself, or at least get a glimpse of his glory. That's the great hope in the Bible: to see God face to face and to live with him (Rev 21:3, 22:4).

David's question is, "Who exactly is fit to come into God's presence?" But why ask the question? If we are made in God's image, will he not welcome us all? You might be thinking, "Forget the answer—I don't like the question! It's the wrong question!"

But with a holy and perfect God, the question must be asked—and it's not the first time David has thought about it. He raises the same issue elsewhere in the psalms:

> For you are not a God who delights in
> wickedness;
> evil may not dwell with you. (Ps 5:4)

> I will look with favour on the faithful in the
> land,
> that they may dwell with me;
> he who walks in the way that is blameless
> shall minister to me.

> No-one who practices deceit
> shall dwell in my house;
> no-one who utters lies
> shall continue before my eyes. (Ps 101:6-7)

The answer

David immediately answers his own question, in verse 2:

> He who walks blamelessly and does what is
> right ... (Ps 15:2a)

Who is able to live in God's presence? The one who is blameless and righteous. But 'blameless' here does not mean 'sinless'. It can't, because the temple was where blood sacrifice took place *for sinners*. The point of the sacrificial system in the Old Testament was to teach people that a sinner can approach God, but only when his sin has been atoned for with blood. So if 'blameless' doesn't mean 'without sin', what does it mean? It refers to that which is 'whole' or 'sound', and describes what God wants from those who approach him once their sin is atoned for.[27] As James Boice puts it, a blameless man is "a person whose character, as we might say, is morally well-rounded and grounded. This person is not just strong in one area and weak in others. He strives to keep all the commandments."[28]

David's answer to his own question is surprising. Who can go into the temple? It is not those who "wash their hands" (Mark 7:3) or give up eating lobster for Lent. David's answer is not a religious answer even though the temple was a religious place. God wants people to *want* to obey him in all parts of their lives; he's not interested in people performing religious rituals in the temple (or at church) while they ignore him for the rest of the week.

God has already told King Saul (David's predecessor) that "to obey is better than sacrifice ..." (1 Sam 15:22). Jesus, quoting Hosea 6:6, declares, "I desire mercy, and not sacrifice ..." (Matt 12:7). You can't have a right relationship with God but not have right relationships with other people, and so at its heart, holiness involves love for your neighbour.

Integrity marks the man whose walk is blameless. He does what is right before God and speaks the truth to his fellow man. The righteous man is consistent in both word and deed. There is no room here for saying your prayers while running two accounting books in your business, or for going to church regularly while being a downright mongrel at home.

David has asked a difficult question and given his answer, and now he describes more specifically what a blameless and righteous man or woman is like.

He does not harm his neighbour

The one who dwells with the Lord is the one who:

> … speaks truth in his heart;
> who does not slander with his tongue
> and does no evil to his neighbour,
> nor takes up a reproach against his friend
> … (Ps 15:2b-3)

Truth from the heart is spoken sincerely and genuinely. It is possible to speak the truth insincerely, or in order to trap people. You can use the truth for your own advantage—it's what the media thrives on. I remember a photo of a senior class from Mt Druitt High School in *The Daily Telegraph*, published because the whole year did poorly. The facts were accurate, but the article shamed those kids. It was not truth from the heart. And remember, Satan used the truth. When he faced Jesus in the wilderness, he quoted the Bible in his attempt to trap Jesus and hijack God's plan to save humankind. This is not truth from the heart.

One of the great joys of becoming a Christian is discovering that the truth is a person. His name is Jesus, and he is the benchmark of truth. Those on the side of truth listen to him, and his great promise is that if you side with him, the truth will set you free.

In becoming a Christian, you meet the God who does not lie (Titus 1:2). Unlike the devil, who is the father of lies, God cannot lie. He cannot make a promise and break it; to do so would be to deny himself. Consequently, Christians tell the truth because we are compelled to be like the God we worship and in whose constant presence we now consciously live.

I soon noticed as a young Christian that by God's Spirit I began to develop a taste for truth. And what a relief! I can still remember the sense of peace that came as I slowly learnt the art of telling the truth. This had not been my normal custom. And the thing about lying is that, sooner or later, you always get caught out—if not for the first lie then for the subsequent lies you use to cover up your original deception. I soon started to enjoy the relief of not having to look over my shoulder waiting to get caught out. It feels so good to live with a clear conscience.

As well as being someone who tells the truth, a blameless person is someone you can trust even when your back is turned. The blameless person does not gossip or flatter, which are opposing ways of harming your neighbour with your mouth. Gossip is what you say behind your neighbour's back but never to his face— because you're ashamed of your words. Flattery is what you say to your neighbour's face but never behind his back—because you don't really mean it. A righteous person understands when a conversation is slipping into gossip or slander, and either steers the discussion in another direction or just walks away from it. Neither option is easy, because you run the risk of being viewed as a prude. But when we refrain from gossip and slander, we serve people and we please God:

> Let no corrupting talk come out of your mouths, but only such as is good for building up, as fits the occasion, that it may give grace to those who hear. And do not grieve the Holy Spirit of God, by whom you were sealed for the day of redemption. (Eph 4:29-30)

John White, the famous Christian writer, told of his mother's way of dealing with anyone who gossiped in her presence:

> I'll never forget the day when the lady next door was dripping vitriol about the neighbour on the far side. My mother took hold of her neighbour's arm. "Come on," she said, "let's go and talk to her about it".[29]

This method took the wind out of the gossiper's sails, and it was amazing how few people were prepared to gossip in Mrs White's company.

Even if you don't initiate gossip, your silence or listening ear makes you an accomplice and fosters a culture that ultimately destroys the church of God. The one who is blameless and does what is right is not naïve about these things.

He is discerning in his assessment of others

> ... in whose eyes a vile person is despised,
>> but who honours those who fear the LORD ...
>
> (Ps 15:4a)

Are you surprised that hating is part of being blameless? We are to despise the vile person—someone who perpetually delights in evil, all the viler when he or she claims to be a Christian. An obvious example is the serial adulterer who justifies breaking his or her promise to forsake all others, and trivializes the pain inflicted upon the rest of the family.

As people who love God, we simply do not hate evil enough. The great passage on love in 1 Corinthians 13 teaches us that love "does not rejoice at wrongdoing, but rejoices with the truth" (1 Cor 13:6). This means that the person who dwells in the presence of the Lord cannot be friends with everyone they meet. In your lifetime you will meet many people who rejoice at wrongdoing, many of whom you will get on with very well. But if your friend influences you for evil more often than you influence them for good, then it may be time to end the relationship. I know many alcoholics who have needed to cut certain people out of their lives in order to stay sober.

Your own spiritual life is not the only reason to take such a drastic step. The protection of God's church is also vital. The Apostle Paul called on the Corinthian church to break fellowship with a man who claimed to be a Christian but was openly engaging in sex with his stepmother. Paul went on to exort them to hate sin:

> But now I am writing to you not to associate
> with anyone who bears the name of brother if
> he is guilty of sexual immorality or greed, or is
> an idolater, reviler, drunkard, or swindler—not
> even to eat with such a one. (1 Cor 5:11)

When we hate what is evil, we protect everybody concerned. In refusing to eat with someone who claims to be Christian but continues in wilful sin, our aim is to bring that person to repentance, to keep the church holy, and to guard the integrity of the gospel. After a long process, there comes a time when such a person needs to be told, "You can't keeping calling yourself a Christian and justifying your sin and maintaining fellowship. You need to stop doing one of the three." This is the neglected grace of church discipline. It's just not Christian to be nice to everybody.

So we despise the vile person. In contrast, we honour those who fear the Lord—and you can be certain that if we don't, neither will anyone else. Our world makes heroes out of self-absorbed musicians, insecure actors, overpaid sportsmen and anorexic models who refuse to smile. We are different. Our heroes are those who fear the Lord.

Let me tell you about two of my heroes. When my friend Peter worked in senior management with a large government agency he regularly travelled the world making billion-dollar deals with CEOs of multinational companies. His position required him to be overseas a lot.

Eventually he demanded to be demoted because he could not run his youth group each Friday night. He knew that teaching those 14-year-old boys about Jesus outranked his high-paying job. Like Jesus, he was downwardly mobile. Peter fears the Lord and he is my hero.

Anther hero of mine is a senior saint who was constantly faithful to her atrocious husband. He eventually ended up leaving her. So vindictive was he that he adjusted his will in order to leave his estate to a cousin rather than to his own wife and children. Years later, despite his treatment of her, she drove three hours to his sick bed to remind him that he could still be forgiven, even at that late stage, if he was prepared to turn to Jesus—which he did. She is my hero. She kept her wedding vows even when it hurt.

He is faithful to his promises

> … who swears to his own hurt and does not change … (Ps 15:4b)

Do you know what vows you will make when you marry? Or if you are married, do you remember the promises you made on your wedding day? The marriage commitment is for better or worse, for richer or poorer, in sickness and in health. These are the terms of reference, the parameters of a marriage. Each marriage is a promise to love even when it hurts.

In the words of James, "let your 'yes' be yes and your 'no' be no" (Jas 5:12). Say what you mean and mean what you say. At the heart of marriage is not love, but faithfulness—two people keeping their word to be faithful to each other whatever the cost.

I recall the story of a man who found out his fiancée had Multiple Sclerosis (MS). Although free to end the engagement, he stayed true to her and they married. It was not long before she was bedridden and he was forced to resign from work, ending his career prospects. For ten years he stayed at her bedside and cared for her until she died. He kept his oath even when it hurt.

People have no difficulty in keeping promises when it's convenient. But that's like loving those who love you back. I suspect Jesus would say, "Big deal!" We who stand in God's presence are to keep our word *whatever the cost*. What is your word worth? What are you prepared to lose to keep your integrity?

Would you be prepared to lose $10,000 to keep your word? Would you be prepared to lose $100,000 to keep a promise?

I knew a woman whose parents asked her to lie in court to prevent the family from being unjustly sued for $150,000. This newly converted young woman felt a great deal of pressure from her non-Christian family to lie. If she lied, the family would be relieved of a great burden. If she told the truth, her family would be cheated out of their hard-earned business and would then turn on her. But she knew the judge would ask her to make an oath before God and man, and to the exasperation of her family she refused to lie.

You do not need to know the end of this story to know that she made the right decision. The rightness of decisions like these is not determined by a happy ending. We are to keep our promises and tell the truth no matter what it costs us.

He does not exploit the poor or oppress the innocent

> … who does not put out his money at interest
>> and does not take a bribe against the
>>> innocent.
> He who does these things shall never be
>> moved. (Ps 15:5)

On view here are the extortionate moneylender and the unjust magistrate who perverts justice for a bribe. God's word is clear—we are not to take financial advantage of those who are powerless and vulnerable:

> "If you lend money to any of my people with you who is poor, you shall not be like a moneylender to him, and you shall not exact interest from him." (Exod 22:25)

The temptation to get something for nothing is strong for all of us. I find that when I sell my car privately, I am forever tempted to withhold information about the condition of the car. I am more interested in getting a good deal rather than a fair deal. But the blameless person will not take advantage of anyone—especially not other Christians, and especially not the poor.

The promise

David answers his own question by describing the person who is righteous and blameless: it is the one who loves his neighbour as himself. God's promise is that such a person will never be moved. He may lose his family, his business, his friends, his job, his money ... but he will not be shaken.

I know a couple who bought a restaurant and four years later had lost all their hard-earned savings. They went from owning their own house on eight acres of land to living in a rented house, bankrupt. Why? It was because they paid their workers properly and would not avoid paying tax.

People who live like this may battle to wear the consequences but they go to bed each night with a clear conscience, ready to meet Jesus when he returns. You can only look forward to being in God's presence if you're right with God, ever mindful of his presence.

Are there things that are not right in your life? Have you gossiped, put people down, lied, given in to corruption, filled forms out incorrectly, or received money you are not entitled to? If Jesus is your Lord, or you want him to be, is it not time to own up, admit, confess, pay back, and stop hiding?

Let me end with a couple of examples of those who came to Christ and began to do what is right.

I know a school principal who received a cheque for $80 in the mail. The note attached said, "Some years ago I was a student at your school. When I was in year 12

I broke a toilet in an act of vandalism. I have since become a Christian and want to put things right. Attached is a cheque for the cost of replacing the toilet bowl."

I know of a man who took the place of his identical twin brother in a nursing exam so his brother would pass. Years later that nurse came to Christ and called up the university to admit to his guilt. The person on the phone in the administration office said, "You are not one of those born-again Christians, are you? We get you guys calling all the time trying to clear your conscience."

The grace of our Lord Jesus is not satisfied in simply saving you; it also transforms you from one degree of glory to the next. Let me be clear: no righteous act or behaviour can in any way earn, merit, buy or contribute to our salvation. Good works do not save us; instead, we are saved to do good works (Eph 2:8-10). We have been commanded to find out what pleases the Lord and do it. The call is to be like the God in whose presence every believer will spend eternity. We are to walk in righteousness in preparation for the home of righteousness.

FOR REFLECTION
- In what areas do you struggle to keep your promises?
- Who are your heroes—those people you want to emulate, and for whom you are grateful to God?
- What sin in your life do you need to confess and repent of?

10 | ONLY THE GOOD DIE YOUNG

Psalm 73

I wonder if Billy Joel had Psalm 73 in mind when he wrote the following words:

> They say there's a heaven for those who will
>   wait
> Some say it's better but I say it ain't
> I'd rather laugh with the sinners than cry with
>   the saints
> Sinners are much more fun …
> And only the good die young.[30]

Billy Joel is appealing to a young Catholic girl to have sex with him. Since only good people die young, he argues, there's no reason to be good and miss out on the fun things in life. He makes a good point: the good die young while the evil prosper, so why bother being good? What is the point of maintaining faithfulness when the unfaithful advance? This is the problem Asaph seeks to address in Psalm 73 as he watches the wicked prosper.

And it's a problem for us, too. We live in the same world Asaph lived in. Children are abused and murdered, while Mafia bosses live to the age of 90 years and then die in their sleep surrounded by a loving family. It isn't fair. A sense of justice tells us that good people should live and prosper, and evil people should suffer and die. That's why so many Hollywood movies end with the sympathetic character vindicated. I've heard of directors re-shooting the end of a film after a test screening because the audience was disappointed with the sad ending. Happy endings satisfy our sense that good people deserve happiness. But life is not often like that, as Asaph makes clear in Psalm 73.

Stumbling over the facts

Asaph led the choir of Israel and wrote 12 psalms. He begins this one by making a claim that he spends the rest of the psalm coming to terms with:

> Truly God is good to Israel,
>> to those who are pure in heart. (Ps 73:1)

The whole psalm hangs on this one important truth about God's commitment to be good to his people—a commitment grounded in his covenant vow at Mount Sinai. Asaph has in mind the nation of Israel and particularly those within who are "pure in heart", who seek to trust and obey God (the kind of people we saw in the previous chapter, about Psalm 15). Asaph knows God has promised to bless those who obey him, but Asaph has come face to face with people and situations that seem to prove that God is not good, and—even worse—that he blesses the wicked.

Picture Asaph giving his testimony to the people of Israel. He begins his story with a sigh of relief—you can almost see him wiping the sweat from his brow:

> But as for me, my feet had almost stumbled,
>   my steps had nearly slipped. (Ps 73:2)

Asaph is aware that he almost fell to his spiritual death. He came close to the worst possible crisis: he almost lost his confidence in God's goodness.

While driving home from a holiday some time ago, my wife pointed out that I had just missed the turn-off. Without thinking, I swung the steering-wheel hard to get back onto the right road. For about four seconds we were locked in on a median concrete strip, heading for a pole that would have certainly killed us. I managed to pull the car back on track in the nick of time. A long silence followed as we realized we'd had a genuine brush with death.

Asaph brushed against something much worse than physical death. He almost abandoned his God, because he thought his God had abandoned him.

Envying the wicked

What made Asaph nearly give up his faith? One simple thing: envy.

> For I was envious of the arrogant
>> when I saw the prosperity of the wicked.
>
> For they have no pangs until death;
>> their bodies are fat and sleek.
> They are not in trouble as others are;
>> they are not stricken like the rest of mankind.
> Therefore pride is their necklace;
>> violence covers them as a garment.
> Their eyes swell out through fatness;
>> Their hearts overflow with follies.
> They scoff and speak with malice;
>> loftily they threaten oppression.
> They set their mouths against the heavens,
>> and their tongue struts through the earth.
>> (Ps 73:3-9)

Do you identify with Asaph? He had focused his attention completely on the prosperity of the ungodly, envying everything that displeased God. He saw that the wicked in their arrogance had it all. Their defiance seemed to be blessed, not cursed, judging by the ease with which they lived their lives and faced death. This group was not marked by the fruit of the Spirit but by the works of the flesh: pride, violence and malicious talk. And yet they enjoyed health, wealth and contentment all the days of their lives. Even their blasphemous sniggering escaped any real consequences.

Everything inside Asaph screamed, "It's not fair!" Everything he thought he knew about God and his commitment to Israel appeared to be lies. At best, God appeared to be ignoring the wickedness of the ungodly. At worst, he appeared to be actively blessing it.

Again, we live in the same world. One student studies hard for an exam and barely passes, while another student cheats and achieves top marks. One person fills out his tax return honestly, while his neighbour brags about how she has successfully avoided paying a $5000 tax bill. And here's a real-life example: my sister and others worked long hours at their own personal cost to keep a small travel company afloat, while the owner quietly embezzled three million dollars and then took off for the USA.

What makes matters worse, Asaph says, is that other people find no fault in what the wicked are doing. In fact, the wicked are praised. They become objects of respect and approval:

> Therefore his people turn back to them,
> and find no fault in them.
> And they say, "How can God know?
> Is there knowledge in the Most High?"
> Behold, these are the wicked;
> always at ease, they increase in riches.
> (Ps 73:10-12)

Where is the justice? The guy who knocks off material from work gets the promotion. The guy who is willing to lie for the boss gets to keep his job at your expense. The woman who boasts of her adultery is envied at the tennis club.

You can see Asaph's problem, and he is not alone. He is saying, "And you're telling me that God is good to those who are pure in heart?" He is so obsessed by it all, and so angry with the way things are turning out, that he begins to think following God has been a complete and total waste of time. All it brings is suffering:

> All in vain have I kept my heart clean
>   and washed my hands in innocence.
> For all the day long I have been stricken
>   and rebuked every morning. (Ps 73:13-14)

Asaph is absolutely right: if God is not good to his own then there is no point in being faithful to him. Without that commitment from God, Christianity is one big con job.

Asaph is like a blind man groping in the dark. Any sense of God's goodness has left him. He is obsessed with one thing and one thing only: the riches of the wicked. Perhaps that explains why he views the wicked so idealistically. Up close you can see the chinks in their armour, but Asaph is too caught up in himself to see reality. He is like the guy in Bob Dylan's song, 'License to Kill':

> Now, he's hell-bent for destruction, he's afraid
>   and confused,
> And his brain has been mismanaged with great
>   skill.
> All he believes are his eyes
> And his eyes, they just tell him lies.[31]

Asaph's faith and experience are out of step. His eyes tell him that the wicked do well, while the Bible tells him that God is good to his people. Asaph's mistake is to believe only what his eyes tell him. But although our faith is not blind (it is based on good reason), we do not live by sight (2 Cor 5:7). Our eyes will lie to us, so we must not believe only what we see.

Asaph also has another problem: he is impatient. He wants to be rewarded for his holiness—immediately! Do you ever find yourself feeling as if you deserve some kind of immediate reward when you obey God? Sadly, in a world of instant credit, instant food and instant messaging, we have lost any sense of delayed gratification.

Asaph has reached his all-time low, and it seems to shock him back into right thinking. He realizes just in time that he is in danger of not only losing his own way but also leading others astray:

> If I had said, "I will speak thus",
>> I would have betrayed the generation of
>> your children. (Ps 73:15)

So he stops in his tracks and tries to understand the dissonance between his experience and the promises he knows God has made. By this stage, Asaph is plumb tuckered out, weary with trying to make sense of what he sees:

> But when I thought how to understand this,
>> it seemed to me a wearisome task,
> until I went into the sanctuary of God;
>> then I discerned their end. (Ps 73:16-17)

Asaph first tries to understand what he sees without consulting God and his word. He sets his mind on understanding the world through his eyes and not through God's eyes.

The light dawns through only when he enters God's sanctuary. Under the old covenant, the sanctuary was the place set apart for the worship of God. So, as Spurgeon put it, "His mind entered the eternity where God dwells".[32] Asaph puts up the periscope from the depths of his claustrophobic obsessiveness.

Many years ago I visited an art gallery, and at the entrance was a large Picasso painting called *Guernica*. It's a huge painting, standing about 3.5 metres tall and 7.8 metres wide. Until Asaph enters God's sanctuary, his perspective on the world is like that of a man who looks at *Guernica* from only three centimetres away and wonders why he cannot make head or tail of the artwork. When Asaph takes a step back, the overall picture becomes clear and his confusion disappears (which, by the way, does not always happen when it comes to Picasso).

Seeing the big picture

Once he consults God, Asaph learns four things that broaden his perspective (and ours).

1. We need to keep the end in mind

The success of the wicked looks a little different in the light of eternity:

> Truly you set them in slippery places;
>> you make them fall to ruin.
> How they are destroyed in a moment,
>> swept away utterly by terrors!
> Like a dream when one awakes,
>> O Lord, when you rouse yourself, you
>>> despise them as phantoms.
>>> (Ps 73:18-20)

Asaph now sees that just as he had almost slipped in his faith, in the same way the wicked are placed on their own slippery ground. Asaph had pictured the life of the wicked as a still photograph rather than as a motion picture with a tragic ending. He had seen their present success but forgotten about their future failure. You may envy an evil man who appears to have it all, but you will never envy a man on his way to destruction—and that is where the wicked will end up if they don't repent.

Asaph had forgotten that God's timing is not Asaph's timing; God is not at Asaph's beck and call. God will finally dispense his perfect justice only on the last day, and the wicked will not escape. They are to be pitied, not envied.

2. We need to take an honest look at ourselves

Asaph has looked at the future of the wicked. Now he looks at himself:

> When my soul was embittered,
>> when I was pricked in heart,

> I was brutish and ignorant;
>> I was like a beast toward you. (Ps 73:21-22)

Asaph has come to his senses; he is seeing himself as God sees him. He describes himself as a man who was bitter and who behaved like a wild animal out of control—not unlike the Babylonian King Nebuchadnezzar who, due to his pride, lost his mind for seven years and was reduced to the behaviour of a wild animal (Dan 4:33).

Notice that Asaph is unqualified in his confession. In effect he is saying, "I was as stupid and senseless and out of control as an untamed animal", and as with any genuine confession there is not a 'but' in sight. Asaph offers no excuses for his behaviour.

Have you ever been so bitter or resentful at some apparent injustice that you just can't stop thinking about it? I'm talking about the things that make you so angry that no matter where you are or what you're doing, you find yourself having the same conversation in your head over and over again. You struggle to stay focused in conversations because there is a great wrong in your life that casts a very long shadow over you. Is it time for you to take an honest look at yourself, and come clean before God?

3. We need to remember that God never lets go

God is good to Asaph. Even though Asaph envies all those things that break God's heart; even though he is like a beast before God, acting out one massive passive-aggressive sulk; even though he is filled with self-pity; astoundingly, God stays right by Asaph's side:

> Nevertheless, I am continually with you;
>> you hold my right hand. (Ps 73:23)

Asaph understands that while he was resentful, God was like a father who takes the hand of a rebellious child and never lets go. Jesus said, "Blessed are the pure in heart, for they shall see God"(Matt 5:8). Asaph sees God not with eyes of flesh but with eyes of faith. He sees that God was always with him even though he thrashed against God.

Asaph finally sees things as God sees them. He sees his own folly and God's faithfulness. He has seen the destiny of the wicked, and now he sees his own destiny.

4. We need to remember our destiny

> You guide me with your counsel,
>> and afterward you will receive me to glory.
>>> (Ps 73:24)

Asaph has remembered where he is ultimately going and, unlike Billy Joel, he shows no hint of disappointment with his destination. When Asaph steps into the glory of the new creation with a resurrected body, he will not be saying, "Hmm, I thought it would be better than this".

Asaph is effectively saying, "It's tough now as I see the prosperity of those who oppose God, but I need to remember where they are going to end up and where *I* am going to end up".

Once you see the present in light of the future; once you see that the unfaithful will be in hell and the pure in heart in heaven; once you see that nothing the wicked have will last; once you know that you will be spending eternity in the presence of God; once you realize all this, you are left with only one thing to say:

> Whom have I in heaven but you?
> And there is nothing on earth that I desire
> besides you. (Ps 73:25)

This is one of my all-time favourite verses, so beautifully clear and simple. Like Asaph, I have to fight hard to maintain this clarity of thought in my life; yet I know this is what centres me as a Christian. When I really think about it, being with God is all I desire. He is all I ultimately need. And in those times when I understand this, it has inspired me again and again to draw near to my Father in heaven.

No-one has expressed this truth better than Jonathan Edwards. He writes:

> God is the highest good of the reasonable creature; and the enjoyment of God is the only happiness with which our souls can be satisfied. To go to heaven, fully to enjoy God, is *infinitely* better than the most pleasant accommodations here. Fathers and mothers, husbands, wives, or children, or the company of earthly friends, are but shadows; but the enjoyment of God is the substance. These are but scattered beams; but God is the sun. These are but streams; but God is the fountain. These are but drops; but God is the ocean. [33]

This does not mean I don't enjoy every one of God's good gifts of creation. It does not mean I don't have deep longings and real needs, which are met by my God-given wife, friends and church, and by creation generally. This verse does not turn me into a hermit or a monk. But it does mean that I don't need a pay-off in this life. Why is that? It is because *God himself* is the pay-off. God is not a means to an end, but the end itself.

Laughing with the saints

At times evil appears to have the upper hand in this world, but Asaph knows this: he is on God's side and God will carry him through. Once you know that God is good to his own, you are magnetically drawn into his safe arms. Asaph now goes out in a blaze of glory:

> My flesh and my heart may fail,
> > but God is the strength of my heart and
> > > my portion forever.
>
> For behold, those who are far from you shall
> > perish;
> > you put an end to everyone who is
> > > unfaithful to you.
> But for me it is good to be near God;
> > I have made the Lord GOD my refuge,
> > that I may tell of all your works. (Ps 73:26-28)

We have now come full circle. In the face of experiences that seem to deny it, we began with a declaration that

God is good to his own. We now end with an affirmation that it is good to be near this good God.

Asaph lived nearly a millennium before God's goodness to us was fully demonstrated at the cross, when God refused to withhold his one and only Son. We live two millennia on the other side of the cross. We have the privilege of being able to see the whole picture of God's plan for salvation, "things into which angels long to look" (1 Pet 1:12). Much more than Asaph, then, should we be able to say, "Whom have I in heaven but you? And there is nothing on earth that I desire besides you."

So why is it that I prefer to be near my TV, my DVD, my computer screen or my iPod instead of my God? How many hours have I tragically lost? How often I have numbed my stress in front of a screen that has stolen my best moments with God. Too often I prefer to make my favourite sitcom my hiding place. At the age of 49, one of my biggest regrets is the time I've wasted. It can't be regained. Oh, that I had read more of God's word, loved more and especially prayed more—not so I could feel self-satisfied, but so I would be energized to tell others of God's goodness:

> But for me it is good to be near God;
>> I have made the Lord GOD my refuge,
>> that I may tell of all your works. (Ps 73:28)

Let me re-write Billy Joel's song:

> I know there's a heaven for those who will wait,
> And so I will wait til I pass through that gate,

> I will not cry with the sinners but laugh with
> > the saints
> for all of eternity ...

Even if sin is more fun in the short term, and even if the good sometimes die young, for me it is good to be near God. I have no-one in heaven but God, and earth has nothing I desire besides him.

FOR REFLECTION

- What earthly things do you desire more than God? How can you change your life so that you put God before these things?
- What do you envy in other people? Will these things last? Will they satisfy you? Do you think they are worth giving up heaven for?

11 | PASSING THE BATON

Psalm 78

W hat do you want to pass on to your children? I want my son, James, to have the watch my father gave me. My wife has some pearl earrings she wants to give to our daughters, Amy and Madeleine (although I noticed recently that they are not waiting for the funeral before they enjoy this part of their inheritance). We are paying off a unit that I want my kids to take. But in the end you want more for your children than jewellery and real estate. Don't you?

I want my children to know some of the stories from my past and my father's past. For example, I want them to know that soon after my dad arrived in Australia from Malta in 1939, as he was cutting down a gum tree in Mackay, Queensland, the axe skipped off the tree and landed on his foot, severing tendons and veins. He described it as a fountain of blood spurting out of his foot. I want them to know that my Dad crawled for three miles to the homestead on his hands and knees to get help. He had to plead with the farmer's wife, who was reluctant to call the ambulance. When it finally arrived, the driver threw my Dad in the back seat of what was really no more than a car. On the way to the hospital the driver decided to stop off for lunch with my father in agony in the back seat.

That's the story of how my dad, at the age of 21, and three weeks after arriving in Australia, came to spend a month in hospital in a foreign country, far from family, alone and with little English. When he told me this story, I said, "Oh Dad, at that point you must really have regretted coming to Australia". Quick as a flash he replied, "No, I always knew this was a better country!"

It's not just the story that I want to pass on to my kids, but also the values embedded within it. I want my children to have a deep gratitude for all they have, and I want them to approach life with my father's optimism in the face of adverse circumstances.

But what I most want to pass on to my children is an inheritance that will never perish, spoil or fade (1 Pet 1:4). That's the most important story for them to know.

There is a hymn we sometimes sing on Sunday mornings, called 'Tell Me the Old, Old Story'. I remember one of the senior saints once asking me in private, "Ray, what exactly is the old, old story?" I answered, "Don, remember the words: 'Tell me the old, old story *of Jesus and his love*'." "Oh!" he said, "Now I get it".

What exactly is the old, old story? I guess it depends on what theological time zone you live in. For Asaph, who wrote Psalm 78, the old, old story began with the Exodus and reached its climax in the raising up of King David as the shepherd king of Judah. And this story needs to be passed on within Israel, from generation to generation.

Don't improvise

Asaph begins with a call for his generation not to be silent about the old, old story. He is doing what he tells them to do:

> Give ear, O my people, to my teaching;
>> incline your ears to the words of my
>>> mouth!
> I will open my mouth in a parable;
>> I will utter dark sayings from of old,
> things that we have heard and known,
>> that our fathers have told us. (Ps 78:1-3)

Asaph is calling on his generation to listen carefully to what he says. Importantly, he speaks only what he has heard. He tells them only what was told to him, "sayings from of old". This is quite unlike the modern era, where new is considered better than old and the past is dismissed as having nothing to teach us. But when it comes to God's word, novelty is not an option. Asaph passes on what his forefathers passed on to him.

It is *so* important that we pass on only what God has

revealed to us in his word. We must not embellish it or deviate from it; we must not "leave the commandment of God and hold to the tradition of men" (Mark 7:8). The Church Father Cyprian (d. 258 AD) rightly said that "custom without truth is the antiquity of error"—that is, a tradition may simply be an error in its old age.[34] Even if 20 generations of people believe a lie, that does not make it true. Sticking to what is revealed is the only thing that matters. Improvisation is not an option.

Every generation of God's people receives the old, old story. Every generation is obliged to pass on the old, old story.

This is no less true for Jesus himself, who quotes Psalm 78:2 in Matthew 13:35 as he makes known the mysteries of the kingdom. Jesus proudly asserts that he doesn't have a single original idea in his head. He says only what his Father has told him to say (John 8:28; 12:29-50; 14:10, 24). Originality is overrated when it comes to God's word.

Whether you are a parent, a grandparent, an uncle, an aunt, a children's worker, a Bible study leader, a youth leader or a preacher, you are obligated before God to hold on to the truth as it has been revealed and pass it on as it has been entrusted to you; nothing more and nothing less. In fact, the word of God was written down for this express purpose: so others may know. We believe a gospel that is "in accordance with the Scriptures" (1 Cor 15:3).

My children joke about how their parents are 'story-repeaters' (I've noticed it is the first sign of old age).

I take it as a compliment because it is what every Christian is called to be: a repeater of the old, old story. The other accusation my children make is that we are 'story-exaggerators'. In every marriage there is usually one story-exaggerator. Each year the tale gets longer and the fish get bigger. But story-exaggerating is off limits when it comes to the old, old story.

Speak up

Asaph articulates a decisive commitment to tell "things we have heard and known" to the next generation:

> We will not hide them from their children,
>   but tell to the coming generation
> the glorious deeds of the LORD, and his might,
>   and the wonders that he has done.
>   (Ps 78:4)

He firmly and clearly vows to tell the next generation of "the glorious deeds of the LORD". We need to make the same commitment. We must not hide the glorious deeds of the Lord from our children. We must tell the next generation and we must refuse to be silent.

I've heard it said that the church is only one generation away from its own extinction. All it would take is the deadly silence of the majority. It is a commonly accepted truth that what is fought for in one generation is taken for granted in the next, and soon forgotten in the one after. What a tragedy it would be if our generation took God's word for granted, or forgot it altogether.

At least three generations are mentioned in Psalm 78: the generation Asaph is speaking to ("my people"; v. 1), their children, "the coming generation" (v. 4), and "the children yet unborn" (v. 6). Asaph's generation is told not to hide the truth from their children, so that their children will in turn tell "the children yet unborn" about the glorious deeds of the Lord. This is how the gospel keeps travelling from age to age until our Lord returns.

We know that the gospel travels along different pathways. For example, it travels from person to person and nation to nation as a result of Jesus' command to "Go therefore and make disciples of all nations" (Matt 28:19). It travels within families from grandparent to parent to child (2 Tim 1:5). It travels as teachers equip teachers, as in 2 Timothy 2:2 where Paul mentions four links in the gospel chain: "… and what *you* have heard from *me* in the presence of many witnesses entrust to *faithful men* who will be able to teach *others* also".

You may be part of a Christian dynasty that reaches back for generations. Thank God for your ancestors who were faithful in passing on the good news of our saviour. It would be tragic if the gospel died with you—strive to make sure that does not happen.

You may be the first Christian in your family. What a great privilege it is to know that you are the head of a new dynasty. And what a dynasty it is: if you have three children, and if each of them has three children, then by the ninth generation you will have nearly 20,000 descendents. If only a third come to Christ, you will end up producing one of the biggest churches in Australia. So take the long view and don't keep silent. Have you ever thought of praying for your great-great-grand-children—that those who carry your name will also carry your faith?

The spiritual giant Jonathan Edwards (1703-1758) ministered in the New England region of the USA during the Great Awakening. Today, hundreds of years later, many people carry both his name and his love for Jesus. Why? Because each generation spoke up, faithfully passing the old, old story on to the next generation.

Tell your children

Passing this knowledge on to the next generation is not just a good idea. God commands us to do it:

> He established a testimony in Jacob
>   and appointed a law in Israel,
> which he commanded our fathers
>   to teach to their children,
> that the next generation might know them,
>   the children yet unborn,
> and arise and tell them to their children …
>   (Ps 78:5-6)

God has not gone to all the trouble of speaking for us to keep it to ourselves. God is not interested in saving just you or your family or your nation or even just the people alive in the world today. God is not a one-generation God.

On the day of Pentecost, the Apostle Peter announced the promise of forgiveness in Jesus to the Christ-killers in Jerusalem. He told them that "the promise is for you and for your children and for all who are far off, everyone whom the Lord our God calls to himself"(Acts 2:39). Peter was not only saying "the gospel is for you and your kids"; he was also saying "it is for your generation and the generations that follow".

A couple of years ago, I heard a man on talkback radio say, "God doesn't need us to speak for him". He was absolutely right. God doesn't *need* us, but he has *commanded* us not to hide the old, old story of Jesus and his love.

The Bible directs fathers in particular to assume this responsibility of instructing children:

> Fathers, do not provoke your children to anger,
> but bring them up in the discipline and
> instruction of the Lord. (Eph 6:4)

Sadly, the Good News translation of the Bible mistranslates the Greek word 'fathers' in this verse as 'parents'. This obscures the fathers' responsibility, which is the last thing we males need. We already find it too easy to step back and allow women to assume responsibility when it comes to the things of God—we don't need any extra encouragement to do so. In my own family it was my mother who taught us the things of God. But the Bible clearly gives men a particular responsibility to teach their children about God.

Understand why this matters

Why exactly does Asaph want his people to pass on the knowledge of the Lord? It is certainly not in order to preserve a quaint religious culture.

> ... so that they should set their hope
> in God
> and not forget the works of God,
> but keep his commandments;
> and that they should not be like their fathers,
> a stubborn and rebellious generation,
> a generation whose heart was not steadfast,
> whose spirit was not faithful to God.
> (Ps 78:7-8)

The ultimate purpose in passing the gospel baton is not simply to transfer information. We speak so that future generations will know and serve the God of Israel. Asaph describes future generations who will trust God and be loyal to his covenant. They will remember God's incredible deeds, giving him due praise and glory. And by trusting God, they will avoid his judgement.

We are to long for the next generation to know God; we are to pray that they will not forget the God who promises to forget their sins. To forget the old, old story is to become like those in the old, old story who ignored God and paid the ultimate price.

Memory loss does not have a lot going for it. At the time of writing, my father is suffering with dementia. In the early days there were some advantages—his favourite movies were like new releases for him. But there is nothing funny about my father driving aimlessly for hours around my suburb, totally lost.

Asaph's warning is clear: remember God or die!

Remember or die

The rest of this long psalm spells out what happens when people forget God. We only have the space here to touch on a few issues, so please make sure you read the entire psalm in your Bible a couple of times.

Essentially, Asaph retells the story of God and his people, from the Exodus and the wilderness, to the conquest of and rebellion in the Promised Land culminating in God's gift of King David. Asaph gives his people the big story. This is not simply a newly discovered antidote to the scepticism of postmodernism. Understanding the big picture has always been the solution to the doubts of God's people. It confronts and challenges their disobedience and disloyalty.

Asaph reminds Israel of the extraordinary signs and wonders of God that led to their rescue out of Egypt:

> In the sight of their fathers he performed
>   wonders
>   in the land of Egypt, in the fields of Zoan.
> He divided the sea and let them pass through it,
>   and made the waters stand like a heap.
>   (Ps 78:12-13)

You can almost see the Israelites running their hands along the wall of water as they walked through the Red Sea. It reminds me of walking through the tunnels of the Sydney Aquarium, but for Israel it was the word of God that restrained the water—not reinforced plastic.

The only thing that matched God's amazing power and mercy was Israel's disobedience. God had rescued them from Egypt and given them water from a rock to quench their thirst, but instead of trusting him they tested him:

> Yet they sinned still more against him,
>> rebelling against the Most High in the
>>> desert.
> They tested God in their heart
>> by demanding the food they craved.
> They spoke against God, saying,
>> "Can God spread a table in the
>>> wilderness?
> He struck the rock so that water gushed out
>> and streams overflowed.
> Can he also give bread
>> or provide meat for his people?"
>>> (Ps 78:17-20)

Although rightfully angry, God responded in mercy and grace, again and again giving the Israelites what they did not deserve:

> Therefore, when the LORD heard, he was full of
>> wrath;

a fire was kindled against Jacob;
his anger rose against Israel,
because they did not believe in God
and did not trust his saving power.
Yet he commanded the skies above
and opened the doors of heaven,
and he rained down on them manna to eat
and gave them the grain of heaven.
(Ps 78:21-24)

God met Israel's sin with mercy, and Israel met God's mercy with yet more sin. Over and over, God forgave Israel's sins and Israel in turn forgot God. But God would not let himself be forgotten:

But before they had satisfied their craving,
while the food was still in their mouths,
the anger of God rose against them,
and he killed the strongest of them
and laid low the young men of Israel.
In spite of all this, they still sinned;
despite his wonders, they did not believe.
So he made their days vanish like a breath,
and their years in terror. (Ps 78:30-33)

This text really has to be God-breathed. What other nation is willing to record such utter failure of its people? What other nation would voluntarily record such total contempt for its own God?

God is slow to anger (Exod 34:6) but that does not mean God is without anger. God is love—but it is a *holy* love. The opposite of love is not anger but indifference, and the God of Israel is anything but indifferent. He takes himself and his people and their rebellion very seriously—hence the need to warn future generations.

It is true that anger is not intrinsic to God's character in the way that love and righteousness are. While love defines the three persons of the Trinity throughout all eternity, God does not experience anger apart from his response to the defiance of humans and angels. But God's anger is a fair and right response to those who oppose him. God's justice springs from his holiness. When you abandon the idea that God has the capacity to be angry, you worship a god made in your own image (i.e. a god you have created). At best, you end up talking to yourself; at worst, you end up worshipping yourself.

Recently on the radio I heard a discussion about what kind of emotions animals experience. During the conversation, the radio host referred to the emotions of anger and jealousy as "base" emotions. But there is nothing more pure, more righteous, or more appropriate than feeling angry in the face of a major injustice, or feeling jealous when your spouse commits adultery. There is nothing base about either emotion, and God clearly feels both.

Knowing that the consequence of forgetting God is death should help us in our commitment to "tell the coming generation" of his glorious deeds.

The old, old story for us

For us, living in the last days, the old, old story continues with the Lion of the tribe of Judah and the son of David: the Lord Jesus. He is the good shepherd who laid down his life for his sheep. At the cross, like a lightning rod Jesus deflected God's anger away from us and on to himself.

This is the old, old story about which we must not be silent:

> For I delivered to you as of first importance
> what I also received: that Christ died for our
> sins in accordance with the Scriptures, that he
> was buried, that he was raised on the third day
> in accordance with the Scriptures, and that he
> appeared to Cephas, then to the twelve.
> (1 Cor 15:3-5)

Without a doubt it is the responsibility of parents and especially fathers to pass this on to their children. Children's workers and youth leaders should only be *assisting* parents in that task. The sad thing is that in some cases they are not simply assisting; in some cases they are the only ones who are doing anything at all to teach the children in their care about God.

On behalf of every pastor who has taken their children's workers, Scripture teachers and youth leaders for granted, I want to apologise for our failure to honour your vital role. Great will be your reward, and great is our shame.

A friend once told me how grateful he was to his Sunday School teachers for putting a stone in his shoe. That stone was the good news of Jesus and his love. Wherever he went, the stone would irritate him. It did not leave him alone until he finally realized that the stone was the rock of his salvation.

We are responsible not only for our generation but for the generations to come. Too much of our ministry planning is short term. We make one-year, five-year, sometimes even ten-year plans. But we need to look to the generations yet unborn and ask ourselves what we need to be doing today to ensure that they will glorify God in the future.

We need to be asking ourselves what we can do so that they will stay centred, able to wholeheartedly join Asaph in his cry: "Whom have I in heaven but you? And there is nothing on earth that I desire besides you."

FOR REFLECTION

- Asaph begins Psalm 78 by saying, "Give ear, O my people, to my teaching". How do you regularly open your ears to God's word and remind yourself of his glorious deeds?
- If you have children, what are you doing (or what could you do) to teach them the importance of God's word?
- If you don't have children, what are you doing (or what could you do) to teach the next generation of the importance of God's word?

Feedback on this resource

We really appreciate getting feedback about our resources—not just suggestions for how to improve them, but also positive feedback and ways they can be used. We especially love to hear that the resources may have helped someone in their Christian growth.

You can send feedback to us via the 'Feedback' menu in our online store, or write to us at PO Box 225, Kingsford NSW 2032, Australia.

NOTES

CHAPTER 1

1. Oprah Winfrey and Eckhart Tolle, 'The Flowering of Human Consciousness' in *A New Earth: Awakening to Your Life's Purpose*, webcast, chapter 1, part 3, 3 March 2008, viewed 11 March 2010: www.opraheckhartvideo.com/Chapter_1.html

CHAPTER 2

2. Mark Twain, *Following the Equator*, vol. 1, Ecco, New York, 1996 (1897), p. 216.
3. Charles H Spurgeon, *The Treasury of David*, vol. 1, Passmore and Alabaster, London, 1888, p. 90.
4. Phillip Adams, *Adams Versus God*, Nelson, Melbourne, 1985, p. 176.
5. By 'evolution' I don't mean so much the notion of natural selection, but the ideology that accompanies this scientific theorem.
6. Eric Lax, *Conversations with Woody Allen*, Knopf, New York, 2009, p. 84.
7. Albert Camus, *The Rebel: An Essay on Man in Revolt*, trans. Anthony Bower, Vintage Books, New York, 1956, p. 100.
8. Martin Luther, *Works*, vol. 29, ed. Jaroslav Pelikan and Helmut Lehmann, Concordia, St Louis, 1955, p. 137.

CHAPTER 3

9. U2, 'When Love Comes to Town', from the album *Rattle and Hum*, Island, Memphis, 1988.
10. Bob Dylan, 'When He Returns', from the album *Slow Train Coming*, Columbia Records, Sheffield, 1979.
11. *The Devil's Own*, motion picture, Columbia Pictures, California, 1997. Distributed by Columbia Pictures and starring Harrison Ford and Brad Pitt.

CHAPTER 4

12. John Stott, *The Cross of Christ*, 20th anniversary edn, IVP, Downers Grove, 2006, pp. 76-77, quoting Plato, *Phaedo*, trans. Harold N Fowler, Heinemann, London, 1914, pp. 117-118.
13. Quoted in John Foxe, *Foxe's Book of Martyrs*, Whitaker House, New Kensington, 1981, p. 24.
14. Lucius Seneca, 'Epistle 101' in *Epistles 93-124*, trans. Richard M Gummere, The Loeb Classical Library 77, Harvard University Press, Cambridge, Mass., 1925, p. 167, quoted in Paul Barnett, *The Servant King: Reading Mark Today*, Anglican Information Office, Sydney, 1991, p. 292.
15. Jean-Paul Sartre, *No Exit* in *No Exit and Three Other Plays*, trans. S Gilbert, Vintage, New York, 1989, p. 45.

CHAPTER 6

16. Hebrew: *bara*.

CHAPTER 7

17. From yet another junk but funny email.
18. Bob Dylan, 'Disease of Conceit', from the album *Oh Mercy*, Columbia Records, New Orleans, 1989.
19. Professor Julian Savulescu, *Enough Rope*, television program, ABC Television, Sydney, 28 September 2008, viewed 11 March 2010: www.abc.net.au/tv/enoughrope/transcripts/s2374638.htm
20. Martin Luther, *A Manual of the Book of Psalms, or, The Subject-Contents of all the Psalms*, trans. Henry Cole, Kessinger Publishing, Montana, 2008 (1837), p. 239.

CHAPTER 8

21. Karl Barth, *Church Dogmatics III.3: The Doctrine of Creation*, trans. Geoffrey W Bromiley, T&T Clark, London, 2004 (1960), p. 472.

22. Francis Schaeffer, *He is There and He is not Silent*, Tyndale, Wheaton, 1972.

23. The NIV translates this verse, "There is no speech or language where their voice is not heard", but the word 'where' is not in the original Hebrew text.

24. For more detail, see John Dickson's *The Christ Files: How historians know what they know about Jesus,* Blue Bottle, Sydney, 2006, and Frederick F Bruce, *The New Testament Documents: Are they reliable?*, 6th edn, Eerdmans, Grand Rapids, 2003.

25. John P Holms and Karin Baji (comps.), *Bite-Size Twain: Wit and Wisdom from the Literary Legend*, St Martin's Press, New York, 1998, p. 61.

26. See www.en.wikipedia.org/wiki/List_of_best-selling_books, viewed 11 March 2010. For those wanting to know which books followed, they are (in order): *Selected Articles of Mao Zedong, A Tale of Two Cities* by Charles Dickens, *Scouting for Boys: A Handbook for Instruction in Good Citizenship,* then *The Lord of the Rings* by JRR Tolkien.

CHAPTER 9

27. In the New Testament, the qualification for a church leader is one who is blameless and above accusation (1 Tim 3:2, 10). In Titus 1:5-9, the nature of blamelessness is further explained—a blameless man is not open to the charge of violence, drunkenness, or greed; he is faithful to his wife and manages his home well; and he holds fast to the word of God.

28. James M Boice, *Psalms Volume 1: Psalms 1-41*, Baker, Grand Rapids, 2004, p. 124.

29. John White, *The Race: Discipleship for the Long Run*, IVP, Downers Grove, 1984, p. 191.

CHAPTER 10

30. Billy Joel, 'Only the Good Die Young', from the album *The Stranger*, Family Productions/Columbia, New York, 1977.

31. Bob Dylan, 'License to Kill', from the album *Infidels*, Columbia Records, New York, 1983.

32. Charles H Spurgeon, *The Treasury of David*, vol. 3, Passmore and Alabaster, London, 1889, p. 343.
33. Jonathan Edwards, 'The Christian Pilgrim' in *The Works of Jonathan Edwards*, vol. 2, ed. Edward Hickman, Banner of Truth, Edinburgh, 1974, p. 244.

CHAPTER 11

34. Cyprian, *The Writings of Cyprian, Bishop of Carthage*, vol. 1, *Containing the Epistles and Some of the Treatises*, trans. Robert E Wallis, *Ante Nicene Christian Library Translations of the Writings of the Fathers Down to AD 325*, ed. Alexander Roberts and James Donaldson, vol. 8, T&T Clark, Edinburgh, 1868, p. 283.

matthiasmedia

Matthias Media is an evangelical publishing ministry that seeks to persuade all Christians of the truth of God's purposes in Jesus Christ as revealed in the Bible, and equip them with high-quality resources, so that by the work of the Holy Spirit they will:

- abandon their lives to the honour and service of Christ in daily holiness and decision-making
- pray constantly in Christ's name for the fruitfulness and growth of his gospel
- speak the Bible's life-changing word whenever and however they can—in the home, in the world and in the fellowship of his people.

It was in 1988 that we first started pursuing this mission, and in God's kindness we now have more than 300 different ministry resources being used all over the world. These resources range from Bible studies and books through to training courses and audio sermons.

To find out more about our large range of very useful resources, and to access samples and free downloads, visit our website:

www.matthiasmedia.com.au

How to buy our resources

1. Direct from us over the internet:
   - in the US: www.matthiasmedia.com
   - in Australia and the rest of the world: www.matthiasmedia.com.au

2. Direct from us by phone:
   - in the US: 1 866 407 4530
   - in Australia: 1800 814 360 (Sydney: 9663 1478)
   - international: +61-2-9663-1478

> Register at our website for our **free** regular email update to receive information about the latest new resources, **exclusive special offers**, and free articles to help you grow in your Christian life and ministry.

3. Through a range of outlets in various parts of the world. Visit **www.matthiasmedia.com.au/information/contact-us** for details about recommended retailers in your part of the world, including www.thegoodbook.co.uk in the United Kingdom.

4. Trade enquiries can be addressed to:
   - in the US and Canada: sales@matthiasmedia.com
   - Australia and the rest of the world: sales@matthiasmedia.com.au